FROM THE CLASSROOM TO THE HEART

AN EXAMINATION OF THE DOCTRINE OF ENTIRE SANCTIFICATION

Paul L. Kaufman, Ph.D.

Professor of Church History and Hebrew
Chair, Division of Bible & Theology

SCHMUL PUBLISHING COMPANY
NICHOLASVILLE, KENTUCKY

THE WORK OF DR. PAUL KAUFMAN in this book is outstanding, and is recommended without question. In an age of noise, he speaks with "no uncertain sound." You will find in these pages the careful, biblical definition of sin contrasted with mistakes and human infirmities. He beautifully paints the importance of salvation as no "halfway work of grace." Questions on anger, impatience, nerves, temptation, competition, inferiority, feelings, emotions and so much more, are all explored. In the final analysis, Dr. Kaufman presents holiness as attainable in a crisis experience and livable in every day life. He, the teacher, has truly brought the message and life of holiness to every sincere student of God's word in a way that can be clearly understood.

JAMES PLANK
Executive Secretary,
Interchurch Holiness Convention

ARE YOU A STUDENT of Scripture; an admirer of Wesley? Have you grappled with the sinfulness of man and the holiness of God? Does the call to live above sin and victoriously Christian resonate with your deepest longing, yet you feel as if the plethora of contemporary voices fail to address the matter or are becoming increasingly ineffective in providing a clear path to do so? Are you looking for the conviction and challenge seemingly lost to the writings of days gone by and wish someone would speak in the same definitive manner that classical Wesleyanism so ably did? If so, the following pages have been tailored for you.

In an era marked by biblical and theological complexity and confusion, Dr. Paul Kaufman offers simplicity and clarity. *From the Classroom to the Heart: An Examination of the Doctrine of Entire Sanctification* provides the reader with a beautiful mixture of interpretation and application. Decades of formal training have been packaged, so as to appeal to the average reader who longs for holiness to step out of the ivory towers of academia and onto the rugged landscape of daily living. Homespun examples and personal illustrations have been sprinkled along the way to add a degree of honesty and practicality that is seldom seen and deeply desired. The result is an incredibly accurate account of Wesleyan theology that is easily readable and difficult to lay down.

Though not offered as such, the book is built squarely on the necessity of a sound systematic theology. Time is also taken to connect the dots, concerning the concept of entire sanctification, from the Church fathers to the Reformers, and on to Wesley, providing historical validity. Through the lenses of theology and history, the Bible is addressed to offer the reader clear answers concerning challenging issues such as sin, secondness, and spiritual fillings. These alone justify Dr. Kaufman's effort, not to mention his handling of misconceptions, maturity, and Old Testament manifestations. The following pages are intended to aid the reader in finding clarity and conviction to "earnestly contend for the faith which was once delivered unto the saints" (Jude 1:3).

C. ADAM BUCKLER
President, Union Bible College & Academy

I WOULD HEARTILY RECOMMEND everyone to read Dr. Paul Kaufman's new book, *From the Classroom to the Heart: An Examination of the Doctrine of Entire Sanctification*. What started out as a simple request for a single article for our church's monthly periodical on the human elements of a holy heart and life, resulted in a series of articles that now has been further refined into this practical handbook on living a holy life.

Much has been preached and written across the years how to obtain the blessing of a pure heart, but there has been a real lack of what this looks like being lived out daily with our human frailties and faults. Many are those that struggle in this area but Dr. Kaufman has provided scriptural and practical answers gleaned from the many years in the classroom where students have had the forum to ask the questions that many of us wonder about. He has the rare ability to take the complex and simplify it so the average reader can readily grasp the truth. His years as pastor, professor, evangelist and Bible teacher, combined with his ability to analyze people, has given him the rare ability to identify vital elements that often confront those wanting to live a holy life pleasing to God. Grounded in Scripture, he corrects misconceptions and misplaced emphases of our present day holiness teachings that have hindered some.

Every generation needs scriptural holiness put in present day language and illustrated with clarity that the average person can easily understand. You will find this book does that and God's Holy Spirit will speak to you through its pages. This work appeals to a wide audience with its practical application for pastors, students, laypeople and new converts. Because very little has been written and taught on how living a holy life appears, many of us have taken years to learn these truths and later have declared, "I wish I had known that before!" and "Why didn't someone tell me this?" Now someone is telling you this in clear, easily understood language with illustrations that will benefit your holy walk with God.

REV. DAVID BLOWERS
*President, The Allegheny
Wesleyan Methodist Connection*

ONE OF THE UNIQUE TALENTS Dr. Paul Kaufman possesses is the ability to connect scholarly, theological concepts with practical, everyday living. In *From the Classroom to the Heart*, Dr. Kaufman draws not only on his vast academic training but also on his rich experience with people as he addresses the subject of Entire Sanctification. Having served as a pastor, evangelist, Bible teacher, and professor at both the college and seminary levels, he has heard the questions and sensed the frustrations of those who struggle to understand and apply this message. So beginning with the all-important definition of Sin, he proceeds to lead his readers carefully from the biblical foundations of this message all the way to the practical application of what it means to have a pure heart and live a holy life in the real world. Thank you, Dr. Kaufman, for putting together such a practical, helpful presentation of this important subject. I can certainly recommend this book to all those who have a deep passion to know, understand, and live the life of holiness.

DR. DANIEL STETLER
*President, Hobe Sound
Bible College*

I SAT IN A PROMINENT CONSERVATIVE holiness camp meeting with my family and grew more frustrated by the service. I attended every service of this ten-day camp and kept anticipating that we would hear a message on our movement's core message, the doctrine of entire sanctification. To my amazement and frustration, the camp meeting closed without a single message challenging us to be entirely sanctified. When Dr. Kaufman suggests that there is a lack of understanding of this precious doctrine, he is undoubtedly correct. What is alarming is that it is not unique to students. In this volume, the author takes his readers from a theological understanding of perfect love to a heartfelt experience and how to obtain, keep it and live it out in a sin-cursed world. This presentation takes the doctrine of holiness and shows us how it looks in practical everyday living.

Each chapter is written in an easy-to-understand format and includes questions that will help the reader teach Sunday School class, have more meaningful family devotions, and enrich their personal walk with the Lord. Dr. Kaufman takes complex material and puts it in an understandable and applicable way that makes the material relevant to his readers. I encourage you to get this book and use it to enhance your ministry, your family worship, and your personal walk with God.

RODNEY LOPER
*President, God's Bible
School and College*

PROFESSOR KAUFMAN HAS MAPPED OUT solid biblical teaching on the way of holiness, informed by decades of his own teaching and dealing with people as well as by centuries of testimony from brothers and sisters in the Lord—people who have wrestled to the same victory. Although Evangelicals in general recognize the carnal heart is a problem for Christians, many of them deny there is deliverance this side of heaven. We proclaim there is cleansing from the sinful nature in this present evil world!

New converts, college students, and people in every stage of spiritual development will benefit from grasping that I John 3:4 teaches that sin is "a voluntary transgression of a known law of God" (Wesley). Belief in the possibility of having a pure heart and living a holy life depends upon this distinction. The more clearly I apply the dual criteria of 1) moral knowledge and 2) consent of the will as I deal with my temptations, my passing thoughts, my mistaken choices, and my infirmities, the greater will be my confidence that I am "walking in the light." Muddy those two distinctions, and I will have cause to question endlessly! Kaufman's footnotes offer a catalog of further sources to study.

If we determine the moral value of an action simply based only on the consequences (teleologically), the same action completed with the same motive (or even in error) could turn out to be either righteous or sinful! Throwing a hammer, he explains, could be either criminal or heroic! Consequences are important, but not defining. On the other hand, if "sins" are actions that are wrong in themselves (deontologically), we obtain a much better grasp on how we should live.

Discerning several "fullnesses of the Spirit" throughout the Bible helps us understand that sometimes God empowered a person to do a task, but that person may not have had a holy heart (for example, Samson and even people who could do miracles in the name of Jesus). "Emotional fullness" is delectable, but not permanent and not life changing. "Ethical fullness" equates with entire sanctification and is transforming, although not always spectacular.

Discovering that "Moral perfection is not faultlessness before one's friends, companions or acquaintances; it is blamelessness before God," we come to understand that Noah was "perfect in his generation," as were also Job, Abraham, Asa, and John the Baptist. As a person's light increases, the implications of blamelessness expand. Pentecost made holiness and holy living possible far beyond anything that preceded that day!

Kaufman offers systematic instruction, biblical clarification, and diligent application. The experiences range from historic Wesleyan writers, to contemporary conservative holiness leaders, and even to individuals outside the holiness movement. Vividly the author illustrates the holy life and helpfully distinguishes what it means to live, not faultlessly, but blamelessly.

Dr. Tim Cooley, Ph.D.
Academic Dean and Professor of
Theology, Penn View Bible Institute

Dr. Paul Kaufman's chapters on entire sanctification are outstanding. His one dealing with Pentecost and its effective cleansing of the human heart from inherited depravity is excellent in its biblical interpretation and theological reasoning. Dr. Kaufman's pen is a vital contemporary instrument in these post-modern times for communicating clearly and compellingly the magnificence of God's sanctifying grace.

Dr. Richard A. Jones, D. Min.

FROM THE CLASSROOM TO THE HEART
AN EXAMINATION OF THE DOCTRINE OF ENTIRE SANCTIFICATION

COPYRIGHT © 2021 BY Paul L. Kaufman
All rights reserved. No part of this publication may be reproduced or used in any form or by any means—graphic, electronic, or mechanical, including photocopying, recording, taping, or information storage or retrieval systems—without prior written permission of the publishers.

Churches and other noncommercial interests may reproduce portions of this book without prior written permission of the publisher, provided such quotations are not offered for sale—or other compensation in any form—whether alone or as part of another publication, and provided that the text does not exceed 500 words or five percent of the entire book, whichever is less, and does not include material quoted from another publisher. When reproducing text from this book, the following credit line must be included: "From *From the Classroom to the Heart* by Paul L. Kaufman, © 2021 by Paul L. Kaufman. Used by permission."

Cover image copyright: <a href="https://www.123rf.com/profile_moredix">moredix / 123RF Stock Photo</a>. Used by permission.
Spine image copyright: <a href="https://www.123rf.com/profile_skymax">skymax / 123RF Stock Photo</a>. Used by permission.

Published by Schmul Publishing Co.
PO Box 776
Nicholasville, KY 40340

ISBN 10: 0-88019-634-3
ISBN 13: 978-0-88019-634-5

Visit us on the Internet at www.wesleyanbooks.com, or order direct from the publisher by calling 800-772-6657, or by writing to the above address.

Contents

Acknowledgements/11

Foreword/14

Introduction/16

1
Perfection and Sanctification in Early Church Writers/23

2
A Correct Understanding of Sin is Vital/38

3
How Does God View Mistakes and Human Infirmities?/49

4
The Ethics of Decision Making/62

5
Initial Sanctification and Entire Sanctification/69

6
Are Carnal Traits Viewed by God the Same as Actual Sins?/86

7
How Does God Deal with Carnality?/98

8
How Does God Deal with Human Traits?/118

9
What about Human Infirmities?/130

10
Sanctification and Temptation/144

11
What about Competition in Sanctified People?/158

12
What are the Various Kinds of Filling With the Spirit?/165

13
Fletcher on Progressive Revelation and Degrees of Perfection/175

14
Sanctification and Danger of Feelings/185

15
Sanctification and Choices/199

16
The Road to Maturity/206

17
If It's Both Crisis and Process, What About the Process?/216

18
Misconceptions about Holiness and Christian Perfection/228

19
The Four Pentecosts in the Book of Acts/238

20
How do I Attain this Glorious Blessing?/263

About the Author/283
Works Cited/284

Acknowledgements

ONE CANNOT RESEARCH AND write a monograph such as this without accumulating a debt of gratitude to those who helped to bring it to fruition. To those who assisted me in finding literary sources and rendered valuable advice in organizing and writing this work, I am deeply in their debt. Also to those who provided the encouragement and prodding needed to keep me moving, I offer sincere thanks. It was Rev. David Blowers, President of Allegheny Wesleyan Methodist Connection, who initially requested me to submit a series of articles on sin, carnality and human infirmities, to be published in the *Allegheny Wesleyan Methodist.*

As the editors of other holiness periodicals became aware of those essays, they requested permission to use some of them in the *God's Revivalist,* IHC's *Convention Herald,* and in other denominational magazines as well. Several of those individuals began to urge me to publish them in a single volume. After months of delay and trying to convince myself that I did not have the time to be involved with publishing another book at this time, circumstances changed radically. In the early months of this year, Covid-19 entered our world. The net effect for me was evangelistic meetings, camp meetings and college classes were cancelled or their mode of delivery was changed to lecturing students in front of the camera in my home office. By mid-summer I had considerable time in which to initiate work on this book. In so doing several gifted individuals came to my assistance.

James Kunsulman, the office editor of the *Allegheny Wesleyan Methodist*, used his literary and editing skills to make my monthly submissions much more readable for the average reader. Once the book began to take shape, I shared each succeeding chapter with my friend, Stephen Mitchem, for his valuable input and corrections. Feeling the need for some help from an academic proofreader, I contacted Professor Elsa Lee who proved to be my harshest critic and to her I am grateful for her merciless critiques. My daughter, Professor Louisa Thomas, has a sharp eye for spotting clumsy wording and unclear writing; to her I offer special thanks. To the editor of Schmul Publishing Company, Curtis Hale, I wish to express special thanks for his direction and execution of bringing the volume to the readership of the holiness movement. Thanks to each of these persons for their advice and encouragement along the way.

Finally, I want to offer acknowledgement and thanksgiving for the prompting and leadership of the Holy Spirit in attempting to write on this topic. There were special moments when I sensed his help in choosing the right words to convey my thoughts to the reader.

All of the helpful input from those listed above does not absolve me of any weaknesses or inaccuracies of this work. Any errors or mistakes are the result of my own humanity. My only purpose in writing is to examine and explain many areas of misunderstanding and erroneous conceptions that students have developed in recent decades about this glorious doctrine of entire sanctification. If this book is helpful in that area, then to God be all the glory. To any who might disagree with me, be assured that I count you as my friend, and some day when we stand before God, all that we now see through a glass darkly will be made plain.

For My Wife

To my wife, Pearl Marlene, goes my deepest gratitude for her unfailing support. She is truly my companion and support through all of life's challenges; I could never make it without her. After fifty-five years together she probably knows me as well as I know myself. She lovingly shared from our time together while I wrote and now I will once again attempt to become a full time husband.

Foreword

WOULD YOU BE MORE LIKELY to trust advice from a shade tree mechanic or one who works day-in and day-out in the shop? How about advice on your health? Would you prefer to trust a relative or neighbor over someone with years of clinical experience?

The author has had years of "clinical" or "shop" experience in the spiritual world. He has pastored, ministered in camp meetings and revivals, and spent years interacting with students on the college and seminary level. Questions have arisen, spiritual impediments have begged for a solution, and every wind of doctrine has blown. In this labor of love, Dr. Kaufman has summarized many of the answers to each of the above.

The striking thing about this new book (just in time for the present distress) is that over and over it addresses spiritual issues "where the rubber meets the road." The author gently corrects misconceptions perhaps held by zealous believers. He stands like a rock for "the doctrine which is according to godliness." He gives practical advice to seekers.

Does God wish to finish the work of sanctification that he initiated in the new birth? Does the obedient, believing soul encounter new light from God's Word as he grows in grace? Is his capacity for God and holiness enlarged, perhaps in time of trial? Does he come to the realization that love cannot completely fill his soul while there remains "self filling" attitudes and motives that, to his great frustration, increasingly become apparent in involuntary reactions?

While this baby believer certainly surrendered to the Lordship of Christ in the new birth, is it possible that he could later become aware of soul areas that require further consecration? While the sinful nature was nailed to the cross in regeneration, has it finally expired in actual experience? Have faith and consecration intersected to produce full reliance on the blood of Christ and the Holy Spirit for victorious daily application of the two great commandments?

New Christians will avoid many a pitfall by reading this book. Seasoned laborers will be much better prepared to lead disciples on to Biblical Christian perfection. All will be enriched by lessons springing from a thorough knowledge of Biblical and historical literature including the original languages.

—Stephen Mitchem
Pastor, Missionary Secretary
Faith Missionary Organization

Introduction

BOOKS AND SERMONS ON THE SUBJECT of Christian perfection or entire sanctification are numbered in the thousands. All major Christian denominations use such terms in their articles of religion, church manuals or confessions of faith. No priest or minister would be ordained without demonstrating a passing knowledge of these concepts. Most religious articles, books and sermons routinely make use of these terms. The average layperson hears them mentioned from the pulpit with great regularity.

But what do these words actually mean? I have found in the classroom, both when I was a student and later, as a professor, these terms have vastly different meanings to various faiths and denominations. For several decades I have taught courses on theology in general and the theology of holiness, in particular. In order to get some understanding of my new students' knowledge of these terms, I have a little routine that I follow. On the first day of class, after I have presented the basics of the course, I ask students to list five sins that they may have committed. Next they are to list five carnal traits that are manifested in unsanctified people, and lastly they are to list five temptations to which they may have been subjected. After giving them several minutes to think and to write, I collect their responses. When the class has ended I retreat to my office to analyze the students' familiarity with these religious terms.

Year after year the results, without fail, constitute for me a major disappointment. Students who have been reared in holiness churches, attended holiness academies, or home-schooled in Christian families, reveal a total confusion as to what constitutes a sin, a carnal trait or a temptation. This little exercise has proven to be quite dismaying for me. The same scenario repeats with every new group of students. Their weak understanding of these critical topics indicates how poorly our teachers and pastors have instructed our youth in these crucial matters. When our own people manifest such limited understanding of these, it is little wonder that those outside our circles lack knowledge of these basic biblical truths.

Another prominent misunderstanding is the erroneous idea that somehow John Wesley invented the teachings of Christian perfection. Nothing could be further from the truth. Wesley, in his eighteenth-century Anglican setting, read and analyzed the preceding Church Fathers of both the Western and Eastern (Catholic and Orthodox) Church Fathers, Luther, Calvin, Pietists and the Moravians. From those forerunners, he subsequently molded his teachings into the Methodist doctrine that swept across England and within another century had spread around the world. From the mid-eighteenth century until the present, Wesley's theology has influenced seekers after heart purity that is taught and preached by the holiness movement of our day. In later chapters we will examine Wesley, his heritage, his teachings and his theological methodology.

The Purpose of This Book

Since most new college students reveal a pronounced weakness in many facets of the topic of Christian perfection, it is my intention to address and correct many of these misunderstandings. In recent years I have been approached by the editors of denominational and other religious periodicals, to contribute articles for their readership — especially articles that focus on matters that pertain to entire sanctification. As those writings began to circulate and appear in other magazines, a number of church leaders urged me to publish them under one cover. Feeling clear to accommodate those requests, I have attempted to organize those into a manuscript that might appeal to a diverse readership across our movement. In each of the following chapters I have expanded the original material, added illustrations, and in general, attempted to organize the various themes into a book that will aid students and newer converts in their walk with the Lord.

This volume is not necessarily arranged in the sequence of salvation, what scholars term *ordo salutis* (the order of salvation), from the sinner's awakening to his ultimate glorification. It is more of a collection of essays organized around topics that frequently arise in the classroom as we study the doctrine of holiness.

Since most of this material originated in the college and seminary classroom, I apologize if some of the words in the text are new to non-academic readers. For those difficult words and theological concepts, I will attempt to provide enough explanation or illustrations to make the topic understandable — and most of all, helpful.

Overview of the Chapters

Chapter one comprises an historical overview of the various streams of religious teachings that shaped the theology of Wesley, i.e., the ancient Church Fathers, both

East and West, the main writers in the imperial church of the Middle Ages, Martin Luther, John Calvin, James Arminius, Philip Spener, Madame Guyon, the Moravians and others. The chapter will also present a discussion of two methodological approaches with which we may understand exactly what the Bible teaches about entire sanctification, i.e., biblical theology or systematic theology.

In chapter two we begin with a discussion of some of the erroneous views of sin that are circulating in contemporary preaching and teaching. This will include some very non-biblical ideas that students hear from popular radio preachers. Others are exposed to false teaching in commentaries and in footnotes of many popular study Bibles. Since so many of the better-known works in circulation present Calvinist theology, our students and laity are constantly exposed to non-Wesleyan-Arminian interpretations. Thus, when they appear in the classroom, their theology is thoroughly confused.

Chapter three focuses on "sins of ignorance" that appear within the Mosaic covenant which raises the issue of the possibility of sinning without being aware of it. This chapter concludes with a discussion of the cities of refuge. The penalties of the manslayer serve to illustrate the consequences of mistakes, mishaps and other unintentional events, in anticipation of the covenant of grace in the New Testament.

Chapter four deals with the process of ethical decision-making and the reader is introduced to teleological and deontological methods employed by philosophical scholars. Once these rather daunting terms are explained, we can then more easily understand how our ethical choices along the pathway of life will determine whether or not we are walking in the light and truly living above sin.

Chapters five and six discuss the differences between the two works of grace and introduce the topic of the "old man" and the ever-present carnal traits that beset the new Christian. We will examine the carnal believers at the church of Corinth and discover Paul's instructions for how to deal with the heart of flesh. In these chapters we will discuss some of the more common carnal traits of the unsanctified and provide some instruction and illustrations to help the readers deal with them.

Chapter seven focuses on Paul's first epistle to the Thessalonians as one of the clearest biblical examples of the two steps involved in the process of entire sanctification. The balance of the chapter examines several types of two works of grace taken from the wilderness wanderings, crossing into Canaan and other similar scriptural examples.

Chapter eight examines the life of the patriarch Jacob to learn of his deceptive nature and his shrewd methods of getting his own way through life, until God finally unmasks him and brings about Jacob's own defeat at the Brook Jabbok. Here we see the man who wrestled with God and in his own defeat, found victory. This entire saga became the focus of Charles Wesley's epic hymn, "Come, O Thou Traveler Unknown," or better known by singing Methodists as "Wrestling Jacob."

Chapters nine and ten deal with more carnal traits, e.g., impatience, prejudging others and a variety of temptations that are common in the unsanctified, and can also be a problem in ascertaining whether or not the sanctified might be guilty of such.

Chapter eleven deals with how competition and legitimate feelings of accomplishment and satisfaction with a job well done might affect one's walk with the Lord and, possibly, his influence with others. Is there a place for any type of boasting in the life of the entirely sanctified?

Chapter twelve is a biblical survey of references to the various "fillings" of the Holy Spirit that appear in both the Old and New Testaments. Students find it confusing when Scripture speak of Samson, living centuries before the Spirit was poured out at Pentecost, yet was filled with the Spirit while he obviously was not living a sanctified life. Drawing on earlier work by Daniel Steele and Delbert Rose, we will develop three different kinds of fillings by the Spirit in Scripture.

Chapter thirteen introduces the students to the various degrees of perfection found throughout Scripture, i.e., Noah and Job were "perfect," Abraham was commanded to "walk before Yahweh and be perfect," and yet these men had never heard of Christian perfection. Drawing from John Fletcher's "Last Check to Antinomianism," we introduce the student to his contributions to the discussion of entire sanctification, and to his concepts of "dispensations."

Chapter fourteen focuses on emotions and feelings that many people think must accompany a work and a walk of holiness. Here the discussion picks up the "prophesyings" by various individuals: godly men, would-be murderers and false prophets of Baal. The work of secular psychiatrists such of Dr. William Sargant reveals the powerful role that emotions play in the lives of people. His findings provide food for thought for how we might respond to stress of mental pressure. This chapter will enable students to understand the critical role that emotions can play in one's spiritual life — even to the extent of bringing about a defeat in the life of the believer.

Chapter fifteen continues the discussion of how carnal traits express themselves, and exposes tactics Satan utilizes in an attempt to keep believers off balance and unsure of their walk with God. Several illustrations from the lives of sanctified leaders will aid students to learn how to maintain a pure walk with the Lord.

Chapter sixteen develops how the road to maturity leads the believer to become "others oriented." In so doing he learns that witnessing reflects his interest in others while it deepens his own walk with the Lord.

Chapter seventeen continues to develop the process of entire sanctification and provides some illustrations of how walking in harmony with the Spirit will not only enable us to live triumphantly, but will lead us as we interact and witness to those around us.

Chapter eighteen is a compendium of misconceptions about entire sanctification that are circulating within the holiness movement— what perfect love will and will not do for the believer, how to walk in the Spirit, how to detect when something seems amiss in the everyday routine of life and other helps for those seeking to be spiritual. This section also shows the pitfall of the teaching "holiness or hell," whether the Holy Spirit dwells in the unsanctified believer, the dangers of procrastination when seeking sanctification, and other similar issues.

Chapter nineteen seeks to clarify many of the erroneous ideas of what actually did transpire in the Upper Room at Pentecost. Since Acts chapter two does not speak about cleansing or purifying the hearts of those present, how can we understand Pentecost as a time of purifying of the heart? The events at Samaria, the house of Cornelius, the experience of the disciples of John at Ephesus, and the conversion of Paul, will be analyzed and discussed.

In the final chapter, we will provide some counsel with specific directions on how the child of God should earnestly seek and find this wonderful deliverance from the carnal mind.

1
Perfection and Sanctification in Early Church Writers

WESLEY DISCOVERED THAT BY the time the New Testament books had been written and the last of the apostles had died, the doctrines of perfection and entire sanctification had been firmly established within the Church. From their writings, men such as Irenaeus, Origen, Macarius and others added their witness to these twin concepts of holiness.

Irenaeus wrote that the believer is subsequently transformed in his essential character, as the Holy Spirit's purpose is to "fit us for God." He insisted that this perfection of heart was not completed when one was converted or baptized, nor was it imputed, but actually imparted after one had been saved. He emphasized that there was a perfection that awaited the believer in this life.

Origen of Alexandria, who was martyred in A.D. 254, viewed sanctification as being given to the believer *in a moment* distinct from the time of justification.

Macarius, the Egyptian monk, recognized that all sin could be washed away, and subsequent to that, a person could be made perfect in the "span of an hour." He also stressed the two-fold nature of entire sanctification as both an act and a process, and went on to point out the difference between purity and maturity, a matter that preachers today often fail to teach to their congregations.

Somehow Perfection and Sanctification became Separated

No one in these early years of Church history challenged the idea that Christian perfection was the norm for God's servants or that entire sanctification was the entrance into it. Unfortunately, these two aspects of the same work of grace began to be separated as the centuries rolled on. Perfection began to be viewed as something that was somehow expected of the saved person, but it tended to evolve into more of an ideal that was somehow imputed to all the redeemed. In addition to that shift away from the teaching of Scripture, entire sanctification was viewed as a glorious event that essentially only happened to very saintly individuals. With the rise of monasticism, such sanctification could only be found in the monasteries, in the lives of those who had virtually dropped out of society and taken vows of chastity and poverty.

Thankfully, God always seems to have a remnant of genuine believers, and within their writings we can find evidence of some of these in earlier centuries, e.g. Gregory of Nyssa, a sainted leader in the Eastern Orthodox Church and, again, Macarius, the Egyptian monk. These men experienced Christian perfection as that perfection of love that God has provided for His children through the process and crises of entire sanctification. Unfortunately, they tended to be viewed as far outside the norm of the Church. When Thomas Aquinas, the thirteenth century theologian of the Catholic Church, wrote on these twin doctrines, he appears to have grasped what the New Testament writers meant, but while he understood the concept of perfection and sanctification, he taught that they only occur through the sacraments of the Church—communion, baptism, confirmation, etc. And so the beauty of what Christ purchased for His Church was essentially hidden away for a few more centuries.

Perfection in the Reformation Era until Wesley

Luther and Calvin, in their quest to refute the erroneous theology of Catholic teachings, both tackled the topic of holiness, but ended up teaching that whatever perfection there was for the justified believers, it would have to await death. Sanctification, they both taught, was imputed to the believer at salvation, but did not actually produce any kind of actual change in one's daily life. For them, we continue to sin every day, while we are actually justified. Not surprisingly, the results of these teachings became evident in the churches those two men formed.

While the light of holiness was still burning, it had unfortunately been buried under the bushel of incorrect teachings. One century after the birth of Lutheranism, its worship services in Germany had become quite formal, sterile, and unable to produce real change in the lives of its adherents. Fortunately, God's hand was on a serious youthful German named Philip Spener. This ardent believer was confident that God could do more for His children than was evidenced in the typical Protestant churches of Germany. In his quest for true spirituality, he gave birth to Pietism (ca. 1675), a movement that developed within Lutheranism that had grown as stagnant and formal as the Catholic Church from which Luther had fled almost a century earlier. God used Spener to initiate Bible studies among sincere seekers. These spiritual exercises led to true seeking after God and genuine conversions. The Pietists found themselves to be closely aligned with a similar group of adherents of the teachings of John Huss, who had been martyred in 1415.

These earnest souls, eventually known as Moravians, gathered together in Bohemia at Herrnhut, on the estate of Count Zinzendorf. John Wesley had not only become a close student of the early Eastern Church Fathers, he also discovered the writings and teachings of these Pietists and Moravians while at Oxford and as a missionary to Georgia in the 1730s. Those writers significantly impacted Wesley's thinking theologically and somewhat influenced his organizing of the Methodists.[1]

Wesley's Discoveries and His Synthesis of Historical Writers

Wesley, an Anglican priest-missionary, who by his own testimony had not been converted during his years at Oxford, began reading the writings of the Eastern Church Fathers. His spiritual quest led him to the writings of Thomas Aquinas, and also to the memoirs of Madame Guyon, a Catholic mystic who appears to have experienced entire sanctification. God graciously led him to discover the New Testament concept that had always been there—perfection of love, e.g., the ability to love God with all of one's heart, soul, mind, and strength, and one's neighbor as oneself. He was convinced that this perfection of the heart occurred at the moment of entire sanctification. As one scholar of Wesley put it, "Right here Wesley rose to mountain heights." So claimed the late George Croft Cell of Boston University. "He restored the neglected doctrine of holiness to its merited position in the Protestant understanding of Christianity."[2]

With that discovery, Wesley set about to reform the Anglican Church and to save a world that he claimed as "his parish." His efforts at reform within his native church met with closed doors; the bishops were not interested in

---

1. Luke L. Keefer, Jr., *John Wesley: Disciple of Early Christianity*, Wesleyan Theological Journal 19: 1, 1984: 23-32.

2. George Croft Cell, *The Rediscovery of John Wesley* (New York: Henry Holt and Co., 1935), 359.

his holiness-of-heart message. So, following the lead of George Whitefield, Wesley resorted to "field preaching," that is, proclaiming the message out of doors, wherever a crowd would listen. While France almost self-destructed in revolution, England was spared massive civil unrest and instead experienced a great move of God, as Wesley and his itinerant preachers blanketed the British Isles with the message of heart purity. As the Wesleyan Revival flourished, it expanded to the shores of America.

Christian Perfection in the Second Great Awakening

At the close of the American Revolutionary War, the Methodist Episcopal Church was organized in Baltimore in 1784, with only a few dozen preachers and was ultimately led by one bishop, Francis Asbury. Taking nothing more in their saddlebags than a Bible, a set of Wesley's sermons, and a collection of Charles Wesley's hymns, these courageous souls set off to win the new continent to a Savior who longed to implant His perfect love in the nation's heart. God so blessed their efforts that from a small band, the Methodists grew to over one million members by 1844. A frequently heard comment on a wintry night became well known, "Well, the weather's so bad tonight, the only thing out are crows and Methodist preachers!"

Unfortunately, from such a lofty position in the eyes of the nation, the Methodist Episcopal Church began to become a dignified, middle class, formal institution with its settled pastors (rather than traveling circuit riders), handsome pipe organs, trained choirs, and sermons devoid of much focus on holiness of heart— and it paid an enormous price. As it began to waver in its commitment to the message of heart holiness, it lost interest in reaching out to the unsaved with the same fervor of its founders. With the advent of abolitionism, secret societies, and a host of other social reforms, the bishops increasingly turned against some of its most passionate and articulate preachers and forced them either to tone down their message or leave. By 1843 the Wesleyan Methodists organized and in 1860 were followed by the Free Methodists. By contrast, in 1844, the Methodist Episcopal Church split into two denominations, one in the South and the other in the North. They have never recovered the spiritual vitality of their founders and serve only as an example of what happens when their clergy and leaders forsake the true message of heart holiness.

So, did the holiness message begin with Wesley? History reveals that there was a broad stream of writers who led to Wesley's theology. Reading and adapting some of the main ideas of those earlier saints enabled him to forge a doctrine that has stood the test of time. And for those who ask sarcastically about Wesley's legacy, a famous response from earlier days answers it quite well: "John Wesley… so what did he do? Well, when he died he left behind a well-worn preacher's gown, twenty pounds sterling (about a year's salary for an Anglican rector), and, oh yes, the Methodist Church."

Holiness since the Second Great Awakening

Students of Church history are nearly unanimous in their agreement that the overarching theology of the First Great Awakening (1720s-1740s), was Reformed theology, e.g., classical Calvinism that promulgated the teachings of the Westminster Confession of Faith. That famous theological framework basically outlines what students know as TULIP. That acronym aids in identifying the five points of Calvinism: T stands for total depravity (every person is born in sin and under the guilt of Adam's sin); U is for unconditional election (God in his sovereignty has selected those going to heaven and leaving the rest to go to hell); L represents limited atonement (Christ died only for those whom he had elected to salvation); I for irresistible grace (those who are elected cannot refuse salvation); and P for perseverance of the saints (the elect are eternally secure and cannot lose their salvation, even though they sin every day in word, thought and deed). Leaders of the First Great Awakening taught, preached and defended this doctrine, e.g., George Whitefield, Jonathan Edwards and other evangelists and pastors. This was the doctrine of the Church of England, under whose auspices John and Charles Wesley were reared and trained. By contrast, it was the Wesleyan-Arminian doctrines of John Wesley that drove the Second Great Awakening.

With the growth and powerful preaching, the Methodist Episcopal Church outgrew its rival denominations and practically became the national church, its influence permeating the developing nation. With its message of free salvation to all, under the powerful influence of Francis Asbury and a host of Methodist circuit riders and class leaders, the doctrines of John Wesley became the overarching theology of the Second Great Awakening. Beginning with the camp meetings of 1801 (Cane Ridge, Kentucky), its doctrines shaped the nation's religious awakening, drawing in Calvinistic preachers like Charles G. Finney, who was raised in a Congregational home (Calvinism), and ordained in the Presbyterian Church (Calvinistic). With the mighty revivals of the first half of the nineteenth century, the message of holiness spread across the nation.

The history of evangelical religion in the middle and later years of the nineteenth century is mainly the history of revivals and camp meetings whose main reason for existence was the promulgation of the doctrine of holiness. Wave after wave of spiritual refreshing continued to wash across the religious landscape during and after the Civil War. Sometimes the revival focus centered in larger cities, e.g., the Urban Revival of 1857; at other times it was the ever-popular rural camp meeting. In both of these instances, every major denomination was well represented. As the end of the century approached, several streams took shape. Most mainline denominations, e.g., Methodist Episcopal, Presbyterian, Congregational, et al, settled for a formal, more liturgical worship style that employed trained choirs, expensive pipe organs and beautiful houses of worship, but sadly, were significantly influenced by liberalism, evolution, deism and the social gospel. By the middle of the twentieth century, factions in these groups had either joined forces with liberal churches or were forced out and evolved into fundamentalism, dispensationalism and evangelicalism.

Holiness and "Come Outers" in the Twentieth Century

On the other hand, "come outer" groups that flowed out of the National Camp Meeting Association firmed up their adherence to the doctrine of Christian perfection while rejecting the emphasis on healing and speaking in tongues that had created problems in several of the new denominations. The Church of the Nazarene and its theologians tended to set the pace in authoring the most influential works on holiness, followed closely by Wesleyan Methodists, Free Methodists and others of similar emphases. An entire literature of classical writings by men such as J. A. Wood, Beverly Carradine, A. M. Hills, H. Orton Wiley, became the core of denominational courses of study and the backbone of most libraries on Wesley's theology. By the mid-twentieth century, Richard S. Taylor and W. T. Purkiser had gained respect as the most astute and accurate interpreters of Wesley's core teachings. Avoiding some of the more extreme and bizarre ideas that had surfaced in various fringe groups, these theologians presented a balanced view of Christian perfection— a presentation that produced the men who have brought the holiness movement to its present form.

Unfortunately, our movement has been influenced by

some scholars who no longer view the deliverance from the carnal heart as biblical; and, even further, they have introduced the idea that sins of ignorance are common in the life of the believer— to the extent that the average new convert cannot be sure if he is living above sin or not. These ideas, of course, reflect the subtle influence of Calvinistic teachings and have caused no end of confusion among our laity, college students and young pastors. Such ideas come from well-meaning professors, but the results are no less deadly. One simply cannot spend years in colleges and seminaries taught by Reformed theologians without being influenced in their theology.

All too frequently I have spoken in a camp meeting or revival on the topic of sin or Christian perfection, only to have a parent or pastor approach me after the message with these words: "The way you just preached that message is the way we were taught when I was in Bible college, but my son or daughter attends a holiness college now, and that's not what is being taught today." What they are saying to me is the cause of the confusion of my students. That accounts partly for their responses to my questions on the first day of class for examples of sin, carnal traits and temptations.

It is my hope that this volume will deal with these and other issues that Satan uses to keep honest seekers in confusion. Like most college professors, I enjoy theoretical discussions in the college and seminary classroom, but in these chapters, my aim is to be a spiritual practitioner, not a theoretician. I wish to assure any reader who might disagree with my theology that the disagreements that he may discover herein are not directed against persons but against doctrines. I trust he senses that he is reading the words, not of an enemy but of a friend and a Christian brother, who writes with a heart full of love, and with a prayer that his words may be both enlightening and helpful.

Biblical Theology or Systematic Theology: Wesley's Method of Arriving at His Theology

Perhaps it will prove helpful to provide the reader with a discussion relative to the methodology of various theologians who have written and are currently writing on theological topics— the matter of whether the writer's approach to truth is biblical or systematic. At first these terms seem overly academic and students wonder why they are even discussed. Every student of Church history understands that the watchword of the Protestant Reformation Era was the Latin term, *Sola Scriptura,* by which the reformers meant that they were turning away from the works-oriented teachings of the medieval Catholic Church. Their intent was to follow Scripture alone; they had had enough of the powerful bishops and popes telling them what was needed to make heaven— just follow the instructions of the Church. In our day we have all heard *sola scriptura* statements from the pulpit in which the speaker states, "Bless God, it says it right here in God's Word and that settles it!"

While such statements have a very righteous and noble ring to them, and may sound quite convincing, the fact of the matter is that the speaker might have taken his thoughts out of the context of his Scripture, and even worse, might have reached his ideas of the passage based upon his own life's experience— be it good or bad. Among scholars today there is the more sophisticated sounding approach used by contemporary college professors who are quite adept at reading Greek and Hebrew, and when they exegete the passage, they will cite no end of possible meanings of biblical words, coupled with grammar tenses, conjunctions, moods and no end of Greek or Hebrew nuances. When they are done consulting a host of grammars, lexicons and analytical tools, the fact is, they can make the text say whatever they need it to say, almost daring anyone to disagree with them.

Potential Weaknesses of Biblical Theology

One of the main problems with that approach is that almost all current theological wordbooks, lexicons and linguistic grammars, have been written by highly trained Calvinists who adhere to the tenets of the Westminster Confession of Faith (Calvinist touchstone of doctrine — see above), so any insights such authors bring to the discussion will conform to their own theological biases. Having taught Greek and Hebrew for almost forty years, I feel compelled to warn my students about the most popular reference books in our libraries. This is not the place, but I could cite many instances in which a Calvinistic commentator has broken basic rules of grammar to force a passage to mean what he needs it to mean, just to bring it into alignment with his own beliefs. Such methods are intellectually dishonest, but his well-meaning, albeit unscrupulous tactics, have deadly effect on the unlettered readers.

Nothing I have stated in the above paragraph should diminish at all our instructing students on developing the necessary tools of the ancient languages as we seek to understand the meaning of any biblical text. This word of caution, however, I feel is absolutely necessary: With adopting the biblical theology methodology, one limits his analysis to only the text and being at the mercy of Calvinistic lexicographers and commentators. He develops into what I term, "every man, his own theologian" — and that can lead to disastrous teaching. The founder of every major cult or incorrect teaching in our world today began with some Bible texts that they chose to interpret to suit themselves, e.g., Mormonism, *glossolalia* (tongues speaking), Christian Science, and a host of other religious isms.

Wesley's Quadrilateral

If biblical theology runs the risk of producing an "armchair theologian," the student may ask, what is the other option for doing one's studies of the Scriptures? The far superior, and much more safe approach, is what Wesley tended to employ and it is known in college and seminary as systematic theology. Such an approach will safeguard students and scholars alike from drawing erroneous conclusions and teachings from biblical passages.

While Wesley himself did not use the term, students of Wesley today are introduced to his method of uncovering the meaning of any given Scripture. It has come to us as the "Wesleyan Quadrilateral." As scholars analyze Wesley's method for discovering truth, it appears that he utilized four different sources in reaching his theological conclusions. His method was first termed the Wesleyan Quadrilateral in 1964 by Albert Outler, a prominent Wesley scholar and Methodist theologian.

Outler observed that Wesley began with a thorough examination of the biblical text, applying his scholarly mind with the Greek or Hebrew tools needed to fully grasp the words that have come down to us from the sacred writer.

Secondly, he surveyed Church history to observe what the ancient fathers had written upon that particular text or topic. Along with that he took into account all of the creeds and rulings of the various Church councils, the writings of Reformation scholars and those scholars living and writing in his day.

Thirdly, Wesley applied the test of reason to his understanding of the text. Was his interpretation rational? Did it make sense in light of other Scripture and common sense, and such like?

Lastly, he used close observation and the test of human experience to determine whether his general conclusions of the biblical passage would pass the test of human experience. To accomplish that he would visit his Methodist bands, classes and societies across England to observe how such teachings were impacting his followers. Did his biblical conclusions actually work in the real world of humankind?

Once he was convinced of the meaning of the Scripture and had applied his four areas of practical analysis, he would write and preach on the subject with divine assurance that he had correctly discerned truth. Employing those steps, he assured himself that he had not fallen into some error as a result of his own subjectivism and limited insights. Using such methodology enabled him to avoid the mistakes of individuals who confine their analysis only to the biblical text.

Before leaving this section it needs to be stressed that while professional scholars do not classify Wesley as a systematic theologian in the proper usage of the term, in his vast writings, he certainly covered every topic that surfaces in the study of theology.

When Did Wesley Expect People to be Made Perfect in Love?

One classic example of Wesley's methodology can be seen when it came to the timing of the believer's reception of entire sanctification or Christian perfection, the term he preferred. Early in his own experience and ministry Wesley held to the idea that one could not be made perfect in love until late in life — near the hour of death. He taught that idea in the earlier years of his ministry. We refer to him during those years as the "pessimistic Wesley." He could not grasp a person being made perfect in love unless he sought for the blessing for half a lifetime or more.

As time went on, however, he shifted in his thinking. He visited numerous Methodist societies and listened to the clear testimonies of members who had found perfect love within days, weeks or months of their conversion. That discovery led him to the conclusion that believers need not expend a lifetime of seeking Christian perfection. As he stated on numerous occasions, "since it is by faith why not now?"[3] With that new understanding, we now see the "optimistic Wesley." Thus we observe how the application of his Quadrilateral can enable one to more accurately understand a biblical concept while avoiding the danger of being overly subjective in his theological understanding.

Wesley's methods, we feel, cannot be improved upon. While many scholars do not tend to classify him as a systematic theologian, the methodology he employed kept him from falling into the error of reaching his own conclusions without consulting earlier theologians and teachers of the Church. Scholars who insist on a pure biblical theology should learn from Wesley's method. His approach has stood the test of time; it has influenced generations of Methodists who will have all eternity to thank him for his methodical, faithfulness to the Word of God.

Chapter Summary

1. The Scriptural truth of entire sanctification and Christian perfection occupied a prominent place in the writings of the Church Fathers, especially the fact that it was a second definite act that took place after one was justified.
2. Unfortunately, several of these early writers began to separate entire sanctification from Christian perfection to the point that only monks in the monastery could achieve perfection.
3. Thomas Aquinas, the official theologian of the Catholic religion, taught that infant baptism was one's justification and confirmation was tied to sanctification.

---

3. Taken from *The Works of John Wesley*. Thomas Jackson, ed. Third edition. 14 vols. Letter #373, 12:362. Reprint 1959. Used by permission of Zondervan. www.zondervan.com.

Thus, one's salvation depended upon, and was controlled exclusively by, the Church.
4. Luther and Calvin both taught a sinning religion that viewed perfection as a goal that was always in the future and not really attainable in this life.
5. Dissatisfaction with the formal worship of Lutheranism led Philip Spener in a return to New Testament concepts of evangelical salvation. His quest led to the formation of Pietism and a group who eventually linked with the Moravians. It was their influence that significantly shaped Wesley beliefs.
6. In Wesley the twin concepts of entire sanctification and Christian perfection were restored to their New Testament teaching.
7. Methodism began to spread in America during and after the Revolutionary War and by 1844 it had grown to one million members.
8. During and subsequent to the Civil War, the holiness message passed from Methodism to the National Camp Meeting Association that subsequently led to the rise of the holiness movement.
9. Wesley's Quadrilateral reflects the superiority of systematic theology over a biblical theology approach. Its advantage is that it is shaped by the orthodoxy of theologians through the centuries, rather than just the ideas of one man.

2
A Correct Understanding of Sin is Vital

WRITING ON SIN, CARNALITY AND human infirmity can prove to be both challenging and controversial. Various ideas and definitions of such a topic have given rise to a host of strange teachings, the result of which has left many believers in confusion, and many well-meaning believers frustrated in their attempts to live a victorious life in Christ. A proper, biblical definition of sin is so important. Students have friends who speak of sinning every day in word, thought and deed. They seem to be nice people and claim to love the Lord, so they wonder what is the problem. Why is a correct understanding of what sin actually is, so important? Richard Taylor's comment sums up the matter quite well.

> The doctrines relating to sin form the center around which we build our entire theological system... And as Christians, if our conception of sin is faulty, our whole superstructure will be one error built on another, each one more absurd than the last, yet each one necessary if it is to fit in consistently with the

whole erroneous scheme. If we are to end right we must begin right...[1]

With his admonition in mind, let us discuss exactly what we mean when we speak of a sin.

As a newly minted Bible college graduate, I was unaware of the many confusing ideas permeating the holiness movement— at that time everything appeared fairly simple and straightforward to me. Now, having served as a pastor, evangelist, and as a Bible college and seminary professor for four decades, I have observed the confusion of both preachers and laymen on these matters. If we are to be delivered from the power and guilt of sin, if we are to live successfully and, even more importantly, if we are to be free of a carnal heart, then it is essential that we speak clearly of these concepts, using terms and definitions that the new convert can understand.

So What is a Sin?

Let us begin with a working definition of sin— what it is and what it is not. Recently, I was conversing with a church leader on this issue and he defined sin to me: "Sin is anything that brings separation from God." While such a statement is certainly true, it really does nothing to define sin; it merely asserts the result of a sin. To illustrate my point from agriculture, a farmer might define locusts or drought as "anything that produces a crop failure." That is no more of a definition of locusts or drought, than my friend's assertion that sin brings separation from God— and certainly provides no help for the inquiring new convert. For anyone who is seeking deliverance from sin, it is essential to know which actions have produced his separated state from God. Otherwise, how will he know what he must do and not do if he is to serve the Lord?

---

1. Richard S. Taylor, *A Right Conception of Sin*, (Nicholasville, KY: Schmul Publishing Co., 2002), 12.

So the unanswered question remains, how can I know if I am living above sin or not? When Satan accuses me of sin, how can I know that he is merely intimidating and falsely accusing me? I must have a means to test my actions, and that is imperative, or else the accuser of the brethren will paralyze me in a life of confusion— just where he wants me. Additionally, if I am to testify to living above sin, how can I know that I am being truthful and accurate? It is essential to have a working definition of sin or else one must live without confidence. To be wrong in this area will directly affect my understanding of the carnal heart. That being the case, let us turn to James 4:17 and consider, "Therefore to him that knoweth to do good, and doeth it not, to him it is sin."

James here is informing his reader that two criteria come into play in this matter of sin. The person must know that something is right or wrong, and when that is clear to him, he must engage his volition (his will) and make the moral choice— to do it, or not to do it. According to Wesley, actions which are contrary to God's perfect will, but of which we are ignorant, are covered by the blood until such a time as we become aware of them. Notice, it is impossible to sin and suffer guilt in the soul unless the will has been involved. Keep in mind, this concept becomes enormously important when we later discuss carnal traits.

Faced with a moral choice, the new convert asks the critical question: how do I know which choice is morally correct? He desires to make the right choice, and is determined to do so— once he determines which choice will please God. Remember what the Epistle of John states: "If we walk in the light as he is in the light, we have fellowship, one with another, and the blood of Jesus Christ, his Son, cleanseth us from all sin" (I John 1:7). What is this "light" in which I am obligated to walk if I wish to retain fellowship with the Lord?

What is this thing that will enable me to know what is morally right or wrong when confronted with a moral choice? Let me suggest an answer.

What is Light?

Years ago in my ministry, I adopted a definition for "light" and ever since I have shared it wherever I go. "Light is God's opinion on any matter." Of course! That is what every Christian needs to know when making moral choices— God's opinion. Since James 4:17 implies that one needs to know to do good (or, negatively, what not to do), then he must get God's opinion on the pending choice. The question immediately arises from the new convert: where do I get God's opinion or "light."

What is Our Source of Spiritual Light?

Most of the believer's light comes directly from God's Word. "The entrance of thy words giveth light" (Psalm 119:130). The vast majority of your light will come directly from Scripture. And it goes without saying that God will never give you a differing opinion on a matter that he has already stated in the Word.

Here is a second source for God's opinion. John writes that "He is the true Light which lighteth every man coming into the world" (John1:9). The Evangelist here informs us that Christ has placed in every person a light, which tends to instruct him on moral matters as to what is right and what is wrong. We call that inherent light, the conscience. This moral indicator, along with the written Word of God, will give very accurate direction in moral decision-making. That is why we must master Scripture, since we derive our "light" from it— and why we must follow our conscience so it will remain reliable. Not following one's conscience will lead to a hardening process that results in an unreliable conscience.

Light May Come as a Personal Conviction

In addition to the two sources of light given above, i.e., directly from God's Word and from the conscience, we receive God's clear direction on certain matters for which there may not be any clear teaching in Scripture. In those cases, that light applies only to the one to whom the Spirit gave it. In those instances we refer to what is commonly known as a personal conviction. Such light applies only to the one to whom it was given and should not be used as a standard to judge others. Personal convictions have unfortunately led to much erroneous teaching and confusion— especially among sensitive souls who get misled by well-meaning preachers and other Christian leaders. Let us consider an example from my own life.

In the early 1970s, just as I was enrolling in Bible college to begin studying for the ministry, we learned that a new Sea World was coming to northeastern Ohio. The local newspaper kept our community informed as to the progress on this multi-million dollar enterprise. For months, many of us waited eagerly for the new attraction to open. Finally the grand opening arrived and my wife and I made our first visit to see all the water shows that it featured. It was great! Each new season more attractions were added. Then came the summer when we visited and this time the new attraction involved speeding boats, water skiing by performers who sped across the waters, some flying with kites behind the boats. The show was labeled, "the Beach Party." In the background, worldly, popular music blared from loud pulsating speakers, and the young actors performed in the skimpiest of bikinis and swimming trunks.

While I was viewing all of this immodest dress and was being bombarded by the music, the Holy Spirit began to speak to me. In His faithfulness, He asked me if I were really enjoying all this worldly display. Then, bringing things a bit closer, He suggested that if Jesus were to return while we were watching this production, would I really want to be there when the Rapture took place? I looked at my wife rather uncomfortably; she returned my glance with a frown. Within a matter of minutes, in the middle of the show, I grabbed my daughter's hand and we got up and left.

At that moment, God gave me a personal conviction on attending Sea World. That venue was just no longer for me. The Spirit made that fact quite clear. To continue attending would constitute my walking against light the Spirit had given uniquely to me. Now I have many friends, students, and relatives, who attend various Sea Worlds that are spread across our country, but I have never gone back. You see, I have a personal conviction against it.

Let me share another illustration. In an altar service at the close of a great camp meeting service, I was praying with a young man whom I knew quite well. "Son," I asked him, "What brought you to the altar, this evening?"

Looking at me with tears flowing down his face, he answered, "It's my music." Here was an honest seeker who wanted to walk in the light and have victory, but apparently had been listening to music that did not meet with God's approval. As a result he was falling behind light (God's opinion on any matter), and now he was facing the matter. He determined at that altar to give up his country and western music, and to my knowledge, has lived without any guilt from failure to listen to God. It became a personal conviction with him, and he would be sinning to go against what the Spirit had shown him.

Actually, no greater joy can fill your heart as you sense the Spirit's leadership in your life. All that God requires of us is that we walk in the light, our light, and great satisfaction fills our hearts knowing that we are pleasing the Savior. Students learn that if they take the time and put forth the effort to know God's will, he rewards them for seeking his leadership. You can seek him for every area of life, e.g., you can stand in front of a mirror and ask the Spirit if he is pleased with your attire. You can look at your library and ask him if he is pleased with your reading. You can sit at your computer or device and seek His approval for what you look at.

Personal Convictions are Not to be Preached as Biblical Standards

Once the Holy Spirit gives you his opinion, you have received light, it becomes your responsibility to walk in that light. If you do so, he has promised that the blood of Jesus will cover you. What a precious place to dwell—under the blood! Thus personal convictions can be observed across the holiness movement. They may be pertaining to clothing, colors that are worn, whether or not to wear a neck tie, what color of neck tie, types of music, or a whole range of issues that surface in the lives of those who are living for the next world.

Unfortunately, much confusion has arisen in our holiness churches and camp meetings when preachers who have such personal convictions, step to the pulpit and preach their personal convictions as the Gospel to their people. Such actions have brought much turmoil into our church and ministers owe it to their hearers not to preach their personal notions and convictions as scripture.

To be sure, I have shared some of these and other similar personal accounts with students and congregations, but I make it clear that I am only illustrating how personal convictions work. I am not condemning anyone who might differ with me on such activities. It is absolutely essential to understand that just because God has dealt with you about such matters, those are for you alone. Of course, if you are a parent, you will very likely hold your children to your standard of behavior, but you dare not judge others who see things differently than you.

We will now consider the first sin in the history of the world to see what happens when we walk against light.

Eve Provides the Classic Example of an Act of Sin

Knowing we must have light on our intended choice, and knowing that we must engage our will and make a choice, we may now proceed with confidence as we seek to avoid sinning. It is helpful to consider the very first sin committed and test our definition for accuracy. When God placed Adam and Eve in the garden, he centrally located an object for testing— the Tree of Knowledge of Good and Evil. Eve, drawn to that tree, lingered and listened to the subtle voice of Satan, pondering that object of their probation.

Observing its pleasant appearance and innocently assuming that in some manner it would make her wise, she concluded the enticing fruit was good for food. Additionally, Satan suggested that partaking of it would not cause death— even worse, he intimated that God, in some manner, was withholding something wonderful from her. Until this point, Eve in the process of temptation could have walked away without sinning.[2]

When interacting with college students my methodology in the classroom is to seek students' opinions on when Eve actually sinned— at what precise point in the temptation process did she cross the line and incur guilt? I typically suggest to the class that perhaps as she reached toward the forbidden fruit, that might be when she sinned. Or, perhaps she actually sinned when her fingers make contact with the fruit. Possibly, she does not sin until she breaks the stem free from the branch and begins to move the fruit to her mouth. Or, she might not actually sin until she chews and swallows the fruit. It is

---

2. Note, it's no sin to be tempted; in fact, it might be an indication that your walk with God has caught Satan's attention and he desires to ruin your fellowship with the Lord. So don't feel badly just because you are tempted.

interesting to listen to students as they come to their various conclusions.

Surprisingly, they are quite diversified in their opinions. Every class has students who opt for each of the various possibilities. Do you know the point at which Eve actually sinned? It's the precise moment she gave the consent of her will to partake of the forbidden fruit. Before she ever moved a muscle to reach for it, she was already guilty in God's eyes! Of course every class has its doubting Thomas, so it is necessary to appeal to the verdict of Jesus to enable them to grasp the concept.

Christ's Teaching on Sin

When discussing the matter of adultery in his wonderful Sermon on the Mount, the Master said this: "I say unto you, that whosoever looketh on a woman to lust after her hath committed adultery with her already in his heart" (Matthew 5:28). What the Lord is saying is vitally important for our definition of sin. He pictures for his hearer the idea of a man who sees a woman (someone other than his wife) and as he looks upon her, his heart is tempted to lust after her. Such a temptation can easily develop in the mind of any man, but knowing that action would be morally wrong and would bring certain guilt, the man immediately dismisses the thought as displeasing to God (and to his conscience). But in Jesus' scenario, the man looks at the woman and in some manner gives the consent of his will to continue thinking thoughts that would lead to outright adultery — if the man could arrange such an event.

In other words, though he knows the deed would be reprehensible and morally wrong, he gives the consent of his will to the idea, though no other person has any idea of what has transpired in his mind. No one knows but he himself — and God! And God alone knows when the man gave the consent of his will to commit the act.

Similarly, when Eve gave the consent of her will to proceed with eating the forbidden fruit, at that juncture she committed sin. If the consent of the will is not given, no sin is committed. Dr. George Peck says, "...when the temptation gains the concurrence of the will, the subject contracts *guilt*. There can be no doubt here... It is equally clear that when the temptation begets in the mind a *desire* for the forbidden object, the subject *enters into temptation*, and so sins against God."[3] Perhaps it will serve us well to consider our spiritual founder's definition of sin.

Wesley's Definition of Sin

> Nothing is sin, strictly speaking, but a voluntary transgression of a known law of God. Therefore, every voluntary breach of the law is sin; and nothing else, if we speak properly. To strain the matter farther is only to make way for Calvinism. There may be ten thousand wandering thoughts, and forgetful intervals, without any breach of love, though not without transgressing the Adamic law. But Calvinists would fain confound these together. Let love fill your heart, and it is enough![4]

Armed with these biblical examples and Wesley's thoughts on sin, we now can arrive at a workable definition of sin. A sin is the result of any act or thought, known to be wrong from God's Word or any other source of light, to which a person gives the consent of his will. Or, we can reverse the negative to a positive and state that any act or thought, known to be right, to which a person refuses to consent, becomes sin. We call that a sin of omission; the former example constitutes a sin of commission.

---

3. Cited in J. A. Wood, *Perfect Love* (Nicholasville, KY: Schmul Publishing Co., 2008), 52.

4. From a letter to Mrs. Elizabeth Bennis, June 16, 1772, *Works of John Wesley*, Vol XII, (London: Wesleyan Methodist Book Room, London), 394.

Nothing then, can be properly termed a sin unless both light has been given and the will has been engaged. Otherwise, he was merely tempted to do wrong and will not be charged with sin. Thankfully, the Holy Spirit can and will enable believers to make moral choices correctly and thus, they can testify to a life free of sin and guilt. Our Savior came to earth to destroy the efforts of Satan to seduce God's children into sin, and by walking in the light ("God's opinion of any matter") believers can live above sin.

Chapter Summary

1. A correct, biblical understanding of sin is critical to establish a correct theology.
2. Any proper definition of sin must include knowledge of the correct moral choice, and must involve a choice of the will.
3. "Light" is "God's opinion on any matter" and without light one cannot be guilty of committing a sin.
4. Light comes from the Word, from one's conscience and from personal convictions.
5. Personal convictions that God has uniquely given to one person must not be preached as binding on others; to do so results in vast confusion within the holiness movement.
6. Eve's actions in the Garden illustrate that she knew God's will and deliberately chose to disregard His will and brought sin onto the human family.
7. Jesus taught that one can sin in the heart without any outward actions, e.g., looking at the forbidden object with lust constitutes the sin of adultery.

3
How Does God View Mistakes and Human Infirmities?

IN THE LAST chapter we learned that in order to commit a sin, one must have light ("God's opinion on any matter") and then he must engage his will and actually reach a decision to do or not to do the act. Walking in the light will enable the believer to maintain fellowship with the Lord. Calvinistic theologians, however, have developed a non-biblical definition of sin. They argue that any act that falls short of perfection constitutes a sin. For them, then, it is their lot in life "to sin every day, in word, thought and deed."

Surely, that error has led to no end of confusion for believers. Those who promulgate such thinking maintain that mistakes, imperfections, or any kind of infirmity that accompanies the human family, can only produce a sinning Christian.

What a confused way of interpreting Scripture! I John 3:8-9 states that "he that committeth sin is of the devil... whosoever is born of God, doth not commit sin." Thank God for salvation that can deliver one from a life of sin!

As a teenager happily serving Satan, I had an opportunity to visit a Baptist (Calvinistic) church. I listened to the preacher as he assured his hearers that a life of sin was all they could expect. As a rebellious youth, that was music to my ears! Wow, I could actually go on in my sin and still go to heaven! But in my heart of hearts, I had enough sense to know that was false teaching. It certainly didn't square with many verses that came to mind, even while I was listening to the preacher.

Recently as I listened to a Calvinistic preacher, I heard a new perspective on how they view sin. After assuring his radio listeners that everyone sins every day, he did provide what he hoped would be assurance that such people were indeed saved. His test for salvation was whether or not one felt badly whenever he sinned. In other words, if as you sinned you felt some uneasiness, then that was proof that you were indeed a believer. If you didn't feel badly, then you probably weren't saved. What a terrible, confused way to try to live a Christian life!

Is it a Mistake or a Sin?

Frequently the matter of mistakes, human error and infirmities cloud the discussion of sin. How are we to analyze deeds that appear quite serious and certainly fall short of we meant to do, but upon reflection they don't meet the criteria for sin. Students are amazed to learn that a believer can actually be guilty of committing a crime without incurring sin. How can that be possible? Perhaps, a personal illustration will be helpful.

FaceTime and Driving

One summer day I was driving to a camp meeting in another state. Traveling down the interstate, it occurred to me that my new smartphone had the capability of permitting me to actually view my wife on the phone as we conversed. Eager to try it out, I called home, gave her instructions on how to prepare the computer at our house to receive my call and presto! Within seconds my wife appeared on my phone, and she could see me as well. It was lovely! Modern technology amazes me! So carefully keeping the speed limit, I drove along enjoying a wonderful chat with my bride. About twenty minutes later, we ended the phone call.

The next day, happily sharing my phone adventure with others at the camp, they looked at me in disbelief and horror. "You did what?" they asked me incredulously. They went on to explain what the fine in that state is for using a cell phone while driving— not to mention FaceTiming my wife. I was completely taken by surprise. As I reflected on my phone call, it occurred to me that I was guilty of a crime in that state— but, interestingly, I was not guilty of a sin in God's sight. Yes, I had given the consent of my will to make the call, but I had no knowledge— or what Scripture would term "light"— that it was wrong. My conscience had not bothered me in the least as I talked with my wife, although I am sure my actions would have bothered a state patrolman.

That incident helps to illustrate our point. In order to sin one must have light and give the consent of the will. And for those who like to tease me— no, I did not make any more FaceTime calls while driving in that state.

Should Christians Pay Their Restaurant Tab?

Another illustration will be beneficial. We have a dear friend, a retired minister, who has a wonderful testimony of saving and sanctifying grace. One evening, he and some friends went out for an evening meal at a popular restaurant in a neighboring town. At the conclusion of the meal, he browsed for a while in the gift-shop area of the facility and then returned home. Preparing for bed that evening, he discovered, to his horror, the restaurant check still in his shirt pocket. He was stunned! How had he left the restaurant without paying? He had committed a crime. He immediately phoned the establishment, explained his absentmindedness, and promised to drive the money to them the next morning.

Now the question arises— did he commit a sin? Absolutely not! My Calvinist friends would declare that he had sinned; after all, walking out of a restaurant without paying does fall short of perfection. But my friend had no motive to cheat the restaurant; he merely forgot to pay. Yes, he chose to leave, but he did so without the "light" that he had not paid his tab. What he had done would be a chargeable crime in any state, no question about it. But his actions did not rise to the level of a sin in God's sight. Both criteria for a sin must be present and, in this case, he was not walking against light, even though he had consented to walking out of the restaurant.

You see how we can correctly judge our actions and know if we are living above sin? C. W. Ruth made this observation: "A mistake is a thing you did when you knew no better; a sin is a thing you did when you did know better."[1] Someone else has stated, a mistake is something you did thinking it was right, but it was wrong; a sin is something you did when you knew it was wrong.

Ever Shoot a Squirrel?

Let us look at one more example of doing something that was wrong, but the one doing it had no idea. Years ago my wife and I decided to build our own home in the woods just a few miles from the college where I was teaching. When the house was complete and we had moved in, my wife had an idea; she wanted us to put up some

---

1. Christian Wismer Ruth, *Entire Sanctification: A Second Blessing, Together with Life Sketch, Bible Readings and Sermon Outlines* (Chicago: Christian Witness Co., 1903), 65.

bird feeders and enjoy watching birds from our window as we ate. My wife is very unselfish and does not ask for many things; thus, when she has an idea like this, I am happy to fulfill her desire.

We drove to the city; found a pet store and purchased the poles, feeders, birdseed and whatever else we were advised to be ready to have some enjoyment watching God's handiwork. We positioned the feeders a short distance across the back yard, filled the feeders with all the things that the various birds would love and got out the binoculars to observe. She even bought a book that described the native birds, their favorite food, and whatever else would make us professional bird watchers.

The first morning after setting things in order, she called up the stairs to me, all excited over the group of bright red cardinals eating at the feeder. She was delighted. On another day she called up the stairs with her voice full of dismay. What on earth was the matter? "Look out there," she lamented. Peering out the upstairs window I saw the problem.

A greedy squirrel had managed to climb onto the perch of one of the bird feeders, enlarged the feeding hole with his sharp teeth and was happily eating the feed as it ran out onto the ground. The effect was somewhat like a drinking fountain as long as the supply of grain lasted. I ran to get my .22 rifle, slid open the upstairs window, placed the crosshairs on him just as he looked at me, and bang! I sent him to the great squirrel-feeder in the sky. I went down and picked him up and threw him on the burn-pile back near the edge of the woods.

That scene repeated itself for a number of mornings until the pile of dead squirrels was growing. I found myself looking forward to each new morning. One day the thought came to me, "I wonder if this is legal?" I convinced myself that surely shooting furry rodents couldn't be wrong; after all, they could get into the attic and chew through the electrical wires or whatever. But as I continued the routine, actually rather enjoying it and looking forward to it, my conscience got the better of me. I was really feeling uneasy about the matter, and since the Ohio State Game Commissioner's office was located right on my way to the college campus, I decided to make the call from my college office in order to keep my home phone from appearing on his caller ID.

That should have alerted me to know I was getting into serious trouble with the Lord. When the local game officer answered his phone, I described the scenario and to my shock, he informed me that shooting squirrels out of season would net me a $500 fine and 30 days in jail! I was horrified and quickly ended the call. I had been regularly breaking the law and had no idea! My squirrel shooting days came to an end.

This incident serves well to illustrate my point; it is possible to be guilty of a crime— but not a sin. You see, I had no light on the law and was operating in complete innocence. Once I received the light, however, I was duty-bound to walk in it.

Let us bring another matter into our discussion of acts committed that do not rise to the level of a sin, properly so called. In the smartphone incident, the unpaid meal check and the squirrel account, we have examples of human infirmities that fall short of the "perfect law of love." In the language of early Methodist theologians, such acts, in some way not fully clear to us humans, require the covering of Christ's blood. Thus, the true child of God frequently humbles himself before God, confessing faults, shortcomings, imperfections and such actions that fall short of actual sins.

Are There Really "Sins of Ignorance" or "Unwillful Sins"?

We have stressed the inability to sin without both knowledge and the engagement of the will, but what shall we say about those mistakes, human defects and infirmities that plague each of us? It is helpful to remember that God's quarrel is not with our humanity, but with our rebellion. In spite of our best intentions, we will make blunders and errors in judgment in a myriad of ways. Such should not be ignored, since as Wesley taught so clearly, those acts and deeds do fall short of the perfect law of love and therefore do stand in need of covering by Christ's blood.

Many tend to term such shortcomings, "sins of ignorance," or "unwillful sin." Wesley, coming from his Reformed theological upbringing, did use the term on occasion, but in our world today, such terms are not helpful. They produce confusion, especially among young people and new converts. Either we sin, or we do not. Most Wesleyan theologians have written in support of our position, "Sin begins whenever the temptation begins to find inward sympathy, if known to be a solicitation to sin. So long as it is promptly, and with full and hearty concurrence of the soul, repelled, there is no indication of inward sympathy, there is no sin."[2]

In defense of using "sins of ignorance" for believers, some appeal to the discussion of the sin and trespass offerings in Leviticus chapters 1-6 and Numbers 15:17-31. Since most of those infractions by Israelites involve ceremonial uncleanness, such as touching a dead body, or giving birth to a child, it is most confusing to younger believers to try to understand sin, using such ceremonial examples from the Jewish law. What application is there to be made in our day when a preacher or teacher points out that when a Jewish mother gave birth, she was unclean and needed to bring a sin offering? That is nonsense to us today.

The writer of Hebrews went to great lengths to show

---

2. R. S. Foster, *Christian Purity*, n.p., 1851, 55.

that the outdated Levitical system was null and void. "For the law having a shadow of good things to come, and not the very image of the things, can never with those sacrifices which they offered year by year continually make the comers thereunto perfect" (Hebrews 10:1).

It is useless for New Testament believers to attempt to define or explain sin in our day by appealing to dead OT theology and examples. We thank God that a more perfect Offering has been made for us, and our more perfect Lamb has been offered and now, our more perfect, great High Priest intercedes for us, before the Father, to enable us to live above a life of sin. Bless the name of the Lord!

What's the Difference Between Law and Grace?

What we are saying is that the manner in which we define sin depends upon which dispensation under which we are living. In defining sin we must remember that we are now under *grace* and not under *law*. "For the law shall not have dominion over you: for ye are not under law but under grace" (Romans 6:11). We understand that the law is impersonal, unbending and cares not for the intentions of the doer.

Take for example the case of Uzzah, the man who put out his hand and touched the Ark of the Covenant, to keep it from falling to the ground. His was a wonderful motive, but that counted for naught; God struck him dead for touching the Ark. The old Methodists had a truism that still stands today: In God's eyes, the motive stands in place of the deed.

Thus, we see that God is more interested in what you intended to do, than what you actually ended up doing. If your motive was right, God judges you as though you had done right. And only God and you know what your motive was. Taylor puts it this way:

> What then must we conclude? Simply that those who insist on rolling mistakes, "sins of ignorance," and

human shortcomings into the same basket as a stubborn spirit and evil affections and conscious choice of evil, and labeling every act that falls below absolute standards of righteousness a true act of sin, are putting themselves *back under the law*. Not only so, but they are themselves the real legalists of modern Christendom; for who is a legalist if not he who defines sin according to the letter of the law rather than the spirit of the law? Yet strange to say, this is the very group which talk so emphatically about being free from the law, and call others legalists. If they wish to be truly scriptural and consistent in their claims, let them forsake absolute law and get under grace in their definition of sin.[3]

What Can We Learn from the Cities of Refuge?

The old covenant should not be completely dismissed and can be helpful, however, in one facet of our discussion. Even though mistakes, human error and infirmities do not rise to the level of sin, they lack conformity to the perfect law of love; they still need some type of covering by the blood. We are referring now to the City of Refuge and its function in ancient Israel. Suppose, in the course of one's work, an accident takes place and someone is killed. In that case, the nearest relative to the deceased person is identified in the Levitical law as the "avenger of blood," literally, the "redeemer of blood."

In this scenario, the one who caused the accidental death must run as quickly as possible to the nearest City of Refuge, one of six such cities dispersed in Israel, three cities on either side of the Jordan River. With the manslayer running toward the city and the avenger of blood on his heels, he reaches the gates of the city and is

---

3. Richard S. Taylor, *A Right Conception of Sin*, (Nicholasville, KY: Schmul Publishing Co., 2002), 63.

immediately granted asylum until the elders of the city can adjudicate his case.

At this point he is safe from his would-be executioner. As soon as the elders can be assembled, the matter is heard. If the accused is found to be guilty, he is thrust out of the city whereupon the avenger is free to execute him. But note, however, if he is found to be innocent of premeditated murder, even though he is innocent, he must remain in the city until the death of the current high priest. There is still some type of penalty to be paid.

The lesson for New Testament believers to be gleaned from a study of the Cities of Refuge is this. Although the offender had been cleared of intentional wrongdoing, the manslayer still had to pay some kind of penalty. For us, then, the lesson is clear; while guilty of a mistake, fault, or blunder, the person will still necessarily face consequences of his actions— broken fellowship, perhaps financial loss, or some other misfortune— just as the manslayer had to remain in the City of Refuge until the death of the high priest.

Similarly, in our discussion of sin and mistakes, even though the deed of the believer does not rise to the level of a sin, it does fall short of the perfect law of love and just as the manslayer must remain in the city, even though innocent of murder, he has some kind of penalty, a price to pay. By the same token, mistakes, blunders, etc., need the atoning blood of Christ. So states Wesley in his *Plain Account of Christian Perfection*,

> ...Not only *sin, properly so called*, that is, a voluntary transgression of a known law), but sin, improperly so called, that is, an involuntary transgression of a divine law, known or unknown, needs the atoning blood... I believe there is no such perfection in this life, as excludes these involuntary transgressions, which I apprehend to be naturally consequent on the

ignorance and mistakes inseparable from mortality... Therefore *sinless perfection* is a phrase I never use, lest I should *seem* to contradict myself... I believe a person filled with the love of God, is still liable to these involuntary transgressions...[4]

Contrast Between Judas and the Other Disciples

Likewise, Judas, the traitor, willfully sinned and our Lord stated that it had been good for him if he had not been born. Conversely, to the sleeping disciples he uttered these tender words: "the spirit indeed is willing, but the flesh is weak." While Judas had sinned, the disciples had merely been overcome by what we can term the infirmity of sleepiness. As Daniel Steele observed, the universal conscience discriminates between a sin and a weakness or an error. There is a huge difference between telling a lie, and falling asleep in prayer meeting, or forgetting to keep a promise. The infirmity brings embarrassment and perhaps a strain on a relationship; but sin brings guilt, shame and separation from God.

Of course, our legal system recognizes a lack of intent, in some cases, e.g., the physician who mistakenly orders the wrong medication and causes extreme harm or even death, or for another example, the guard who falls asleep and faces execution. In that we see that the law of God is more merciful than the statutes of human government. Still we must note, that a well-intentioned mistake does not defile the conscience or bring condemnation and guilt. That notwithstanding, when the mistake comes to light, it still requires an apology, any amends that are possible and, of course, the covering of the blood.

---

4. John Wesley, *A Plain Account of Christian Perfection,* (Nicholasville, KY: Schmul Publishing Co.), 46.

Some Helpful Advice

In closing this section I have some advice that might assist you in how you deal with sins and mistakes in your life. To help sort through the difference between these I have offered this advice. If you have committed a sin against someone, when you are dealing with that person, ask that one to forgive you. On the other hand, if you have done something that was unintended against that one, ask them to accept your apology. Simply put, seek forgiveness for a sin; apologize for a mistake. If you can keep this in mind, it will sharpen your theological thinking.

How often have we heard the song leader call out the wrong page number in the hymnal and when he corrects his error, he says, "Forgive me, that's the wrong page number." Actually, he doesn't need forgiveness; he has not sinned. His will was not involved; it was simply a human error. If you are late to class or you have forgotten someone's birthday, don't ask for forgiveness. All you need to do is to apologize. What you have done is a human infirmity, a simple mistake and was not sinful and will not bring guilt or shame. A mistake may bring embarrassment and humility, and might even cause a strain in the relationship, but it has nothing to do with walking in the light or severing your relationship with God.

Chapter Summary

1. A correct, Biblical understanding of sin is critical to establish a correct theology; a failure to have a correct definition will confuse students in their attempt to differentiate between mistakes, human error or infirmities that plague all of us.
2. Breaking the civil laws of the land may get one in trouble with the judge, but may not bring guilt and condemnation with God.

3. All mistakes of the head fall short of the perfect law of love and need the atoning blood of Christ, because not every mistaken action is a matter of morality.
4. Under the Law of Moses, mistakes needed some type of atonement, i.e., a penalty still had to be paid.
5. Sins of ignorance were generally ceremonial matters such as touching a dead body or some matter of uncleanness; these were used to show that no mercy obtained under the Law.
6. The New Covenant makes application of a penalty entirely based upon one's motive; God does not look upon the outward, but upon the heart, e.g., one's intentions.
7. Learn to seek forgiveness for sins and to apologize for mistakes.

4
The Ethics of Decision Making

BEFORE LEAVING OUR DISCUSSION on sin, light and choices, it will be helpful to consider this matter of making moral or ethical choices. Life involves countless choices every day, many of which have no moral value attached to one's choice. To add another dimension to our learning, let us now consider how philosophers and ethicists discuss this matter of decision-making. Our discussion will take us beyond the common realm of the laity and into the world of professionals.

As part of their preparation, persons in these fields have been required to take college courses that focus on the ethics of making decisions— many of which have life or death implications. Similarly, those in the discipline of law, accounting and other professions, must complete courses that provide direction for making ethical decision. So this matter of making choices impacts our world in many ways beyond our spiritual and theological interests.

When teaching on this matter of ethics, which is a subdivision of philosophy, I introduce students to two approaches we use when making an ethical choice: *teleological* and *deontological*. These two terms often seem quite daunting at first mention in the classroom, so let me define and illustrate them for you. We will begin with an incident that actually happened to an individual many years ago. From this account we will draw some conclusions that should aid in our understanding of the process of decision-making.

This individual worked as a hired hand on a large dairy farm. Not long after he was converted, he and the farmer for whom he worked were in the barn replacing boards on the deck of a large hay wagon. Both were driving the same number of nails into each board, working across the wagon from each other. The project turned into a little contest — the hired hand against the farmer. Neither man termed it a contest, but it had turned into the farmer against the hired hand. Who was the faster carpenter of the two? When it became obvious that the farmer was falling behind in the undeclared race, in his embarrassment he announced, "Okay, it's time to go feed the chickens."

Knowing that the farmer was too proud to admit his defeat in the little contest somehow angered the hired hand. In his anger he took his heavy carpenter's hammer and angrily threw it at the barn door, hard enough to splinter one of the boards. Immediately, his awful reaction filled him with shame and he sheepishly retired into a nearby field and kneeling down, he talked to the Lord about what he had just done. He was troubled, not knowing what had caused him to respond in such an un-Christlike manner. He asked God to forgive him and later apologized to the farmer.

The account of my newly saved friend's first encounter with anger does provide us with an example of this matter of ethical decision-making. (I will point out that by his own admission, his action happened so quickly that he did not actually make a choice about the hammer, he merely reacted in anger without even thinking what he was doing.) Let us now consider a discussion that transpired with a prominent holiness preacher regarding this incident.

While discussing the topic of whether venting one's anger constitutes an actual sin or not, my friend set up a hypothetical scenario. Arguing that the throwing of the hammer did constitute an actual sin, he put forth this sequel to the hammer incident. "Let us say," he suggested, "that a mother was pushing her baby in a stroller outside the barn just as the angry hired-hand threw his hammer through one of the barn windows." To make his point he added, "The result was that the tool struck the infant and caused the baby's death. Why he would be guilty of murder," he concluded, satisfied that he had proven that throwing a hammer in anger rises to the level of an actual sin.

To counter his point, I offered an alternate scenario to him, "Let us suppose the mother and child were outside the barn, and a mad, rabid dog was about to attack the infant— and the hammer struck the dog, killed it, and saved the baby's life. Now the hammer thrower becomes a hero!" How do we solve this problem of determining whether or not a sin had taken place? Obviously, we cannot decide if an act is correct or wrong based on the outcome of the action. Once that concept is introduced to students, they find a new source of helpful information that is needed to decide the rightness or wrongness of any ethical decision. Let's look more closely at these two ways in which ethical decisions are made.

What Factors Govern Our Ethical Decision-Making?

The word "teleology" comes from a Greek word, *teleos,* which means, "to reach the goal." In the field of ethics, that means that one makes a decision or choice, depending upon the ethical goal or outcome he wishes to achieve without considering God's opinion on the issue.

By contrast, the other word, "deontology" means "duty oriented," i.e., one understands what duty (or for our study, light) demands that he perform in a given situation. For the Christian, this means that Scripture, or conscience or some other source of spiritual light, dictates one's duty. Explaining to my class the concept of deontology versus teleology, I then proceeded to point out that one cannot judge the rightness or wrongness of an act based only on its outcome — in this case, killing the dog or the infant.

Deontology is defined as an ethical concept that determines the morality of an action, whether that action itself is right or wrong, based upon understood principles or absolutes, such as Scriptural injunctions or rules or laws, rather than based on the consequences of the action. In the case of the believer, "light," i.e., "God's opinion on any matter," dictates to him the correct choice, and in so doing, he is content to have God lead him. I have often used this little aphorism: "I can trust the consequences of my obedience to God." How true that is! Do whatever duty (Scripture or your light or your personal conviction) demands, and God will be pleased with you and will take care of the consequences of your obedience. Now, let us return to the hammer, the child and the dog.

Applying the teleological method of judging the rightness or wrongness of an ethical choice will not be helpful — especially to the child of God. Whether the hammer struck the child, causing a death, or if it struck the dog and saved the baby's life, one cannot determine the correct decision from a teleological framework — especially in view of the fact that we cannot know the results of our choice before the choice is made.

The deontological choice says, "It's wrong to throw hammers in anger," period. End of discussion. Duty (deontological approach) dictates the correct moral and ethical choice; God will take care of the results. (In a later chapter we shall take up the matter of whether the one throwing the hammer in anger actually made a choice at that point, or was it the involuntary reaction of an unsanctified heart.)

Lest you get confused it should be pointed out that in the course of a day or a lifetime, we often resort to making decisions utilizing the teleological approach, and that is fine in cases where one is making *non-ethical and non-moral decisions*. A simple example will make the point. Let's say you are planning a busy day's activities and you need to accomplish certain tasks, make certain purchases, all with an allotted period of time. So you carefully plan which stops to make, where you need to be at a certain time and hopefully, by the end of the day, you have followed your outline and reached your goal at the end of the day— just as you had planned. So you made and followed your plan and accomplished all that was needed. In this case no ethical choices were involved and the teleological approach enabled you to meet your goal and that is fine. But, one dare not make ethical decisions using such thinking— that of trying to manipulate events to achieve a desired goal. The following will illustrate.

Doing One's Duty will Insure Walking in the Light

Let us consider an example of employing the teleological model, "goal-oriented" to make a decision. A university student discovers that she is pregnant. In her panic she reasons that she needs to finish her education, i.e., her preparation for life. Besides, she reasons, she is not equipped to be a mother— and her boyfriend, also a student, is pressuring her to take the life of the unborn child. Allowing herself to be influenced by worldly friends and secular professionals, she reasons that aborting the baby will solve her problem. Such a terrible choice will selfishly enable her to achieve her college goals while ignoring the clear teaching of God's Word. She foolishly opts for an abortion and justifies murder to achieve her desired outcome. That is making her choice using the teleological approach which holds that the end justifies the means.

By contrast, however, if she uses a deontological basis for her decision, she recognizes that opting for abortion is wrong, since it involves taking a life. As desperate as her plight appears to her, duty tells her that taking a life is murder. Knowing this, she decides either to keep the child and raise it, or place it for adoption. Walking in the light of an absolute principle from Scripture, she makes the correct moral choice. That is adopting the deontological (duty oriented) approach. When we do that, we do what is morally right and we will be aware of pleasing God by walking in the light. That action will assure our continued fellowship with the Lord.

Perhaps one more example taken from Scripture will help. In Numbers 22, we have the account of Balaam. He offers a clear example of someone who made his choices from a teleological position. God had clearly warned Balaam, "Do not go beyond what I tell you to do," and every time, Balaam tried to anyway. He failed to heed God's warning at every turn because he wanted his own way. He wanted the gold, the honor, and the reputation he would have by cursing Israel (who had defeated mighty Egypt and most of the nations they came in contact with).

This approach reveals his major character flaw, one that many in the world also have. He believed that the end justified the means. He was willing to set aside principle (if he had any) to achieve his goals. He functioned by self-interest rather than by beliefs or standards. His standard was "anything that is good for Balaam," which is self-righteousness and self-interest. These were the principles by which he felt he could live a successful life. He did not base them on anything godly or even ethical but strictly on human reason. Herein we can see someone making ethical choices using a teleological approach.

Learn to heed the voice of conscience and always walk in your light, and you can live with the blessing of the Lord upon your life. Herein is to be found true happiness.

Chapter Summary

1. One can never determine the rightness or wrongness of an act based upon the outcome.
2. Ethical choices based upon what one understands to be his moral duty (deontological approach) will always do the right thing regardless of the outcome or result.
3. To make one's moral choice based upon the desired outcome (teleological approach), is really saying that the end justifies the means. Such choices, more often than not, lead to breaking the moral law and result in sin.
4. Our example of throwing the hammer in anger demonstrates that even though something positive resulted (killing the mad dog), the unintended result does not justify the temper tantrum.
5. The child of God must always act upon what he knows to be his moral duty regardless of the outcome. Even though we can never know in advance the outcome of our choices, rest in the knowledge that God may turn things in a different direction to reward us for doing the right thing.

5
Initial Sanctification and Entire Sanctification

PROBABLY ONE OF THE GREATEST AREAS of confusion that surfaces in the classroom centers around the difference between the two works of grace, i.e., what does God actually do for a saved person, why isn't that good enough, how is that different from the second work of grace, and why doesn't the Lord do both works at one time? In one form or another these questions keep coming up for discussion.

In 1972, Mildred Bangs Wynkoop, a Wesleyan-Arminian Nazarene scholar, raised the issue in what she termed "the credibility gap." Fully aware of the confusion that develops in the mind of poorly instructed students and laity, she discussed the lack of understanding about the two works of grace in which she raises the question as to why Wesleyans speak of two works of grace rather than only one, or perhaps three or even one hundred works of grace. She then proceeds to ask how one is to know one work from the other, or if a person loses out with God, which work was lost? In an almost mocking manner she continues with questions such as which part of the sin problem is solved in the first work, if God can justify a person, why cannot he finish the work in one stroke? Why is a crisis experience necessary when one is sanctified wholly? If one is saved, is he not ready for heaven? If so, why a second work? And so she continues as if intentionally trying to confuse new converts and honest seekers. She then moves to definitions: what does "saved" mean? What is perfection? Sanctification?[1]

Professor Wynkoop's series of questions surfaces many times in one form or another in my classroom discussions; they deserve to be answered. Any new convert who attends services within holiness churches will hear these terms and concepts with great frequency in a typical sermon, Sunday School discussions or in the college classroom.

Since these are significant concepts, I will devote a considerable portion of this chapter to these questions. As you read, keep in mind that man can explain and teach to the best of his ability and training, but the Holy Spirit will become the Revealer of Truth to the earnest seeker. When He speaks, things become clear beyond any explanation by humans. Prior to our actual discussion it will prove helpful to consider some contrasts between justification and entire sanctification as listed by C. W. Ruth, one of the founders of the Church of the Nazarene:

> In Justification there is life.
> In Sanctification there is life more abundantly.
> In Justification there is love.
> In Sanctification there is perfect love which casteth out fear.
> In Justification the "old man" is repressed.
> In Sanctification the "old man" is destroyed.
> In Justification there is "peace with God."

---

1. Mildred Bangs Wynkoop, *A Theology of Love* (Kansas City, MO: Beacon Hill Press, 1972), 46-47.

In Sanctification there is "the peace of God."
Justification gives us the right to heaven.
Sanctification gives us the fitness for heaven.
In Justification we "put on the new man."
In Sanctification we "put off the old man with his deeds."
In Justification there is joy— intermittent joy.
In Sanctification there is fullness of joy— abiding joy.
Justification includes pardon, which is a judicial act.
Sanctification includes a cleansing, which is a priestly function.
Justification comprehends adoption; making us children of God.
Sanctification comprehends anointing; making us kings and priests unto God.
Justification separates us from the world, so we are no longer of the world.
Sanctification takes the world out of us along with worldly desires and ambitions.
Justification has to do with sin as an act— sins committed.
Sanctification has to do with sin as a principle— the sin nature we inherited.
Justification restores us to favor with God that we had lost through our one disobedience.
Sanctification restores to us holiness or the moral likeness of God, which we had lost through Adam's disobedience.
Justification is the impartation of a spiritual nature, bringing us into possession of eternal life.
Sanctification is the crucifixion and destruction of our carnal nature, making us dead indeed unto sin.

Justification destroys the "shoots" of sin.
Sanctification destroys the "roots" of sin.[2]

The above group of comparisons and contrasts generally reflect early-twentieth century Wesleyan-Arminian teachings on how Wesley and his followers viewed the contrast between what God does in the heart of the justified person and what he further accomplishes in the lives of those who follow the Spirit into the blessing of entire sanctification.

As we have observed earlier, teaching or preaching about these concepts may fall into the error of attempting to make the second work of grace so glorious that they tend to reduce the significance of God's initial work of salvation. Such misplaced emphasis leads not only to students misunderstanding justification, but that error results in even more confusion and discouragement. Let us look more closely at the life-transforming work that takes place at salvation. Such is not a half-salvation or even a partial sanctification (a term that more recently has come into usage in some areas of the holiness movement). It is initial sanctification.

Justification is Not a Halfway Work of Grace

When my great uncle graduated from Houghton College in 1917, the faculty described his sanctified state in the college annual as him having "received salvation in two installments." A member of the faculty or administration apparently chose those words that appeared on his senior page in the yearbook, and they captured my attention— receiving salvation in two installments. The writer was simply pointing out that although it is one great event in the penitent sinner's life, it takes place in

---

2. Christian Wismer Ruth, *Entire Sanctification: A Second Blessing, Together with Life Sketch, Bible Readings and Sermon Outlines* (Chicago: Christian Witness Co., 1903), 31-34.

two steps. When the Holy Spirit awakens a sinner, that event constitutes a significant moment in that person's life. From his earliest awareness of himself as a moral creature, capable of making ethical choices, he has essentially lived for self, giving way to temptations and has become what Wesley termed, a willing servant of sin.

God Awakens the Sinner to His Need

Such persons in that condition are generally carefree, happily going through life without ever thinking about eternity, the judgment, or any sense of any accountability to God. Under the influence of godly parents, a gifted teacher, a faithful pastor or any person whom the Lord chooses to use, that soul becomes awakened to spiritual verities. He awakens to the fact that he is mortal, he is accountable to a higher Being, he will appear at the Judgment and eternity is real and eternal. As Wesley would say it, dreadful light breaks into his world and things shift into an entirely different context. He becomes restless, sleep might evade him, and he becomes mightily concerned about his position in God's light and decides to change. His status has changed from a "willing servant of sin," to now become what Wesley termed, an "unwilling servant of sin."

What is happening to this awakening sinner is really the work of the Holy Spirit who is tasked with convicting sinners and inviting them to the foot of the cross where they may find salvation. He alone can fully awaken and convict of sin and of righteousness and of judgment. This action of the Spirit is a high act of mercy and without it no one will be genuinely converted. On many occasions I have prayed with seekers who were not fully awakened and convinced of their need. The result was that they did not find victory in their time at the altar.

The Willing Servant of Sin Becomes an Unwilling Servant

As the awakened one attempts to reform, however, he becomes aware that he is not nearly as free as he had envisioned. He begins to feel the weight of his chains that are preventing him from two things: (1) enjoying his life of sin and, (2) breaking loose from the habits of sin— his outright slavery to Satan. The apostle delineates this condition thusly:

> I find then a law, that, when I would do good, evil is present with me. For I delight in the law of God after the inward man: But I see another law in my members, warring against the law of my mind, and bringing me into captivity to the law of sin which is in my members. O wretched man that I am! Who shall deliver me from the body of this death?
> —*Romans 7:21-24*

I have observed the efforts of some who, once awakened, attempted to reform themselves with a goal of finding some relief. Some begin to pay tithe, some start attending Sunday evening services or mid-week Bible study. Any type of reform efforts, while good and perhaps helpful, will not bring about salvation. At some point the decision must be made to seek God in earnest.

Perhaps seated in the church service, standing during the altar call, or walking in the field— it matters not where, the now fully awakened, unwilling servant of sin, convinced that Christ is his only hope, turns toward the Savior for deliverance.

The process leading to salvation need not be complicated; several steps are usually involved. The first move is that of humbling himself. He must, in his heart, bow at the feet of the Lord. It's of no consequence where this takes place. I am convinced that for some, the mere act of stepping out into the church aisle and walking to the altar signifies true contrition and humility. Perhaps for some, that act alone breaks the spell of a rebellious heart and begins the wheels of salvation turning. From that penitent state one moves into the next phase, that of confession.

Confession Alone Won't Save You

Confession is an interesting word that literally means, "to say along with." In other words, as the Holy Spirit brings up the sinful areas in the seeker's life, the proper response is to say along with, or confess to the charges heaven has lodged against you. If the Spirit says, "You are a liar," you respond in your heart, "I am a liar." If He says, "You are a thief," you agree, "I am a thief." It's essential to continue to seek until you have confessed all known sin. Ask the Spirit to search out your heart in order to reveal any hidden areas that need to be exposed to the atoning blood of the Lamb. However, as important as humility and confession are to the process, those alone will not save you. You are now ready for the all-important step that follows.

Repentance is the Crucial Turning Point

Repentance can be a bit tricky due to the fact that two slightly different Greek words are both translated "repentance" in the KJV. One term, *metamelomai,* means "to feel remorse for." We find that word in Matthew 27:3-4,

> Then Judas, which had betrayed him, when he saw that he was condemned, repented himself, and brought again the thirty pieces of silver to the chief priests and elders, Saying, I have sinned in that I have betrayed the innocent blood. And they said, What is that to us? see thou to that.

The writer has stated that Judas, seeing that his plans had gone seriously awry, in his guilty mind felt a wave of remorse wash over his being and tried to undo his awful deed of betrayal. Of course, his actions hope to bring about a change, but that is not the basic meaning of the word "repent" as used here.

The other word for repentance surfaces many places in the New Testament. It's the Greek word, *metanaeo,* and essentially means "to change," or "to turn." The Hebrew counterpart to that word is *shubh,* and it means "to turn" or "to return." With this word we observe a deliberate change of mind that results in a changed life.

When the humbled penitent has confessed every known sin, he arrives at the threshold of repentance, i.e., he tells God he is going to change, even as he prays. He is convinced that the old life must go; he is done with it and he is changing.

Repentance encompasses at least five distinct things: a consciousness of sin and guilt; a deep heart sorrow for sin; the confession of the sin; restitution to those whom he has wronged; and the total abandonment of sin. Without the complete commitment to change, salvation will never be reached. Many examples of that can be observed.

It's All About Change

A few years ago my wife and I were in an auto accident that necessitated some physical therapy in the weeks that followed. Scheduled as a camp evangelist in a distant city, we found ourselves in an outpatient facility a few miles from the campground. Our therapist approached us in the waiting room, introduced herself and led us back to the treatment rooms. As we were following her, she turned to me and asked, "Are you a believer?"

I answered in the affirmative, somewhat curious as to why she asked, and then countered, "How about you?"

"Oh, yes," she replied, "I was raised Presbyterian,

married a Baptist fellow, was baptized and now I am a believer."

Entering what was to be my treatment, I asked, "Christine, since you became a Christian, how have you changed; what's different about your life?"

She replied, "I'll have to think about that." I admit I was a bit disappointed at her rather vague answer. Surely the Lord had wrought a wonderful change in her life. Why did she need time to think about it?

She positioned the treatment machine and left for about fifteen minutes to care for my wife in another room. When she returned she said, "I have been thinking about your question and I will share at least one change in my life since becoming saved."

Eagerly I awaited her testimony. She stated to me, "I don't drink as much as I used to." I was stunned! After what should have been a glorious life-changing event in her life, all she could come up with was drinking somewhat less.

The point is that when you repent and God graciously grants you release from the old life of sin and makes you a child of God, more will change in your life than a mere lessening of your drinking habit. Christ's atoning blood at Calvary purchased you more than that! I have often stated from the pulpit that when a person claims to have been saved, the church has a right to see a changed life. If there's no change, there's no salvation!

It is Time for Faith to Reach Out to God

Let's return to the process of salvation. After you have completely repented, the last logical step remaining is quite simple — it's only necessary to believe. When you have laid the foundation of humility, confession and repentance, faith is almost automatic. Saving faith is a gift of God, one that he longs to bestow on the prepared seeker. Only God can know when you have reached that point. No one can talk you into it and certainly, no one can talk you out of it. In your heart of hearts a sweet consciousness will cause you to know that something has happened to you. You will become aware that the guilt and defilement are no longer there!

> There is therefore now no condemnation to them which are in Christ Jesus, who walk not after the flesh, but after the Spirit. For the law of the Spirit of life in Christ Jesus hath made me free from the law of sin and death. For what the law could not do, in that it was weak through the flesh, God sending his own Son in the likeness of sinful flesh, and for sin, condemned sin in the flesh.
> —*Romans 8:1-3*

Four Simultaneous Aspects to Salvation

In that glorious instant four things have transpired in your heart, all in one split second.

First of all, you have been justified, i.e., your long record of sin on the books of heaven has been wiped clean. The word "justified" is a legal or forensic term that changes your record and your legal standing in God's sight. I have often told students that justification is better than a pardon (although we do often use that term). When the governor pardons a person, he may be freed from prison, but the record of his crime is still on the books and could be held against him in future brushes with the law. With justification, however, it's just as if the sins had never happened.

Another aspect of that event happens at the same moment of justification and it's found in Romans 5:1-5.

> Therefore being justified by faith, we have peace with God through our Lord Jesus Christ: By whom also we have access by faith into this grace wherein we stand,

and rejoice in hope of the glory of God. And not only so, but we glory in tribulations also: knowing that tribulation worketh patience; And patience, experience; and experience, hope: And hope maketh not ashamed; because the love of God is shed abroad in our hearts by the Holy Ghost which is given unto us.

These verses are vitally important to establish that the Holy Spirit has entered the heart of the believer. Notice that Paul, the writer, speaks of justification, and the glorious benefits that accrue to the new babe in Christ. He then finishes this section by pointing out two important items: the love of God, e.g., the *agape* (that lofty love from God that only Christians possess) is poured into the heart and also, the Holy Spirit is given to the new believer. There can be no doubt as to this glorious event and what it has accomplished! There is nothing partial or halfway about it.

The second thing that happens at the new birth is regeneration, a term that means, "to have or begin a new life." The miracle of God's transforming power produces in you a brand new beginning; new life is imparted to the penitent seeker— all things are passed away and all things become new! He becomes a brand-new person in Christ. One Wesleyan scholar has described this new life thusly:

> The dead soul of the sinner is brought to life; the graces or qualities of this new life are all planted in the believer. This new life is in infancy, as a newborn babe, and is capable of growth. This new creation is perfect in its kind... At the same time that the new life is planted in the soul, God begins the cleansing of sin. The power of sin is broken. Man is made holy, pure, clean, but not entirely so. This cleansing work is the beginning of sanctification. It is holiness begun. It can be called initial because

it is just a beginning. This new life exists where some evil is still present.[3]

Thirdly, with adoption, the new babe in Christ becomes part of the spiritual family of God; Jesus Christ is now his elder Brother; God is now truly his Father! The significance of this feature of salvation cannot be overemphasized. Psychologists stress that one of the basic essential needs of every human being is the need for community. It was never God's intention that we live in a world of isolation. We need friendship, companionship and a social group with whom we may interact. With the advent of this adoption that takes place at the moment of salvation, the new convert has a new spiritual family, beginning with his new Father and Brother. In addition he is now a member of the family of God and that explains why so many enjoy the chorus, "I'm so glad I'm a part of the family of God."

The fourth thing that happens at the moment of salvation has presented a puzzle to many folks. Wesleyan theologians have used various terms to identify this phenomenon: initial sanctification, provisional sanctification (that is, it's provided by Christ), or positional sanctification.

It is this initial sanctification that gave rise to Wynkoop's list of questions we observed earlier in this chapter. As the heading of this section asks, is this glorious first work of grace merely a "half-way work of grace," i.e., is it deficient in some manner; was the seeker cheated out of a significant victory?

The answer is a resounding, No! Any work accomplished by the Holy Spirit is a gracious act and perfect to the extent that it was intended. So many students assume that since there is more ground to gain as the seeker learns of Christian perfection yet ahead, there must be some-

---

3. Leo Cox, *John Wesley's Concept of Perfection*, (Salem, OH: Schmul Publishing Co., 1999), 90.

thing deficient with his salvation. Still others ask why God doesn't do it all in one work. It will be helpful to consider this analogy.

Justification is a Perfect Event but the Work is Not Complete

When God began his work of creation on the first day of creation week, what he accomplished on that day was perfect, but creation wasn't finished. Again, on the second day his activities were perfect, but he wasn't finished. And so it went every day until on the sixth day when he made man, his work was perfect, but it was also finished. Thus, God rested from all his work of creation.

The same analogy holds true when God saves a person. The work is perfect, but he's not finished until the new believer is made perfect in love. There remains no need for a newly saved Christian to feel slighted or shortchanged— the Holy Spirit has formed a brand new creature in Christ and that is glorious. His record is clean in heaven, his sins are forgiven, he now enjoys fellowship with his Lord and with his Christian brothers and sisters, and the work of sanctification has begun in his heart. The guilt of his past sins is gone, and frankly, at that moment, he probably cannot imagine how things could be any greater.

His task now is to deal with the necessary restitutions that the Spirit has prompted him to recall as he was seeking to be saved. This business of restoring all the sins of the past, those that involve past sins against others, will consume considerable time in the immediate days ahead. Some restitutions will involve money; if he lacks the amount to repay debts owed, the best thing is to contact those involved, apologize and seek forgiveness from them and then arrange to make payments when possible. Most folk will be very understanding until funds are available. Never forget, as long as you are walking in your light, your credit is good with the Lord.

Restitutions and Apologies: Do Them Right

As you make your restitutions, be sure you apologize for what you did. Many people fail to care for this matter properly. Three things enter into an apology: (1) tell the person you are sorry, (2) accept the fault and the blame, without excusing yourself or qualifying what you did, and (3) ask what you can do to restore your relationship back to a good footing. I am confident if you will practice the three steps anytime you feel the need to apologize, you will meet with success, you will feel good about yourself, and doing so will go a long way toward not needing to do it all over again. God will be pleased and he will go with you and help you as you care for your restitutions.

The important thing for you to keep in mind is this: as a new convert, you have now qualified for heaven, vis-à-vis Hebrews 12:14, "Follow peace with all men and holiness without which no man shall see the Lord." You have initial sanctification; holiness has been planted in your heart. Note, the verse does not say, "Follow peace with all men and two works of grace without which no man shall see the Lord." If the thief on the cross could make it into paradise on that first Good Friday without two works of grace, then any saved person can— if they keep walking in the light. We can say that with confidence because by walking in the light, new believers will walk right into the light of holiness, i.e., having their heart made perfect in love.

Two Steps in Healing the Blind man at Bethsaida

Let us consider two incidents in the life of our Lord that illustrates his sovereign discretion to do things in his own manner. Even more importantly for our discussion, we observe his timing in the process. To those students who are slow to grasp the concept of Christ doing things in one or two steps, these two accounts offer an interesting example of him healing in one or in two steps. First let us observe the restoration of the sight to the blind man in Bethsaida.

> And he cometh to Bethsaida; and they bring a blind man unto him, and besought him to touch him. And he took the blind man by the hand, and led him out of the town; and when he had spit on his eyes, and put his hands upon him, he asked him if he saw ought. And he looked up, and said, I see men as trees, walking. After that he put his hands again upon his eyes, and made him look up: and he was restored, and saw every man clearly.
> —Mark 8: 22-25

Here we have a most interesting account of a healing that our Lord chose to perform in two steps. Just as at creation God chose to perform his work in six days, here Jesus opted to do this healing in two steps. As Clarke points out,

> Our Lord could have restored this man to sight in a moment; but he chose to do it in the way mentioned in the text, to show that he is sovereign of his own graces; and to point out that, however insignificant means may appear in themselves, they are divinely efficacious when he chooses to work by them; and that, however small the first manifestations of mercy may be, they are nevertheless the beginnings of the fullness of the blessings of the Gospel of peace. Reader, art thou in this man's state? Art thou blind? Then come to Jesus that he may restore thee. Hast thou a measure of light? Then pray that he may lay his hands again on thee, that thou mayest be enabled to read thy title clear to the heavenly inheritance.[4]

---

4. Adam Clarke, *Clarke's Commentary*, (Nicholasville, KY: Schmul Publishing Co., 2019.), 5:315.

Instead, he performed the healing in two steps. Joseph Benson noted that

> By a second imposition of Christ's hands he received a clear sight of every object in view. Our Lord's intention in this might be to make it evident that in his cures he was not confined to one method of operation, but could dispense them in what manner he pleased. In the meantime, though the cure was performed by degrees, it was accomplished in so small a space of time, as to make it evident that it was not produced by any natural efficacy of our Lord's spittle or touch, but merely by the exertion of his miraculous power. Christ perhaps intended, by restoring the man's sight gradually, to signify in what way those who are by nature spiritually blind, are generally healed by his grace. At first, their knowledge of divine things is indistinct, obscure, and confused; they see men as trees walking; but afterward, by a second or third imposition of the Saviour's hands, a further degree of spiritual discernment is communicated, and they see all things clearly. Their light, like that of the morning, shines more and more unto the perfect day.[5]

The Timing is in God's Hands, Not Ours

Both Clarke and Benson have laid out for us the fact that it is within our Lord's prerogative to speed up the process or delay it; to perform it in one, two or more steps — it's at his discretion. So for the student who wonders why a person is not saved and entirely sanctified at the same instant, these biblical examples demonstrate that Christ is not bound by any timing, sequence or pattern, when he does his work. We will observe in a later chapter

---

5. Joseph Benson, *The Holy Bible, Containing the Old and New Testaments (according to the Present Authorized Version) with Critical, Explanatory, and Practical Notes* (New York: Lane & Tippett, 1846), 4: 286.

that for the Apostle Paul, both works were accomplished within three days. Wesley mentioned the case of a woman who professed to be saved and made perfect in love at the same moment and her life testified not to the contrary but that she had been.

Chapter Summary

1. Two works of grace may be thought of as salvation in two installments. Since the seeking sinner cannot be fully aware of the need for a cleansing of the carnal heart, he is in no position to seek for entire sanctification.
2. Modern theologians who deny entire sanctification have belittled the first work of grace to the point of confusing seekers.
3. Wynkoop's "credibility gap" betrays her conflict with orthodox Methodist teaching, probably resulting from her years of studying under Reform theologians.
4. Wesley's description of sinners as "a willing servant of Satan," is amazingly insightful; his term "unwilling servant of sin" beautifully reflects the awakened sinner of Romans chapter 7.
5. Humility and confession are essential to salvation, but it is repentance that brings about a changed heart, and makes faith easy.
6. At salvation one is justified, regenerated, adopted and initially sanctified — all in the same instance at the moment of faith.
7. When God does his work in steps, that doesn't mean his work is imperfect; at creation he had six days of perfect works, but his plan wasn't complete until the sixth day. Anything God does is very good; but it may not be complete.
8. Restitutions and apologies need to be done correctly; the only thing worse that making a restitution is making the same one twice due to improper handling of the problem when the first restitution was attempted.

6
Are Carnal Traits Viewed by God the Same as Actual Sins?

WRITING ON THE CONTRAST between carnality and human infirmities can prove to be both challenging and controversial, whether inside or outside the college classroom. In past chapters we have dealt with the problem of discerning between temptations, mistakes and actual sins.

Consider the matter of, and the influence of, what Paul calls "the old man" (Romans 6:6). Here the apostle refers to original sin, that phenomenon that is the basis for every moral problem in our world today. When Adam fell in the garden, not only did he become deprived of God's leadership and holiness in his life, he came to discover an inner nature that he had not possessed prior to his rebellion. When he lost God's holiness, he lost something in his inner man that he needed, and, tragically, he gained a corrupted nature that inclined him away from God. It will be helpful now to discuss the importance of the Presence of Yahweh within the new believer.

God's Presence is What Makes Things Holy

The word holiness is often misunderstood. Actually, holiness and love are the very essence of God, not attributes he possesses — they are who he is! They constitute his very being. When we speak of this, we are speaking of his presence within that which he indwells. Nothing is holy without the presence of the Holy. The land of Canaan was just a location, but with God's presence, it became the Holy Land. Jerusalem was just a stronghold of the Jebusites, but with God's presence, it became the Holy City. The tabernacle was just a tent, but when God occupied it, it became the Holy Place. Likewise, the Holy of Holies was just a room, until God's presence came and dwelt in it, on the lid of the Ark of the Covenant and then it became the Holy of Holies. God can take ordinary places, things and people, and fill them with his presence and that makes them holy.[1] Thank the Lord! So, when Adam and Eve sinned, God withdrew from them and they became sinful. Deprived of his wonderful presence, they retreated into a life of sin, an existence controlled only by their own selfish desires.

We observe this bent toward sinning in Adam's son, Cain, who in a fit of jealousy and anger slew his younger brother Abel. Every person born, upon reaching the age of moral accountability, finds himself under the control of the carnal heart. The human family knew of no way of defeating this enemy of the soul, until Jesus, "that he might also sanctify the people, suffered without the gate," became our Deliverer. Thanks be unto God!

While all orthodox Christian theologians agree that original sin exists in all mankind and has ruined our

---

1. Kinlaw provides an excellent discussion of the impact of God's Presence in his *This Day with the Master: 365 Daily Meditations*. (Zondervan, Kindle).

world, they do not agree on the remedy— or for that matter, whether a cure for the problem actually exists in our world.

What Changes Occur in the Life of the Saved Person?

Let us now consider the matter of carnal traits, those hateful manifestations that govern all sinners and continue to cling to the new convert and are so readily observed by those with whom we live and interact. When the Lord enables one to truly repent of his or her life of sin, a wonderful change takes place.

Carnal Christians, but Not Sinning Saints

Let us begin by noting that when a soul is regenerated, all the elements of God's holiness are imparted to it, or, we might say, the graces produced by the Holy Spirit are implanted in it, in complete number, but not in their fullness. The ultimate perfection of these graces is entire sanctification. The babe in Christ loves but possibly not with total consistency. Evidences of the remaining carnal nature, not only remain but these "uglies might seep through the cracks" involuntarily. The result is that a weak believer could even succumb to temptation to willful actions or words contrary to love, i.e., contrary to divine nature.[2]

We observe, then that entire sanctification does not take place in regeneration, for the graces implanted in the believer are not then perfected. This fact is clearly taught throughout the Scriptures. We will look, now, to a passage found in Paul's letter to the Christians at Corinth:

> I, brethren, could not speak unto you as unto spiritual, but as unto carnal; as unto babes in Christ. Ye are yet

---

2. I am indebted to Stephen Mitchem for his helpful metaphor that in the life of the unsanctified certain "uglies might seep through the cracks" of an unsanctified heart.

carnal, for whereas there is among you envyings and strife, are ye not carnal?

—*1 Corinthians 3:1*

This is precisely our point. It is certain that the persons here addressed were believers, justified and regenerated. How else could Paul address them as brethren? Much more, how could he expressly declare them to be "babes in Christ"? Is it possible to be a "babe in Christ" without justifying and regenerating grace? Surely no one can think so. These new believers at Corinth were in Christ. They were born again. But what was their level of spiritual development? Were they entirely holy? Free from sin, inward as well as outward? Paul does not say so; on the contrary, he expressly says they were yet "carnal."

Paul, as a result, could not speak to them as completely spiritual, but as carnal. He describes what of carnality he found remaining among them, and impairing their spirituality or holiness; "for whereas there is among you envyings and strife, are ye not carnal?" Are not these "envyings and strife" evidences of a sinful nature? Expressed outwardly, with the consent of the will, they have the potential to become actual sins. This passage then fully corroborates our expressed views, and authorizes us to say that evil propensities, opposed to perfect love, remain in the hearts of persons who possess justifying and regenerating grace.

Countless volumes have been written to discuss carnality and the havoc that it can wreak in the lives of saved people prior to their being delivered from its hideous influence. It will not be necessary to spend much time describing inward and outward manifestations of inbred sin. One reason for not doing so is that some will read our examples and then, with a sigh of relief declare, "Well, that particular trait is not my problem." You will not, however, advance very far in your walk with God until your unsanctified heart will begin to manifest itself in some way that you will understand is foreign to the new spiritual life that you have been enjoying since God saved you. Permit me to give an example from the early ministry of Dr. Delbert Rose, who taught at Asbury Theological Seminary and then later helped to found Wesley Biblical Seminary.

New Converts are Not Aware of a Deeper Need

When serving as a student pastor in Iowa many years ago, he met a man with a wife and five children. The man was given but two years to live by his doctors. On a cold winter night, the man wept and prayed to God and the Lord both saved the man and healed him that same night. For the next eight months the man lived in ecstasy, so happy in his salvation and in his healed body. Whenever Dr. Rose would preach about advanced steps of grace beyond conversion he would say, "Why, the Lord did all of that for me the night he saved me!"

After those eight months of almost continuous joy over sins forgiven and conscious fellowship with the Lord, the man came off the mountain of his spiritual ecstasy and entered into some real temptations and testing. There, within a few hours or days, his evil tempers showed up and the selfishness of his ambitions and a basic "proneness to evil" which he had been denying finally began to manifest itself. At a Sunday evening altar service, this brother came hurriedly to the front and in less than three minutes on his knees arose to spontaneously witness to the purifying flame of the Holy Spirit that had entered into his spirit.

More than three decades passed and the man still witnessed with clarity and joy to both his conversion and the spiritual ecstasy that was his for months; but also that, without backsliding, he moved subsequently into the baptism with the Holy Spirit, which was accompanied with his own special fullness. This illustrates well the teaching of Wesley who wrote, "A person may be *sincere*, who has all his natural tempers— pride, anger, lust, self-will. But he is not *perfect*, till his heart is cleansed from these, and all its other corruptions."[3]

Some contemporary writers argue that Wesley did not teach two distinct works of grace but that is not accurate. In writing to Miss Jane Hilton in 1776 he stated, "It is exceedingly certain that God did give you the *second blessing*, properly so called. He delivered you from the root of bitterness, from inbred as well as actual sin."[4]

So let us be quite clear on what Scripture is teaching us: every unsanctified person has a carnal heart that will seek to hide itself and then will, under the right provocation, manifest itself in such a way that it will humiliate, embarrass and undermine that saved person. Only when he seeks and finds deliverance will he be free. The extent of cleansing according to the Scriptures includes the complete removal of all sin. Sin is to be cleansed thoroughly, purged, extirpated, eradicated and crucified; not repressed, suppressed, counteracted or made void, as these terms are commonly used.

Sin is to be utterly destroyed. Any theory, which makes a place for the existence of inbred sin, whatever the provisions made for its regulation, is unscriptural. In a later chapter, we will examine the process of how God leads his children to a place of deliverance from the carnal heart.

Does God Judge Carnal Manifestations as Actual Sins?

In this segment of our study let us address the difficult matter of those awful carnal traits in the life of the unsanctified child of God. These will produce no end of discouragement, embarrassment, broken fel-

---

3. John Wesley, *A Plain Account of Christian Perfection*, (Nicholasville, KY: Schmul Publishing Co.), 74.
4. John Wesley, *Works*, 18:45.

lowship, and trouble, until the Holy Spirit reveals and solves the problem. Only He can lead the obedient believer to deliverance from the "old man" that had been inherited from Adam.

The Decalogue (the Ten Commandments), the Gospels, and many of the New Testament epistles, list a whole host of sins that will bring separation between God and the offending sinner. About these willfully committed acts there is no debate among theologians; one simply cannot indulge in such actions and maintain a saved experience with the Lord. Nevertheless, classroom discussions often take place relative to carnal manifestations and how they might impact one's relationship with God.

In the classroom one might ask, "If I manifest a carnal trait, have I sinned and become a backslider?" The key in answering this troubling issue need not be difficult to find, if we keep in mind our definition of an actual sin. To be guilty of sin, one must have light on the matter being contemplated, and then one must give the consent of the will to commit the act. Unless both criteria are present, no sin can result. We have illustrated that truth earlier with the example of Eve. She knew that to eat from the tree would be wrong. After her conversation with the serpent she gave the consent of her will and that is when she sinned. Let us consider some examples of wrong attitudes and actions that may not rise to the level of sin and cause one to backslide.

Is Jealousy Sin?

For the sake of illustration, let us imagine a new convert sitting in the church sanctuary on a Sunday morning. While awaiting the beginning of the service he glances through the church window at a new, expensive automobile pulling into the parking lot. Sitting and admiring that beautiful car, his mind begins to imagine how great it would be to own such a car, if only he could afford one.

But his mind and heart move into a jealous mode. His carnal heart suggests something like, *Just who does that fellow think he is, driving such a fancy car?*

Such subtle thoughts may continue to lurk beneath the surface as the carnal nature manifests itself. If we were to ask this fellow if he knows that envy and jealousy are wrong, he would quickly agree that such behavior is definitely wrong. For our discussion, it is essential to note that the man never gave the consent of his will to engage in such jealous behavior. He was not even aware of his thoughts until the Holy Spirit began to chide him. Perhaps, the Spirit whispered to him, "Son, what's going on here? You are envious over that car and its owner, and have even allowed jealous feelings to cloud your mind. Such action is not pleasing to me, Son. I could rescue you from such an attitude, if you would just permit me."

We learn from this scenario that it is possible for the believer to find his mind and heart being drawn into wrongful thinking, and yet he is not even aware of it until the Holy Spirit begins to deal with him about his thoughts. Are envy and jealousy sinful actions? Of course, but just because envious thoughts passed through this man's mind, did he really commit sin? We would answer resoundingly, No! Remember, to commit a sin, two criteria must be met: light and approval of the will. Were they met in this example? No, the man never gave the consent of his will to such thoughts. In fact, he was not even aware of them until the Spirit faithfully pointed them out to him.

Wesley lists four things to keep in mind regarding sin:

> He that is, by faith, born of God, sinneth not (1.) By any habitual sin; for all habitual sin is sin reigning; But sin cannot reign in any that believeth. Nor (2.) by any willful sin; for his will, while he abideth in the faith, is utterly set against all sin and abhorreth it as deadly poison. Nor (3.) by any sinful desire for he continually

desireth the holy and perfect will of God; and any tendency to an unholy desire, he, by the grace of God stifleth in the birth. Nor (4.) Doth he sin by infirmities, whether in act, word, or thought; for his infirmities have no concurrence of his will; and without this they are not properly sins. Thus, "he that is born of God doth not commit sin:" and though he cannot say, he hath not sinned, yet now "he sinneth not."[5]

Thus we can see that carnal traits in general do not have the consent of the will and do not rise to the level of actual sinning. Of course, such carnal actions bring chagrin, embarrassment, grief, and a whole host of human responses from one's family, friends and associates—but do not necessarily bring separation from God so long as the will is not involved.

Here we are on sound theological and biblical ground. The man no doubt was embarrassed and chagrined to discover that his heart was capable of such thinking. He surely would not want his friend to know what he had been thinking about his new automobile. That leaves us with a classic example of a carnal trait, not a willful sin or a "sin properly so called" as Wesley would term it. Was it a wrongful attitude? Yes, of course. Would it send him to hell as a backslider? This would depend on his response to the Spirit's dealing. Read on. This is a case of the Spirit revealing to a man the depths of his unsanctified heart and doubtlessly pointing him to the cure— entire sanctification. Now, let us consider a scriptural example from the writings of Saint Paul.

Are Carnal Christians Sinners?

In I Corinthians 3 the apostle identified believers who were overcome with envy and thereby were causing strife and division in the church at Corinth. He

---

5. John Wesley, *Works*, 5:11-12

termed them "babes" and "carnal," while making it quite clear that they were believers in Christ. He did not label them as backsliders or such like. He merely points out their carnal traits and how they were negatively impacting the congregation of which they were a part.

Many students have discussed these types of actions with me, fearful that God had cut them off or fearing that they had backslidden. Attempting to live with carnal traits will produce much grief in the life of the unsanctified. Those will result in strained relationships, hard feelings, broken fellowships, and in the case of the Corinthian "babes in Christ," even potentially, a division in the congregation. The question is this: do carnal traits cost a person his salvation?

What About Throwing Skillets?

An example of a believer struggling with carnal anger will illustrate our discussion. Anita, a new convert and a young mother with two preschool children, was married to a rough fellow, a heavy equipment mechanic who proved to be a mean, temperamental person, and was no doubt unbearable to live with. He bullied his wife and wasn't much of a father to their little girls. Once, when Anita and the girls were at church, he remained at home. The family pet dog "got on his nerves" with its incessant barking so he got his rifle and shot the poor animal. When Anita returned home, her husband informed her of how he had handled things. Such was her life with a bitter, angry man.

One night he came home after a long day at work. The children were in bed, and he seated himself at the table to eat a late supper. Anita was at the sink washing dishes. For whatever reason he began to berate her in a loud voice and an argument began. Anita's anger was getting the best of her. Pulling a heavy iron skillet out of the sink, she drew it back to throw it at her husband. Just at that point, she testified later, the Holy Spirit said to her, "Anita, I can deliver you from this anger if you will let Me." Recognizing the voice of God, she placed the skillet back in the sink and let her husband's remarks pass. She further testified that her act of obedience seemed to break the spell of that anger, and soon after that incident God entirely sanctified her. She was able to testify to a pure heart.

In this case, she had been struggling with anger, and God had been dealing with her about it. Had she refused to seek the cure for her malady she would have been guilty of a sin of omission, and that would have led to backsliding. Once believers become aware of the ugly fruits of the carnal heart, they not only have the privilege of seeking the cure, but it also becomes their duty. We will say more about this in a later discussion.

If you are unsanctified do not give up in discouragement and quit. When carnality rears its ugly head, take your case to the only source of deliverance— the sanctifying blood of Christ. Once you have learned of your disease, begin immediately to seek the cure.

Chapter Summary

1. The tendency of newly saved people in holiness churches is not to fully enjoy what God has done for them. Under poor counseling they may tend to feel unsatisfied when they hear about how wonderful entire sanctification is. Never belittle what the Lord has done when he saves a sinner.
2. Newly saved individuals will soon feel the residue of original sin in their lives; God permits this to reveal the deeper need of the heart.
3. Carnal manifestations do not rise to the level of sin properly so called; we do not believe in sinning saints,

but we are well aware of carnal Christians, e.g., the believers at Corinth.
4. It is essential for justified ones to understand that carnal traits will be manifested, but most of these do not lead to outbroken sin, unless the will is involved. An example is jealousy; one may be experiencing a jealousy toward someone and not even be aware of it until the Spirit reproves them. This is important so he doesn't feel like a backslider every time a new carnal trait surfaces.
5. Once the believer learns of carnality and refuses to seek deliverance, it is at that point he will become guilty of a sin of omission— not for the carnal heart but for refusing to seek the cure.
6. Sometimes God will permit certain provocations to emerge just to reveal to the unsanctified heart how desperately a pure heart is needed.

7
How Does God Deal with Carnality?

As we continue our discussion of this all-important subject, we will need to engage many misunderstandings that sincere people bring to the topic. The idea that one can be justified, regenerated, and adopted into God's family, and still manifest characteristics that are less than Christ-like, is too much for some to grasp. The fact is that the new believer possesses the Spirit of Christ, but not in his fullness.

In my classrooms, that concept gives rise to many questions, such as how can one receive the Holy Spirit, but not in his fullness? How can you divide up the Spirit, or why doesn't God both save and entirely sanctify a person at the same moment of time?

The truth is that the work that God performs in the heart of a sinner is really one huge event that takes place in two installments. To borrow from the language of John Wesley, the father of Methodism, some are "saved," and some are "fully saved," meaning their hearts have been made perfect in love, or as we commonly call it, entirely sanctified. The problem from humanity's point of view is this: we are dealing with two aspects of sin, committed sins (termed, "acquired depravity") and the sin nature (termed, "inherited depravity"). Knowing this to be the case, New Testament writers employed a number of passages to urge believers to complete the second installment of salvation.

When it comes to God's communications to believers of all generations, we read many exhortations: warnings and promises intended to motivate new believers to move on (after the new birth) to receive all the grace necessary to fulfill His eternal purposes for us. We are called to the action of faith. "Follow [*pursue*] holiness"; "*Go on* to perfection"; "*Perfecting* that which is lacking in your faith"; "Having therefore these promises, dearly beloved, *let us cleanse ourselves* from all filthiness of the flesh and spirit, perfecting holiness in the fear of God"; "...let us *lay aside* every weight, and the sin which doth so easily beset us." "*Be* ye therefore *perfect*, even as your Father which is in heaven is perfect." "For the *perfecting* of the saints." "...Warning every man, and teaching every man in all wisdom; that we may *present every man perfect* in Christ Jesus"; "Herein is our love *made perfect*, that we may have boldness in the day of judgment: because as he is, so are we in this world." "To the end he may *stablish your hearts* unblameable in holiness before God, even our Father, at the coming of our Lord Jesus Christ with all his saints." (emphases added)

As we have stressed earlier, when one is truly born again, there comes a consciousness of the presence of Christ within that new spiritual life. As we begin to enjoy that new relationship and as that fellowship deepens, we become conscious of how deeply our sinfulness has permeated our personal being. We realize that it is one thing to have our sins forgiven, and another matter to have our inner heart cleansed. Theologians, unfortunately, have not always been clear about the power of Christ's blood, through the work of the

Spirit, to purify and sanctify individuals deep within. But there have always been some who have probed the depths of grace and found that Christ's words, "Blessed are the pure in heart, for they shall see God" (Matthew 5:8) are a promise as well as an admonition.

Two Installments in Salvation at Thessalonica

Paul's first Epistle to the Thessalonians is one of the clearest examples of the two steps involved in the process of entire sanctification. Let us consider the spiritual experience of that new body of believers as the apostle unfolds it in his letter to them, i.e., what qualities did they possess that would indicate that they were believers?

The first quality the reader observes is that as Paul prayed for these believers, he thanked God for them—not burdened down about them, but rejoicing (I Thessalonians 1:2). Notice at least three things in that prayer.

> We give thanks to God always for you all, making mention of you in our prayers; remembering without ceasing your work of faith, and labour of love, and patience of hope in our Lord Jesus Christ, in the sight of God and our Father.
> —*I Thessalonians 1:3-4*

Here we can see these believers had faith that motivated their work; their labors were motivated by love, and they exhibited the patience of hope. As one commentator has stated about their patience of hope, "It is the spirit which can bear things, not simply with resignation, but with blazing hope."[1]

Another quality to notice about these Thessalonian believers is the manner with which Paul addressed them, he referred to them as "brethren beloved"; "Knowing,

---

1. William Barclay, *A New Testament Word Book* (London: SCM Press, 1955), 60.

brethren beloved, your election of God" (I Thessalonians 1:4). As one scholar pointed out, "the practical evidence of the Spirit in their lives showed that God had willed to enroll them among his chosen people."[2]

The Apostle continues his evaluation of them when he states that the gospel had reached them, "in word... but also in power, and in the Holy Ghost, and in much assurance" (I Thessalonians 1:5). Clearly they were to be counted as new converts; and then they progressed to the point of serving as role models, "And ye became followers of us, and of the Lord, having received the word in much affliction, with joy of the Holy Ghost: so that ye were ensamples to all that believe in Macedonia and Achaia," and even stated that they "became followers of us, and of the Lord, having received the word in much affliction, with joy of the Holy Ghost" (I Thessalonians 1:3-8).

Anyone who reads Paul's description of the believers in that church would have to acknowledge those people as unquestionably followers of Christ. It is as though the apostle cannot speak too highly of the transformation that the gospel had wrought in their lives. As one scholar evaluates these, "Although these believers had not as yet experienced the advanced state of entire sanctification, they were nevertheless basking in God-given faith, assurance, divine love, and 'joy of the Holy Ghost.'"[3]

All of this commendation notwithstanding, this church had some spiritual deficiencies. Paul found it necessary to warn them against fornication (I Thessalonians 4:3), fraud (I Thessalonians 4:6), and apparently, noisy meddling (I Thessalonians 5:11). Their greatest lack however, was perfect love — entire

---

2. W. Robertson Nicoll, ed. *The Expositor's Greek New Testament* (Grand Rapids, MI: Wm. B. Eerdmans Publishing Co., n.d.), 4: 24.

3. Joseph D. McPherson, *Exploring Early Methodism: Discoveries of Spiritual and Historical Value* (Evansville, IN: Fundamental Wesleyan Publishers, 2018), 110.

sanctification. And that brings us to the pivotal verse in the book.

In Thessalonians 3:10, the writer lays bare his heart to them in this manner: "Night and day praying exceedingly that we might see your face, and might perfect that which is lacking in your faith." After bragging on them as their teacher and mentor, he brings them to the main issue that yet eludes them; there is something missing in their walk with the Lord— a pure heart. As a skillful orator, he has laid his groundwork, setting them up to see that there still existed a lack in their life. "For this is the will of God, even your sanctification" (I Thessalonians 4:3). This is what Paul was telling the Thessalonians when he prayed for their heart cleansing. He knew they could never sanctify themselves. That is why he concludes, "Faithful is he that calleth you [to holiness], who also will do it" (I Thessalonians 5:24). Take note that the call to a holy heart is also a promise.

Matthew 10 declares that "Whoever finds his life will lose it, and whoever loses his life for my sake will find it." Having taught that, Christ became the ultimate example of dying to live, with his death on the cross. And that is why the Apostle Paul was faithful to inform the believers at Thessalonica, that there was still something significant lacking in their faith. For the inquiring heart, the Scriptures are replete with examples of the two steps involved in reaching the beautiful experience of entire sanctification.

Other Symbols and Types of the Carnal Heart

The Two Crossings of Israel

Students find the typology of two works of grace in the Scriptures to be helpful. The Old Testament provides many such examples. Let us now consider the two crossings of the Israelites as they journeyed toward Canaan. In the first incident they had just concluded the first Passover and left the land of Goshen sometime after midnight. When Pharaoh discovered their departure he assembled his army in pursuit. Crying to the Lord for deliverance, Moses led them across the Red Sea to safety even as the Egyptian army drowned. This marvelous deliverance stands as a type of what God does when he rescues sinners from the awful bondage of sin and works for them a wondrous deliverance. Note, they are not leaving Egypt because they love Jehovah; they are fleeing for their lives with the swords of Pharaoh's army at their backs. So it is with the sinner. He is fleeing the bondage of Satan and seeking to avoid an eternity spent in hell and desperately needs freedom from his chains. Here we can observe a type of regeneration, the first work of grace.

When Israel reaches the Jordan River, it's an entirely different scenario. No one is pursuing, there is no great fear; now they are being drawn by the milk and honey of Canaan. The spies have returned with glowing reports of what awaits them and they are ready to cross over and take possession of the land. Thus it is with the justified believer who has been rescued by Christ from a life of bondage, misery and sin. When the wonderful news of a Canaanland experience comes to him, he is ready to step into the Jordan by faith and inherit that second rest that awaits him in the joy of entire sanctification. In an obedient step of faith he follows the Ark of the Covenant into the flooding Jordan and then onto the western bank, soon to possess the Promised Land. What a wonderful type of the second work of grace.

Two Chambers in the Tabernacle

The tabernacle beautifully illustrates two steps in the process of reaching entire sanctification. God had a special reason for designing its layout as he did. In our churches we do not have special areas for certain people; the entire congregation is welcomed into the sanctuary or chapel. In the tabernacle, however, the Lord told Moses to make two chambers or rooms: the Holy Place and the Holy of Holies. Outside, in the courtyard where any Israelite was free to enter, was the altar of burnt offering where the blood was sprinkled, and the brazen laver where the priest washed. Those two objects typified the blood of Christ and the washing of regeneration and were the prerequisite for priests to enter the Holy Place, i.e., the outer room.

Three pieces of furniture placed in that chamber provide beautiful types: the table of showbread— the Bread of Life; the menorah or lamp stand— the Light of the World; and the altar of incense— the ascending prayers to heaven. Only priests, descendants of Aaron, could minister within the outer room and then only after proper preparation. Here is a type of the first work of grace. Beyond the veil, however, lay the centerpiece of Jewish worship, the very Presence of Jehovah.

The Holy of Holies whose dimensions formed a cube that was half the size of the outer room. It contained no light, no windows, nothing but the Ark of the Covenant. In that sacred chest were a pot of manna from the Wilderness wanderings, Aaron's rod and the two tablets of stone, which contained the Decalogue (Ten Commandments). On the solid gold lid had been cast two cherubim (which are always associated with deity) who faced each other with their enormous wings outstretched, and in some mysterious manner, the Presence of God, the *Shekina* (Hebrew, "dwelling"), rested on the lid, or Mercy Seat, as it was termed.

On one day of the year, Yom Kippur ("Day of Atonement"), the high priest was permitted to enter to wave the golden incense burner and to sprinkle the blood that procured forgiveness for the entire nation. Before he could enter, he must put on holy garments and be washed by immersing in the brazen laver, a type of regeneration. Entering this chamber presents us with a type of a second work of grace— the holiest of all. Then he must take sacrificial blood, Hebrews 9:6-10,

> Now when these things were thus ordained, the priests went always into the first tabernacle, accomplishing the service of God. But into the second went the high priest alone once every year, not without blood, which he offered for himself, and for the errors of the people: The Holy Ghost this signifying, that the way into the holiest of all was not yet made manifest, while as the first tabernacle was yet standing: Which was a figure for the time then present, in which were offered both gifts and sacrifices, that could not make him that did the service perfect, as pertaining to the conscience; Which stood only in meats and drinks, and divers washings, and carnal ordinances, imposed on them until the time of reformation.

When Christ died the veil between the two chambers was torn in two, and Paul informs us that we are to enter the holiest of all in a spiritual relation with our Savior.

> Having therefore, brethren, boldness to enter into the holiest by the blood of Jesus… Let us draw near with a true heart in full assurance of faith, having our hearts sprinkled from an evil conscience.
> —*Hebrews 10:19, 22*

In the same manner, the sinner has passed the brazen altar, washed in the laver of the washing of regeneration, enjoys spiritual food, light and a prayer life, and as such, is qualified to enter into the full salvation provided by Christ within the veil. What a beautiful type of two works of grace!

The Burnt and the Sin Offerings

Another beautiful type of the two necessary steps to achieve the state of entire sanctification can be viewed in the Levitical system of sacrifice vis-à-vis I John 1:7 and 1:9. Let's examine the relationship between the burnt offering of Leviticus 1 and the sin offering in Leviticus 4 and 5.

The Book of Leviticus has been termed the "Holiness Code" by biblical scholars for good reason; its purpose is to provide instruction on how Israelites may worship Yahweh and have access to his presence. The entire first chapter is devoted to the burnt offering.

> And the LORD called unto Moses, and spake unto him out of the tabernacle of the congregation, saying, Speak unto the children of Israel, and say unto them, If any man of you bring an offering unto the LORD, ye shall bring your offering of the cattle, even of the herd, and of the flock. If his offering be a burnt sacrifice of the herd, let him offer a male without blemish: he shall offer it of his own voluntary will at the door of the tabernacle of the congregation before the LORD.
> —*Leviticus 1:1-3.*

Students learn that the one bringing the offering and the offering priest each perform three actions. First the one needing to offer must select and bring his animal; he then placed his hands on the head of the offering; and then he must slay the animal with his own hands.

At that point the priest sprinkled the blood on the brazen altar, cut the victim into pieces and then placed them on the altar.

Two things must be noticed about the burnt offering: it is to be wholly consumed on the altar. The priest or the one bringing it are to get none of the animal. For that reason the burnt offering is identified in the Septuagint (Greek Old Testament) as the *holocaust* (a word that means "all burnt"), and in the Hebrew Scriptures, it is termed the *Calil*, which means, the "all offering."

We observed then, that this offering is a type of what Paul spoke of in Romans 12:1, "I beseech you therefore, brethren, by the mercies of God, that ye present your bodies a living sacrifice, holy, acceptable unto God, which is your reasonable service." Here the apostle is calling for the believer to bring his entire person to the cross of Christ. It truly becomes an "all offering," what he later terms, "your whole spirit, soul and body." Just as the Jew bringing the offering observed the entire animal going onto the altar of burnt offering, in like manner, the seeking believer yields his entire self to Christ as a living sacrifice.

However, there remains one more lesson to be derived from the burnt offering. It cannot be offered until first a sin offering is given.

Which Offering Comes First?

"But," the observant student will ask, "if one must do the sin offering first, why does it not appear until the fourth chapter?" That is an excellent question and part of the answer can be found in John's first epistle. Let us consider an interesting phenomenon in Scripture. Whenever a theological point is to be established by the sacred writer, he often will state the most important fact first, and then he drops back and presents the steps leading up to that most significant point. Such is what Moses did when he began Leviticus with the most important offering — the "all offering," the "all-burnt offering" — and then gives subsequent directions for the sin offering, which actually is offered first. The main goal in the Mosaic system was to be able to bring that crucial burnt offering — after a sin offering (or a trespass offering if financial damages were incurred when one sinned).

Another example that roughly parallels this concept of

the most significant being stated first, though not in chronological order, can be seen in many of the Psalms. Often, David will state the conclusion of his truth in the first verse or two of a psalm, then he will drop back and state what got him to that truth in the subsequent verses of the psalm. In other words, he establishes his point, and then develops the steps that got him to whatever his truth was in the first verse. It is a Hebrew way of thinking that became a literary style.

Psalm 34 will illustrate this point. In the first three verses, David establishes the fact that God is worthy of our praise all the time, despite any circumstances we might be facing. Then in the balance of the verses of that psalm, he presents a list of challenges that he had faced and God had caused him to triumph over them all. Thus, God is worthy of praise continually.[4]

Another example of God teaching a proper order of sequence can be seen when Moses was given instructions for building the Tabernacle. Between chapters 25 through 31 of Exodus we find all the various components of this portable structure as the Lord directed. Interestingly, rather than begin with the poles and curtains, the bronze altar and the golden altar of incense, the table of showbread, the menorah, etc., God began with the most important object in the entire worship center— he began with the Ark of the Covenant, Exodus 25:10-22. Thus, the Lord continued his pattern of beginning a sequence with the most important item first (the Ark), just as he did with the order of the sin and the burnt offering as we noted above.

Let us now observe how John demonstrates knowledge of that sequence in his epistle.

This then is the message which we have heard of him,

---

4. We can see a similar strategy in the courtroom where the prosecutor initially states the charges against the accused and then takes hours or even days to prove the validity of those charges.

and declare unto you, that God is light, and in him is no darkness at all. If we say that we have fellowship with him, and walk in darkness, we lie, and do not the truth: But if we walk in the light, as he is in the light, we have fellowship one with another, and the blood of Jesus Christ his Son cleanseth us from all sin. If we say that we have no sin, we deceive ourselves, and the truth is not in us. If we confess our sins, he is faithful and just to forgive us our sins, and to cleanse us from all unrighteousness.
—I John 1: 5-9

After introducing his reader to "light," John informed his readers that those who walk in the light enjoy fellowship with one another and enjoy the benefit of being covered by the blood of Jesus, and they are cleansed from all "sin." Here we have a view of entire sanctification: the believer enjoys all the benefits of a pure heart and has been, and is being cleansed from all sin (notice the singular). Almost all theologians and Bible scholars agree that when sin appears in the epistles, it refers to original sin, that that we inherited from Adam. A. M. Hills informs us "twenty of the world's great commentators tell us that the noun for sin (*hamartia*) in the singular number with the article 'the' before it means 'the sin-principle.'"[5]

Here we observe the Apostle John first describing one who has been purged from the carnal nature of "sin." This verse thus reflects an antitype of the burnt offering that appears as the first offering in Leviticus and is a type of Romans 12:1.

Now it is appropriate to look at I John 1:9. Here John informs the reader what he can expect when he confesses his "sins" (notice, the plural in the NT almost always means committed deeds of sin; the singular of "sin"

---

5. A. M. Hills, *Fundamental Christian Theology* (Salem, OH: Schmul Publishing Company, Inc., 1980) 2:168.

means the carnal heart or original sin) the Lord is faithful and just to forgive the sins. Beyond that the Lord will cleanse the believer from all unrighteousness, e.g., from the guilt and pollution of acquired sins— those committed before his being saved, or, of course, of any he might commit after his justification, should he lapse into committing any further sins.

What we have learned from John's epistle is simply this. In verse seven he speaks of the ultimate level of New Testament Christianity, the top rung of the spiritual ladder. He then steps back in verse nine and deals with the subsequent step that is an antitype of the sin offering in the Mosaic offerings.

We conclude this section by pointing out that this sequence is noted throughout the Levitical practices of the first section of the Book of Leviticus. Any time a burnt offering was being used for cleansing it was almost always preceded by the sin offering. One simply cannot present the "all offering" of total consecration, until he has properly dealt with his sins by bringing the sin offering.

Two Types of Servants: Bond Servant vs. Love Slave

The Mosaic Law was much more extensive than the Decalogue. Three chapters of further instructions appear in the Book of Exodus. That section is referred to by scholars as the Book of the Covenant. Let us consider the case of two types of slaves as presented by Moses in Exodus 21:1-6.

> Now these are the judgments which thou shalt set before them. If thou buy an Hebrew servant, six years he shall serve: and in the seventh he shall go out free for nothing. If he came in by himself, he shall go out by himself: if he were married, then his wife shall go out with him. If his master have given him a wife, and she

have born him sons or daughters; the wife and her children shall be her master's, and he shall go out by himself. And if the servant shall plainly say, I love my master, my wife, and my children; I will not go out free: Then his master shall bring him unto the judges; he shall also bring him to the door, or unto the door post; and his master shall bore his ear through with an awl; and he shall serve him for ever.

Before considering these instructions, students need to understand how slavery functioned under the Mosaic system. The term "slavery" for most of us usually conjures up in the student's mind the awful curse of human bondage that plagued the South in the antebellum years prior to the Civil War. In ancient Israel, however, in the Mosaic era, people might find themselves in financial trouble. What to do? Since there were no banks or lending institutions in those days, the debtor could "mortgage" himself to the one to whom he owed money. In that status, his lifestyle would be someone like an apprentice to a master; he would in effect work off his debt to that person.

Biblical Slavery and Indentured Servants

Such arrangements are well known to students of American colonial history. For example, if someone in Old England desired to migrate to America, but had no resources, he might contract with a shipowner and secure passage to the New World by agreeing to work off the cost of his transportation. Such persons were termed "indentured servants." They served in that capacity with limited freedom, usually for a period of three to five years, depending upon their agreement. Similar agreements were often made in Israel; recall how Jacob agreed to serve for seven years to earn Rachel.

To return to our Scripture, Moses instructed that in

such types of bondage, e.g., the "slave," could be forced to serve for a limit of six years. He further stipulated what property the released servant was entitled to take with him upon his departure. Then Moses raised a fascinating concept. If during his period of servitude, a servant had become attached to his master and to the household, he had a beautiful option. He would approach his master and declare that rather than take advantage of his freedom, he had reached a decision to remain with the master — not for another six years, but forever.

His love for his master and his condition within the household had won his love and he desired to become what we will term a "love slave." Two points must be made at this juncture. Can you imagine the feelings that must have come over the master to discover that his treatment of the servant had completely won him over to his master! What love the master had to have felt for his servant! What a beautiful type of the regenerated believer who to Jesus has fled for refuge! As a slave fleeing the bondage of Egypt, he has found safety and protection in his new Master as a bondservant. However, after falling completely in love with his service in the spiritual family of God, this one catches the beauty of a life of eternal devotion and longs for an even better position. He seeks to become a love slave forever, and willingly and completely devotes his life in full consecration to the Master. Now he is not fleeing Egyptian masters; he has fully counted the cost of perfect love and he yields to the position of a love slave, and his Master is delighted and seemingly withholds no blessings upon him.

The Mark of the Awl

But it gets better. Note the rather strange ceremony that ensues. Scholars for centuries have written all manner of possible explanations for taking a servant to the doorpost where his ear lobe was pierced through with an awl. Paul says in Galatians, "From henceforth let no man trouble me: for I bear in my body the marks of the Lord Jesus" (Galatians 6:17). The word for mark here is στιγμα — *stígma*. This term is from a primary στιζω — *stízo* (to "stick", i.e. prick); a mark incised or punched (for recognition of ownership), i.e. (figuratively) scar of service. In ancient cultures it might be a mark pricked in or branded upon the body. To ancient oriental usage, slaves and soldiers bore the name or the stamp of their master or commander branded or pricked (cut) into their bodies to indicate what master or general they belonged to, and there were even some devotee's who stamped themselves in this way with the token of their gods. Thus, in Mosaic usage this servant became marked as belonging to the master whom he had come to love.

We find that earlobes have some significance and as such are featured in another place in the Torah, in the consecration of priests:

> Now this is what you shall do to them to consecrate them, that they may serve me as priests... you shall kill the ram and take part of its blood and put it on the tip of the right ear of Aaron and on the tips of the right ears of his sons, and on the thumbs of their right hands and on the great toes of their right feet, and throw the rest of the blood against the sides of the altar.
> —*Leviticus 8:1*

Here we discover that priests are consecrated to the Lord by a ceremony that involves their ear, thumb and great toe being made holy with blood from the sacrifice. How fitting is that typology for the love-slave ceremony with the boring of the ear lobe of the new love slave!

For years I had pondered a possible explanation for this rather bizarre procedure until I located the field report of an archaeological excavation in modern Israel. To my delight, I discovered that the family registry was carved into the doorpost of the Jewish home. Just as the family tree used to be filled into the family in grandma's Bible, so the members of the family were chiseled into the *mezuzah*, i.e., the doorpost. To glean the full teaching of this beautiful account, let us make a few observations about the doorjamb or doorpost.

Lesson from the Love Slave

The analogy of the bondservant becoming a love-slave prefigures the rich insights the Apostle Paul shared with his readers, "...so now yield your members servants to righteousness unto holiness" (Romans 6:19). The longer you walk with the Lord the more your desire to be entirely possessed by him will increase. In that God-shaped vacuum, your hunger for him will become an overarching theme of your life and of your daily prayer. Those who lack this hunger will eventually fall by the wayside and become spiritually weak and ultimately lose out with God. The old devotional hymn expresses the situation quite well,

> Make me a captive, Lord, and then I shall be free.
> Force me to render up my sword, and I shall conqueror be.
> I sink in life's alarms when by myself I stand;
> Imprison me within thine arms, and strong shall be my hand.[6]

There remains yet one more lesson to learn from the love slave teaching in Exodus 21 and that is this. The doorpost where the servant's ear was bored through with an awl was known in Hebrew as the *mezuzah*. We first learn of the *mezuzah* when Israel prepared for the Passover in Egypt. We typically think of that term as the doorjamb on which the door swings. It was there that the blood of

---

6. George Matheson (1890), "Make Me a Captive, Lord," *The United Methodist Hymnal*, no. 421.

the Passover lamb was stricken and served to protect the Jewish family inside from the destroying angel.

But we are not finished. Recent archaeology field reports reveal that the family's genealogical records were often carved into the doorjamb, much like grandma's Bible had the family tree written out for all to see. So, we may conclude that when the master placed the awl through the ear of the love slave and into the *mezuzah* he was actually adding to the family register— he was now one of the family. Hallelujah! That is exactly what the Lord does for his love slaves!

Crucifixion and Death as Symbols of Entire Sanctification

As we read the New Testament, we have noted that sacred writers use many types, symbols and metaphors to enable readers to get a grasp on the nature of the remaining carnal nature that lurks beneath the surface of the heart of the new believer. In Romans 6:6, "Knowing this, that our old man is crucified with him, that the body of sin might be destroyed, that henceforth we should not serve sin," Paul speaks of crucifying the "old man" as a way of describing how the Holy Spirit begins the process of ending the carnal nature. When the apostle speaks of destroying the "old man" he does not intend merely to weaken, to suppress or to weaken. He means destruction— to put an end to the carnal spirit that resides in the unsanctified.

Paul's death symbolism continues in Colossians 3:5, "Mortify [put to death] therefore your members which are upon the earth," and in Galatians 2:20, "I am crucified with Christ: nevertheless I live; yet not I, but Christ liveth in me: and the life which I now live in the flesh I live by the faith of the Son of God, who loved me, and gave himself for me."

Crucifixion, not to be confused with execution, was designed by the Romans to begin a death process, one that would take an extended period of time so that passing observers might learn the reality of what happens to criminals who defied the might of the Roman government. Others have noted that a criminal might agonize in the throes of death for several hours, or even days, but process of crucifixion was an event that eventually did culminate in death and the criminal was no longer a threat to society. Correspondingly, the Spirit will initiate a process within the new believer that will fasten the "old man" to a cross in such a manner that will lead to its death.[7] We are well aware that preaching about "death route holiness" is not popular in many religious circles, but we will see it certainly is a biblical concept.

One of the most profound truths found in Scripture is the fact that life is always preceded by death; no death, no life— it is as simple as that. In John 12, as Jesus responded to the request of the Greeks, he taught this fundamental lesson from the "corn of wheat," that before there can be life, there must be death. In the same way one must destroy the firewood to enjoy the warmth of a fire, we, too, must die to self in order that we might live again in Christ.

Admittedly, this spiritual truth does not fit with our world's concept of success. Our society teaches that in order to get ahead in life one must work hard, step on others, scheme and manipulate one's way to the top. But Christ teaches just the opposite from this world's thinking. In his teaching on the "corn of wheat," the way up is the way down. Just as a the seed must fall into the ground, shrivel up and die, in order to grow, so the believer must fall into the furrow and die to him/herself, in order to really live in Christ. That is our Lord's way of saying that in "dying" to our own plans and desires we thus can gain the life that God truly wants us to live. Do we believe in "death route" holiness? Absolutely!

---

7. Donald S. Metz, *Studies in Biblical Holiness* (Kansas City, MO: Beacon Hill Press, 1971), 143.

Chapter Summary

1. The Holy Spirit will permit circumstances in the life of the unsanctified with the purpose to reveal the deep need of the heart.
2. Wesley utilized helpful terminology to discuss the matter of the unsanctified heart. Some of his terms were better understood within his eighteenth-century context, e.g., terms such as "saved," and "fully saved," are not part of our theological vocabulary when we speak of regeneration and entire sanctification.
3. A review of scriptural passages reveal both the need and the cure for an unsanctified heart.
4. An analysis of Paul's letter to the Thessalonians is a very helpful example of how the two steps are discussed.
5. An understanding of the meaning of the burnt offering (*holocaust offering*) in Leviticus 1 will enable the student to connect its meaning to Romans 12:1-2. Properly grasped, one can see its significance in the Mosaic offerings, and that one cannot bring such an offering until after he has performed a sin offering by way of preparation.
6. Two works of grace can be seen in the Mosaic ordinance that deals with the bondservant and the love slave. A proper understanding of the mark of the awl and the ritual at the doorpost (*mezuzah*) beautifully anticipates the New Covenant.
7. God has a sequence and a proper order in dealing with things that require a series of steps. The burnt offering, symbolical of entire sanctification, follows the sin offering, symbolical of the first work of grace, but is placed first in Leviticus. Other examples of this sequence can be seen in Scripture.
8. Roman crucifixion and death typify the death of the old man and the life of entire sanctification.

8
How Does God Deal with Human Traits?

Wrestling Jacob: "Come, O Thou Traveler Unknown"

IN OUR DISCUSSION OF the lives of believers as they walk in the beautiful light of God, it will be helpful for us to consider one of Charles Wesley's most meaningful hymns. Of all of the wondrous songs that he penned, perhaps these lyrics have impacted the development of Wesleyan theology more than any other. We have introduced students in the classroom to these words, and have been delighted at the response of those who are genuinely seeking a deep spiritual walk with the Lord. We have preached in revivals and camp meetings from the account of Jacob as he struggles with what symbolically represented his carnal nature and discovers the ultimate blessing that God wishes to bestow upon his children. In numerous cases, God has honored that preaching with precious seekers.

Fleeing Jacob's First Encounter with God

Students generally know the essential facts of Jacob's life. In Genesis 25, we are introduced to the twin sons of

Isaac and Rebecca. Esau, whose name derives from a similar word for "goat," due to his extreme hairiness at birth, became the father of the Edomites, having bartered away his birthright for a bowl of "red, red" soup (as the Hebrew reads, probably some type of red lentil bean).

Jacob, the younger twin, apparently as he passed through the birth canal, extended a flailing hand and feeling the foot of his brother, by way of reflex, closed the palm of his hand around the other's heel. The midwife must have informed the parents of what she observed. Since the heel in Hebrew is termed the 'aqab (from a verb that means "crooked") they named him 'Ya'aqob or "heel grasper," which in English is the name Jacob. Genesis 27:36 employs the term "supplant" to describe what the deceitful brother had done to Esau. Since the bottom of the human foot is referred to as the plantar surface, it is easy to understand the concept of taking or tripping (supplanting) someone by grabbing the bottom of the foot—not a complimentary name. What an apt metaphor for the deceitful carnal heart! Jeremiah uses the term in the passage that declares, "the heart is deceitful ('aqab or "Jacob") above all things and desperately wicked" (Jeremiah 17:9).

Esau, early on, demonstrated his disregard for significant matters in his culture, bargaining away his birthright, the most important thing in his life within the Patriarchal world. The writer of Hebrews refers to him as a "profane" person (12:16) using a word from Latin that literally means "outside the temple," i.e., to take something sacred that belongs in the temple, and drag it outside the temple into the secular realm. That is what happens when someone takes God's sacred name and uses it to swear. They thus profane the name of the Lord. Esau profaned his birthright, something to be considered sacred, by selling it to his cunning brother for a bowl of pottage, just as people today sell their spiritual opportunities for some meaningless, secular trifle.

We then discover that Jacob deceived Isaac into giving him the "birthright blessing" and fled from his home to escape Esau, who had threatened to kill him for his actions. On the way, Jacob stopped for the night, had the dream of the ladder to heaven with the angels ascending and descending. He saw the Lord at the top of the ladder and at that juncture, God recounted the same covenant to Jacob that had been given to Abraham and Isaac. Somewhat startled with his heavenly encounter, he awakened and subsequently named the place Bethel ("house of God"). He then promised to pay tithes if God would protect him and continued his journey. This is Jacob's first encounter with God and may serve to provide as a type of salvation, in our vernacular, an initial work of grace.

After twenty challenging years of life with Laban's household, after acquiring two wives, two concubines, eleven sons and one daughter, and a huge fortune in flocks and herds, Jacob headed back to Canaan, where he soon learned of Esau's coming to meet him with what appears to be a small army. Fearful of the prospects of that meeting, Jacob initiated a plan to save his own life and as much of his wealth as possible. The setting for Genesis 32 is near the fording place of the Jabbok, a tributary stream that flows into the Jordan River, which Jacob had crossed twenty years earlier when fleeing home.

Understanding his actions is the key to grasping the truths that Wesley has built into the words of "Wrestling Jacob." And for our purposes, those insights will enable us to view with our spiritual eye what God has planned for his children who sincerely want their hearts made perfect in love.

A Fearful Jacob's Second Encounter with God

Fearful of what might happen when Esau arrives, Jacob sends an enormous gift from his flocks and herds to his advancing brother, divides his remaining company into smaller groups, in order to cut his losses in case fighting were to break out. He then settles down for the night on the Jabbok.

What the student will realize is that God has ordered the events of that night, just to force Jacob into a situation in which he cannot save himself. God is doing this for Jacob's own good, much like the Lord will order the events of your life that he might reveal to you that he is your only hope— that you, on your own, cannot achieve the degree of spirituality that you seek, i.e., entire sanctification. God often does this by emptying you of your props and things that you might otherwise rely upon to accomplish in your own strength.

Interestingly, the name of that place, Jabbok, derives from a Hebrew word that means "to empty out." As hikers know, when a stream flows through a narrow channel it tends to be more swift and deep. When it "empties out" into a wider place, it flows more slowly and becomes shallow, a place where the hiker may cross without danger— he fords the stream at that wide, "emptied-out" location.

Spiritually, that is what the Lord was doing to Jacob; God was emptying him out of himself, his abilities and his own strength. Sometimes I tell my students, it's as though God has Jacob upside down by his ankles and was emptying him out— just as the Lord will symbolically do to the seeker of perfect love. It's a necessary step that God utilizes to divest us of our self-sufficiency— and we will make no spiritual progress until that happens. In the next section we shall discover how God brought Jacob to a point of total surrender, the greatest event in the life of the patriarch.

Jacob Wrestles with God

God has emptied him of all his self-confidence and carnal traits and brought him to a point of total surrender— a place at which he can bless him. In doing so, we shall consider some of the beautiful words of Wesley's immortal hymn, "Wrestling Jacob," to achieve a better grasp on the theological issues that are symbolized. I point out to my students that Isaac Watts was so moved by this hymn that he stated these poetic words of Wesley were worth more than all of his own hymns! While we often sang this song when I was a youth, today I scarcely find anyone among believers who have even heard of it— much less, have sung it! Let's observe how Wesley intertwines his poetry with the scriptural account.

Terrified of a possible disaster when he meets up with Esau, Jacob has sent gifts of appeasement to him, hoping to avert bloodshed. Encamped on the near side of the Jabbok, he retires for the night. However, he cannot sleep and decides to send over the ford "that he had," i.e., the balance of his material holdings and his wives, concubines and children. Totally alone, he faces the most memorable night of his life, a night that will change him forever. It becomes necessary to learn in seeking the fullness of God that you must come completely to an end of all your human self-reliance. God will order the events of your life in order to maneuver you into that place, just as he did for Jacob. You see, God is desirous to "bless" him, but must bring him into total surrender in order to gain the desired blessing.

Mysteriously, with no advance warning, a "man" appears on the bank of the Jabbok and apparently initiates a struggle, a kind of wrestling match with Jacob. Genesis 32:24 and 25 simply state, "And Jacob was left alone; and there wrestled a man with him until the breaking of the day. And when he saw that he prevailed not against him, he touched the hollow of his thigh; and the hollow of Jacob's thigh was out of joint, as he wrestled with him." The sacred writer omits many details we should like to know. He only informs the reader that a struggle is taking place and continues until "the going up of the dawn."

"Come, O Thou Traveler Unknown"

Wesley fittingly terms this opponent as the "Traveler Unknown," although with further study, the identity of the opponent becomes more clear. Hosea 12:3 and 4 state that "He took his brother by the heel in the womb, and by his strength he had power with God: Yea, he had power over the angel, and prevailed: he wept, and made supplication unto him: he found him in Bethel (a type of the first work of grace), and there he spake with us." We see that he is termed here as "the angel" and as "God." Clearly, this is what theologians term a "theophany," e.g., an appearance of God in human form. Most conservative scholars view this as a pre-incarnate appearance of Christ.

> Come, O thou Traveler unknown,
> Whom still I hold but cannot see;
> My company before is gone,
> And I am left alone with thee:
> With thee all night, I mean to stay,
> And wrestle till the break of day,
> The break of day.[1]

Interestingly, the Hebrew word "wrestle" literally means "to raise the dust," as struggling men would

---

1. Charles Wesley, "Wrestling Jacob," *Wesleyan Heritage Hymns* (Salem OH: Allegheny Publications, 2008), 110-112.

tend to do in that location. Obviously, a seeming life-or-death struggle transpired throughout the early pre-dawn hours of the memorable day.[2] Thus it is that when God, in his mercy, shows you your need and then isolates you from all your supports and props, you too will engage in a spiritual showdown until he grants you the blessing of perfect love you desire.

With the arrival of the first dawn of light, the heavenly combatant proceeds to the next step by "touching" the hip of the patriarch. He chose the hip due to that joint's powerful strength and muscles. Understand that the Hebrew translated "touch" really carries the meaning of "to strike." As the finality of your seeking approaches, God who knows all things, will locate your stronghold of resistance and will expose that to you in order to get you to acknowledge your main source of carnal resistance. At that point, victory is within reach!

Names in Scripture are Important

Seeking to disengage from Jacob, who has now apparently just thrown his arms around the body or neck of his opponent, the Lord insists on being freed, for the day was dawning. But this close to victory, the exhausted seeker declares his resolution and adamantly refuses to quit until that which he seeks is found.

One more step needs to be taken; he must confess his name. Of all the questions that he did not want to address, that must have been the one. Again, the Lord touches a sensitive area, and it's for Jacob's own good. God, as the term Jabbok implies, is going "to empty" this one out, until nothing is left that might weaken his spiritual life down the road. Thankfully, God does a thorough job on the one who would be pure in heart!

---

2. Jesus somewhat reflects the urgency of the spiritual battle when he warned his disciples, "The kingdom of heaven suffereth violence, and the violent are taking it by force," Matthew 11: 12.

At that point, he admits that his name is "heel grasper," and then inquires as to his opponent's name; but it's not time for that revelation to Jacob — that will come in due time.

> I need not tell thee who I am,
> My sin and misery declare;
> Thyself hast called me by my name,
> Look on thy hands, and read it there;
> But who, I ask thee, who art thou?
> Tell me thy name, and tell me now, and tell me now.

With those lines, Wesley begins to unpack the deep theology that encompasses the seeking believer, and continues to expand the meaning.

> In vain thou strugglest to get free,
> I never will unloose my hold:
> Art thou the Man, that died for me?
> The secret of thy love unfold:
> Wrestling, I will not let thee go,
> Till I thy name, thy nature know, thy nature know.

> Yield to me now, for I am weak,
> But confident in self-despair;
> Speak to my heart, in blessings speak,
> Be conquered by my instant prayer:
> Speak, or thou never hence shalt move,
> And tell me if thy name be Love, thy name be Love.

Just as soon as Jacob acknowledges his name and all that it represents, it's like a whole new world begins to open up to him. The sacred writer states the event thusly:

> And he said unto him, what is thy name? And he said, Jacob. And he said, Thy name shall be called no more Jacob, but Israel: for as a prince hast thou power with God and with men, and hast prevailed. And Jacob asked him, and said, tell me, I pray thee, thy name. And he said, wherefore is it that thou dost ask after my name? And he blessed him there.
> —*Genesis 32: 27-29.*

His new name fascinates my students and opens up some thoughts about its significance. Permit me to explain it in this manner. To fully understand the new name, we will begin with the wife of Abraham, whose name was *Sarah*, which in Hebrew means "princess." The masculine form of that would be *Sar*, a "prince." In the patriarchal world, if one wanted to be qualified as a "prince," he must prove his status by defeating any who would challenge his strength. When I was a lad, any time a new house was built in our neighborhood, there would usually be a large mound of dirt beside the newly dug basement. Boys cannot resist an old game, "king of the mountain," in which all the boys on the block took their turn in claiming and defending his mountain.

Similarly, in the Patriarchal world, any man who desired to achieve the status of a prince *(sar)* must show himself a strong man by defeating all challengers. The Hebrew verb "to wrestle" literally means "to raise the dust, to contend, to prevail." With this insight into the original language, one might translate his new name "Israel" as "one who has successfully wrestled (prevailed) with Elohim." Again, Wesley develops his analogy, but now begins to focus on the concept of pure love that only the Savior can bestow:

> 'Tis love! 'tis Love! Thou diedst for me;
> I hear thy whisper in my heart;

> The morning breaks, the shadows flee:
> Pure universal Love thou art:
> To me, to all, thy mercies move;
> Thy nature and thy name is Love, thy name is Love.

The Triumphant Cripple: A Marked Man

This nocturnal episode finally ceases with a formerly, self-confident, self-sufficient son of Abraham, limping across the Jabbok to reunite with his family. He soon learns that the Lord has taken care of the advancing Esau and the sun rises on a new man, as it were. Yes, he is a marked man who now possesses an awkward, shuffling gait that will be with him until death. But of what consequence is that? What does it really mean? Simply this: he has prevailed with God and can, with confidence, face any future foes— just as can the newly sanctified heart. The last verse concludes with:

> Lame as I am, I take the prey [battlefield spoils];
> Hell, earth and sin, with ease o'ercome.
> I leap for joy, pursue my way,
> And, as a bounding hart [deer], fly home,
> Through all eternity to prove,
> thy nature and thy name is Love.

Shouting Methodists have reveled in the sublime truth of those immortal words. Saints today find comfort and solace in them. In a recent camp meeting, praying with a seeking young man, I observed him remove a copy of this hymn we had distributed in the service from his pocket and read, pondered over and wept, as he sought for a pure heart. Curiously, I later asked him what he found helpful in those lines, to which he responded, "Wrestling, I will not let thee go, Till I thy name, thy nature know." It wasn't long after that interaction until the Lord witnessed to his heart being made perfect in love. My advice to any searching soul is to secure a copy of this beloved hymn of the Church and ask the Savior to open those words to your heart. Methodists have testified for over two hundred years to the veracity of Wesley's insights. Blessed be the Lord!

The wonderful sequel to this account presents two facts, "And Jacob called the name of the place Peniel: for I have seen God face to face, and my life is preserved. And as he passed over Penuel [same as Peniel in Hebrew] the sun rose upon him, and he halted upon his thigh" (Genesis 32:30-31). From Jacob's perspective, he has seen God. That is amazing since to see God meant instant death. That fact alone bespeaks Jacob's assurance that he has linked his life with deity, and that had resulted in a changed person.

It is helpful to observe that as Jacob limped upon a dislocated thigh, he had become a marked man. Many saints have observed that the sanctified life will produce a life that is uniquely "marked" by God.

Chapter Summary

1. Jacob at Bethel depicts his first yielding to Yahweh after his encounter following the dream of the ladder between earth and heaven; he promised to pay tithes of all that the Lord would bless him.
2. Life under Laban proved to be difficult and upon his determination to return home, God ordered all the subsequent events to place Jacob in a position where his only hope was God. Under great fear of Esau and his separating himself from all his goods and family at the Jabbok, God encounters him in a wrestling match.
3. Unable to defeat the angel, his hip is dislocated by the Opponent, and in his apparent defeat, Jacob finds the

victory he so desperately sought. Limping away from the divine encounter, wrestling Jacob, now a marked man, serves as a type of entire sanctification.
4. The patriarch Jacob provides one of the clearest attestations of two works of grace during the Patriarchal Period prior to the Mosaic Law.
5. Charles Wesley, Methodism's great hymn writer, captures the details and theological ramifications of the events at Peniel, i.e., "the face of God."

9
What about Human Infirmities?

Let Patience Have Her Perfect Work

WRITING ON THE CONTRAST between carnality and human infirmities can prove to be both challenging and controversial, for all earnest seekers. Earlier we have dealt with definitions of sin, as well as discussing carnal traits and how we may distinguish between them and natural infirmities that plague each of us. This discussion is necessary since our spiritual enemy, the devil, exerts great force to keep us in a state of doubt as to our spiritual condition, or to discourage us into thinking that we have unwittingly offended God.

Our case is somewhat analogous to that of Job as he confronted his friends who were convinced that he must have sinned since such severe calamities had invaded his life. I encourage students to understand that being ignorant of Satan's devices and of our own human infirmities often leaves us in a weakened position in which we are not strong in the Lord and in the power of His might. The lack of a proper understanding of what New Testament writers have in mind is essential if one is to remain settled in his experience of Christian perfection. Some sensitive soul may hear a message on the topic of patience and may be tempted to discredit his own experience of heart holiness and end up in darkness and doubt.

Many factors enter into a sanctified life that might produce moods, emotions, and acts that might be termed impatience, but these might not be the result of carnality, and are not actually impatience in any sense of the term. It thus becomes essential to discriminate between the carnal and the human, the physical and the mental.

An overtaxed nervous system will produce moods and emotions that are not due to any moral lack. Those are the result of physical conditions, not any spiritual deficiency. Weary bodies and tired minds overloaded with the stress of a long day's work or a short night of sleep will not produce an excess of religious joy. The nagging of small children, endless questions, a pan boiling over on the stove, a household full of sickness, broken automobiles and a host of other examples may lead to a hastily spoken word or the lack of a perfectly placid spirit. But that is not necessarily an indicator that there is a spiritual need—rather the need of a good night's rest. Of course, the devil will attempt to convince you that you have forfeited your heart made perfect in love, but quite likely, that is not the case at all. Let us consider the matter of impatience.

Is Impatience a Sign of Carnality?

How many times have students offered an example of carnality as a situation when one is running late and then, through no fault of their own, is delayed by conditions that they could not avoid? For example, what if someone sitting in the car waiting for their mate to get into the car for her doctor's appointment, feels frustrated and impatient, especially since they are already behind in the schedule? If the poor husband sits in the car, nervously tapping the steering wheel until his wife arrives, does that indicate that he is carnal? Does any reader really believe that the uneasy husband should sit in the car and get blessed as the minutes tick past, as opponents of holiness have charged? That would be utter nonsense and certainly there is no state of grace available to us that would take away any concern for being late.

The issue at hand is not whether one should get blessed while the clock is ticking; the larger issue is how one reacts as the pressure builds. When the late person finally arrives, do I roll my eyes, give a withering look, and then give them a piece of my mind? Whatever response is offered, it will be tempered, seasoned and guarded with perfect love. There is an old aphorism that is helpful to keep in mind: "I can afford to be wrong, but I cannot afford to be unkind." Scripture reminds us "love suffers long, and is kind." A sanctified heart will give the late person the benefit of the doubt and will consider that the offending party may have taken an emergency phone call or in some manner was providentially hindered on the way. The carnal heart will assume the worst-case scenario and blame the late one for being careless, unmindful of the time or worse. Your reaction will be determined by the state of your heart.

Let us consider the scenario in which a child holds the door open while the rain is pouring into the room. Will our response be one of perfect peace and tranquility? Any reasonable soul would not fault the parent who shouted to the careless child to hurry and shut the door. Is that carnality? Surely it is not.

How should we analyze those kinds of incidents? Does a lack of perfect peace and tranquility reveal an unsanctified heart?

How You Respond Reveals Much

Let me recount an incident shared by one of the most respected ministers in our denomination. The late Rev. H. E. Robertson, Sr., who conducted the noon fast and prayer at Stoneboro Camp for many years, gave an account that happened in his retirement years. I recall him sharing this account in a revival service he preached more than fifty years ago. He and his wife had returned to their home with several bags of groceries just as it began to rain. Hurrying to the side door as the rain increased, she fumbled with the key in the lock, and he, frustrated, urged her to hurry; the bags were getting wet and about to tear open. A second time he spoke with more intensity for her to hurry. Finally, she got the door opened and they entered. He set the bags on the sink and turned to go to his study.

As he passed through the dining room, a Voice spoke to him about his demeanor at the door. Knowing the gentle voice of the Holy Spirit, he turned back to his wife in the kitchen, placed his arms around her and apologized for the tone of his voice at the entry door. "I know you were frustrated, hubby, and don't you worry about it," she responded. That godly prince of a man and his companion demonstrate well that while the tone of one's voice and the urgency with which one speaks could be debated *ad infinitum,* what really matters is how one reacts to the dealing of the Holy Spirit when such situations occur. When Paul speaks of patience as a fruit of the Spirit, it is doubtful that he meant to imply that being late to the doctor's appointment should not bother real Christians.

Far more likely, the apostle has in mind our attempting to hurry up God's plans. In our humanness we might tend to rush forward. For example, let us assume that a student feels called to the mission field, and grows impatient to get there. I know of some cases where a student decided to quit college and hurry to the mission field, without waiting for God's timing. Such actions provide a more accurate view of the impatience biblical writers have in mind. Hebrews states that we are to "be not slothful, but followers of them who through faith and patience inherit the promises" (Hebrews 6:12).

Another example of waiting for God is provided. "For ye have need of patience, that, after ye have done the will of God, ye might receive the promise" (Hebrews 10:36). We might consider servants of the Lord who are chafing under some affliction, not waiting until God's timing delivers them from the present burden under which they are suffering. Such might be an example of impatience; after all, Paul instructs us to be, "Rejoicing in hope; patient in tribulation; continuing instant in prayer," Romans 12:12. The Psalmist provides helpful advice when feeling the urge to hasten forward, "Rest in the LORD, and wait patiently for him," Psalm 37:7.

Godly John Fletcher's Impatience: Could it Be?

Perhaps it will be helpful to notice that even great saints of God, men we highly esteem, sometimes manifest a level of impatience. Consider a letter written to Charles Wesley on July 26, 1763:

> My Dear Sir,
> I have for two months waited impatiently for some news of you, but in vain. Are you alive, paralytic, gouty, slothful, or too busy to write a line to your friends at Madeley? If you have not leisure to write a line, write a word, "I am well," or, "I am ill." God grant it may be the former![1]

Those lines, written by none other than the saintly John

---

1. John Fletcher, Familiar Letters, *The Works of Reverend John Fletcher in Four Volumes*, (New York: Lane & Scott, 1849) 320.

Fletcher— yes, the one about whom John Wesley wrote that he was more of an angel than a man— illustrates that patience is a trait on which we all can improve with the help of the Lord.

It is commonly agreed that when everything is going our way, patience is easy to demonstrate. The true test of patience comes when our rights are violated; when another car cuts us off in traffic; when we are treated unfairly; when God's timing seems to be so far behind our schedule. Unsanctified folk think they have a right to get upset in the face of irritations and trials. To them, impatience seems like a holy anger.

Patience, however, will reveal our faith in God's timing, omnipotence, and love. Peter Marshall shares some helpful advice, "Teach us, O Lord, the disciplines of patience, for to wait is often harder than to work." Wesley states that "Humility and patience are the surest proofs of the increase of love." It is well to keep in mind, "Patience is not the ability to wait but the ability to keep a good attitude while waiting."

George Croly, an Anglican priest, in the last line of this verse of his devotional hymn, penned the central point of my comment on patience, when he wrote:

> Teach me to feel that Thou art always nigh;
> Teach me the struggles of the soul to bear.
> To check the rising doubt, the rebel sigh,
> Teach me the patience of unanswered prayer.[2]

Just as we must develop patience in our daily walk and in our interactions with others, we will learn patience when we have asked our Father to consider a prayer need when the answer is delayed.

---

2. George Croly, "Spirit of God Descend Upon My Heart," *Psalms and Hymns for Public Worship* (London: N.P., 1854), np.

What about the Lack of Patience?

Perhaps one other point should be made. Patience can be learned and developed. It is not something that can be sought and found at the altar. "My brethren, count it all joy when ye fall into divers temptations; Knowing this, that the trying of your faith worketh patience. But let patience have her perfect work, that ye may be perfect and entire, wanting nothing" (James 1:2-4).

Here James, the brother of Jesus, instructs us to treat our trials as a reason for great joy, the reason being that trials have the potential of producing positive results, depending upon our reaction to them. Trials have the possibility of making us bitter, instead of better. Our response will determine their long-term effects upon our walk with the Lord. Properly responded to, trials can develop spiritual maturity. God, knowing that patience can be developed in his children, probably demonstrates greater understanding toward this imperfection than we humans.

Since we live in a world where iniquity seems out of control and is abounding, we must heed the warning of the Lord for the need of endurance, Matthew 24:12-13.[3] The concern for James was whether or not they would produce perseverance in each of us. Actually the word "patience," while an acceptable translation, would be better rendered "perseverance" or "endurance." The original Greek word, *hupomone,* carries the idea of waiting for something to come to pass, not merely in a passive sense, but to actively participate in what he is enduring.

Barclay defines *hupomone* as "having the quality to stand, facing the storm, struggling against difficulty and

---

3. "But he that shall endure unto the end, the same shall be saved. And this gospel of the kingdom shall be preached in all the world for a witness unto all nations; and then shall the end come."

opposition." That means that one is to make progress vis-à-vis his trial, not just to wait it out, hoping somehow to live through it. James stresses that such trials really are a test of our belief and trust or faith. Also the matter of hope that derives from faith further enables us to endure the struggle with which we are faced in life. The sanctified believer must face his trials with the idea that he will emerge successfully, and more mature and wise for having been through them.

Patience Often Means Simply Waiting on God

One other aspect of our discussion on patience needs to be addressed. For many of us, the issue revolves around our willingness to wait for God's timing as he leads us along. It is most human to want things to occur according to our timetable. I have often discussed this matter with students who are preparing for ministry. But some tend to get in a hurry and find it very difficult to wait for God to open the door for their next step in life. In our day of fast food, instantaneous emails and text messages, it becomes very burdensome to wait for things. For so many, they want it to happen— and they want it now. The following study illustrates my point.

The Stanford marshmallow experiment provides for students an interesting study on the topic of delayed gratification. This experiment was conducted by psychologist Walter Mischel, a professor at Stanford University. In his study, a group of children were offered a choice between one small but immediate reward, or waiting and receiving two rewards. Preschool children were brought into the room in which various snacks (marshmallows, pretzels and candy) were placed on a table. Instructions were given to the children. When the adult leaves the room the child may take one of the treats, but if they will wait for about twenty minutes, when the teacher returns, they can have two marshmallows. Not surprisingly, some did not wait and immediately grabbed a treat. Others tried to divert their thinking until the teacher returned and then received twice the reward. There is a fascinating sequel to this experiment.

The researchers followed each child for several decades and interestingly, the group of children who were willing to wait patiently for the second marshmallow met with greater success in their later years. They fared better financially, in their professions, and even in controlling their BMI (body weight). By being willing to delay their gratification, they found success in various areas of their life's pursuits.

There is a remarkable parallel with believers who are willing to wait patiently for the doors to open as God leads in their lives. We, as God's children, know we are promised wonderful rewards if we will develop patience and deny ourselves the immediate gratification that the world is offering.[4]

Jesus Demonstrated the Ability to Wait

An example from the life of our Lord will prove helpful. When Jesus was tempted by Satan in the wilderness, in the second scenario he was invited to jump off the Temple at Jerusalem. To do so would prove to be a grand design of God's power as well as to reveal his Messiahship. In the human, that would be a wonderful boost to Christ's earthly ministry, but the will of the Father was for Christ not to reveal that he was the Messiah until later in his ministry. It was necessary for him to show restraint and patience until God's timing and means would be revealed to him. So we observe that even our Lord developed patience, "though he were a Son, yet learned he obedience by the things which he suffered" (Hebrews 5:8). And the entire Scriptures reveal how painful waiting defined the

---

4. Walter Mischel, *The Marshmallow Test: Why Self-Control Is the Engine of Success* (New York: Little, Brown and Company, 2014).

life of many of the saints, "that ye be not slothful, but followers of them who through faith and patience inherit the promises" (Hebrews 6:12).

I recently learned of a group of wives who had not been able to conceive. They desperately wanted children and they formed this group as a means of encouraging and supporting each other. These believers met regularly to pray about their intense longing and to discuss their disappointments. They were learning to wait and to be patient. Over a period of time and one by one, they conceived until, amazingly, each of them became joyous mothers. They often spoke of their need for patience as they wrestled with their plight, and God, in his time, granted them their desire. No fair observer would accuse them for being carnal or impatient. It was a matter of awaiting God's perfect will— as well as his timing.

Daniel Steele observes that infirmities may entail regret and humiliation, but not guilt. Of course, if one were to override the checks of the Spirit in the matter of impatience, that person moves dangerously close to sin. Another evidence that patience is not gained in a moment at the altar can be seen in Paul's instruction to newly saved ones. "And not only so, but we glory in tribulations also: knowing that *tribulation works patience*" (Romans 5:3, emphasis added).

Thus we observe that most biblical comments on the matter of patience place this phenomenon in the realm of something that can be developed and improved upon, and certainly falls short of actual sin, unless of course one's impatience produced an angry, non-loving response when the pressure is on. Thankfully, the Holy Spirit will provide faithful direction to the earnest child of God.

Is it Anger or Righteous Indignation?

Students, sooner or later, bring up the topic of anger. We have already discussed some issues involving this problem. No one likes the trait of anger. For most it conjures up the red-faced loudmouth, blowing his top, yelling, throwing things. Then there is the other approach to this emotion in which someone attempts to rationalize a carnal, self-defensive anger that gets explained away as "righteous indignation." Wesley, well aware of two sides to this matter, on one occasion stated that "there is an anger which is not sinful, a disgust at sin which is often attended with much commotion of the animal spirits," but acknowledged, "I doubt whether we can well distinguish this from sinful anger but by the light of heaven."[5]

W. T. Purkiser very astutely observes that in few other areas of human experience are individual differences more evident than with the subject of anger. Such is the case because folk differ so widely in how their emotions are expressed, All have different temperaments and various nervous responses to pressure. Some react faster than others; some with greater intensity, from the newly saved person to those with more maturity. How a child is reared, what was modeled before him, and what type of Christianity was professed by those early shapers of his personality, all become factors in how he will respond to certain situations in later years.[6]

Of course, most will justify anger if they see some type of injustice done to someone else, as long as they are not the objects of the one venting the anger. As William Cessna put it, "Injustice should evoke the emotions of anger whether the injustice is against us or someone else." As Wesley stated, only the light of heaven, i.e., the Holy Spirit brought to bear on the matter, will reveal if the response was carnal anger or righteous indignation.[7]

---

5. W. Curry Mavis, *The Holy Spirit in the Christian Life* (Grand Rapids, MI: Baker Book House, 1977), 22.

6. W. T. Purkiser, *These Earthen Vessels* (Kansas City, MO: Beacon Hill Press, 1985), 63.

7. Ibid.

What about Nerves?

Closely related to the anger issue is the matter of what is termed nervous irritability. I recall a brief question put to me by a church member in the vestibule at the close of the service. Her question had to do with whether or not bad nerves were equal to carnality. I assured her that one did not necessarily imply the other. The poor soul totally misunderstood my response and later admitted that for almost an entire year that she had some bad feelings toward me because she thought I was telling her that if she had a nervous condition she must be carnal. In retrospect, it appeared rather clearly to me that bad nerves or not, she did have a problem with holding a grudge.

We are all constituted differently. Some people I have known are placid and phlegmatic (i.e., they are calm, easygoing people) and are not plagued with the emotional outbursts, exaggerated feelings, anger, bitterness or unforgiveness, as are other temperaments. It would appear that nothing bothers them. Those people, however, struggle in other areas. Merely observing the external actions of our friends and neighbors does not reveal everything they are battling. That fact reinforces the concept that we dare not judge the other person, but must leave them with the Lord.

Even the Saintly George Mueller Battled Nerves

A passage from the diary of George Mueller, the Christian evangelist and the director of the Ashley Down orphanage in Bristol, England, illustrates my point. By his testimony he had entered what he termed, "the full surrender of the heart," subsequent to his initial surrender to the Lord. This great paragon of faith wrote spoke of being in a distressed state of mind that hindered his ministry, apparently caused by nerves, and led to an irritability of temper and other attacks from the enemy. In his frustration he prayed that God would take him home rather than permit him to bring dishonor the cause of Christ.[8]

The challenge for the student when reading this account of Mueller is the idea of his irritability of temper. What are we to make of his words? It is very possible that his problem was a deeper spiritual need, an unsanctified heart and even walking behind light. Or was it just a satanic darkness with which the enemy had blanketed his soul? Here again we run the risk of judging his situation by either excusing carnality or for condemning one who is in the throes of satanic oppression.[9]

Permit me to share some advice that can help you to determine how you might respond if this is your experience. If you are unsanctified you will have a distinct tendency to explain away those feelings and refuse to deal with them, to bring them into the light of the Holy Spirit. If, however, you are in a good relationship with the Lord and such feelings arise in your heart, your reaction will be to know the worst of your case, confess what you are feeling, and ask the Holy Spirit to reveal exactly where you are. Unsanctified folk always want to excuse away their reactions; sanctified people always throw open the door of their heart and invite the Spirit to reveal to them any need they might have. Without fail, the earnest child of God can determine how they are doing in their walk with the Lord based upon whether or not they are open to divine inspection.

---

8. Purkiser, 64.

9. Part of Mueller's problem was that he had embraced the doctrine of election and the final perseverance of the saints, which are part of Calvin's theology, and he may have lacked proper instruction in deliverance from a carnal heart.

Chapter Summary

1. Patience is often misunderstood to mean that we should never feel concern if we are running late.
2. Many times impatience as discussed in Scripture conveys the idea of waiting for God's perfect timing.
3. Some of the most spiritual people demonstrate that patience can be greatly affected by danger, fear of injury or damage and these things really do not diminish from one's purity of love. One's natural temperament also influences his response.
4. Laboratory research demonstrates how the ability to wait patiently (delayed gratification) can significantly affect one's actions later in life.
5. How you respond to pressure situations after the crisis has passed reveals much about your state of grace. Do you excuse it away or do you invite the Spirit's searching of your heart?

10
Sanctification and Temptation

QUESTIONS FREQUENTLY ARISE in classroom discussions relative to temptations and the sanctified life. Most discussion has been generated in trying to decide if sanctified believers undergo different types of temptation, i.e., are their temptations external only, as opposed to unsanctified who must battle inner, as well as outer temptations. Such debates tend to be more academic and really provide little direction for believers whose only goal is to be victorious when tempted and thereby keep walking in all of their light.

Looking to the Garden of Eden, we remember that the original couple were as holy as only God could make them. They faced a temptation that appeared to be an external issue, but it did involve an inward battle. Tragically that battle was lost. It goes without saying that a sinful heart responds quite readily to solicitations to evil. Wesley described the unsaved one as the "willing servant of sin," who had no power nor desire to fight off temptation.

The truly saved person must fight against temptation

while warring against an inner corruption that weakens the one who is battling temptation. By contrast, the entirely sanctified person possesses the dynamic of the now-reigning Holy Spirit with which to combat those ever-present temptations that beset all of God's children. We do well to keep in mind that temptation is not our lot because we are sinful. It becomes our lot because we are human and we live in a fallen world in which even the most natural or normal desire has the potential to corrupt innocent desires and lead to outright disobedience to God.

Wiley points out the dangers that remain in us— normal human proclivities and appetites— that not properly guarded can lead to problems, including typical bodily appetites, desires and passions. These are God-given instincts and desires that are part of being one with Adam's race and while innocent enough in themselves, these must with diligence and God's grace be kept within bounds.[1]

James 1:14,15 provides the source of temptation. "Every man is tempted, when he is drawn away of his own lust, and enticed. Then when lust hath conceived, it bringeth forth sin..." Students typically assume that lust bespeaks something immoral, but the word simply means any desire that opens the door to temptation. Bishop Foster adds this explanation:

> Sin begins whenever the temptation begins to find inward sympathy, if known to be a solicitation to sin. So long as it is promptly, and with full and hearty concurrence of the soul, repelled, there is no indication of inward sympathy; there is no sin.[2]

---

1. H. Orton Wiley, *Christian Theology* (Kansas City: Beacon Hill Press, 1952), 2: 500.
2. R. S. Foster, *Christian Purity*, (n.p., 1851), 55.

Christ's Temptation Reveals that Holy People are Tempted

The temptation of our Lord in the wilderness reveals how proper and right objectives have the potential of leading to sin. We may be tempted through God-given desires and instincts that are morally neutral, while we recognize that improperly realized they could become defiling and sinful. We need to note the legitimacy of the temptations that Satan used to appeal to Jesus. Certainly there is nothing wrong with eating when one is hungry, but Satan did not merely tempt Jesus to eat. He wanted Jesus to step out of God's will for him, and so he invited Jesus to use divine power to satisfy his hunger.

Many of our temptations are attempts to get us to use God's gifts, given to us for service to others, for the satisfaction of our personal needs. In Christ's second temptation Satan pressed him to show God's power to quickly and powerfully reveal to the world who he was. This seemed to be an effective way of proving his divinity. Yet Jesus refused to accomplish God's purposes without using God's intended means and timetable.

Our point here is to call attention to the fact that the sinless Jesus faced temptation in every way that we do. So to expect that temptation will end with a pure heart is simply wrong. Students frequently will argue that, as the Son of God, he possessed a defense that is not available to us today. Actually, Jesus became a member of the human family to be our example and in so doing did not resort to supernatural help that is not accessible to us. In his humanity, each of the three temptations was real and appealed to his human nature, but using only the assistance of the Holy Spirit, unlike our first parents, he rejected Satan's offers.

Entire Sanctification does not Preclude Temptation

In other sections we have considered that entire sanctification does remove unholy appetites. Other holiness writers have used terms such as "extirpate," "crucify," "remove," and "eradicate," to describe that subtraction from the heart of all that is unholy. With that defiling element out of the way, when temptation does appear, the battle that takes place within the mind and heart of the tempted person does not have an ally on the inside, i.e., a carnal heart. That does not make the temptation any less real, but it results in a strong defense against that which is offered by Satan, and just like his Master he is enabled to reject the offer of what I will term "the solicitation to evil."

The point here is that it is not helpful to try to take one's spiritual pulse or to determine one's level of progress by attempting to assess whether the temptation was external or internal. The pathway of duty remains the same: "resist the devil and he will flee from you."

We all tend to talk to ourselves — at least we become aware of thought processes that almost seem like an internal conversation. Actually, we can almost diagram or chart how temptation is presented and observe how a person reacts. I have found it most helpful to let Wesley walk us through the series of steps that David took as he lost his battle with temptation when he viewed Bathsheba on that fateful evening in Jerusalem. Let's listen to Wesley as he walks us through an account from one of his important sermons:

The Unquestionable Progress of Grace to Sin

> [David] was walking upon the roof of his house, (2 Samuel 11: 2) probably praising the God whom his soul loved, when he looked down, and saw Bathsheba. He felt a temptation; a thought that

tended to evil. The Spirit of God did not fail to convince him of this. He doubtless heard and knew the warning voice; but he yielded in some measure to the thought, and the temptation began to prevail over him. Hereby his spirit was sullied; he saw God still; but it was more dimly than before. He loved God still; but not in the same degree; not with the same strength and ardor of affection. Yet God checked him again, though his spirit was grieved; and his voice, though fainter and fainter, still whispered, "Sin lieth at the door; look unto me, and be thou saved." But he would not hear: He looked again, not unto God, but unto the forbidden object, till nature was superior to grace, and kindled lust in his soul.

The eye of his mind was now closed again, and God vanished out of his sight. Faith, the divine, supernatural intercourse with God, and the love of God, ceased together: He then rushed on as a horse into the battle, and knowingly committed the outward sin.

You see the unquestionable progress from grace to sin: Thus it goes on, from step to step. (1) The divine seed of loving, conquering faith, remains in him that is born of God. "He keepeth himself," by the grace of God, and "cannot commit sin." (2) A temptation arises; whether from the world, the flesh, or the devil, it matters not. (3) The Spirit of God gives him warning that sin is near, and bids him more abundantly watch unto prayer. (4) He gives way, in some degree, to the temptation, which now begins to grow pleasing to him. (5) The Holy Spirit is grieved; his faith is weakened; and his love of God grows cold. (6) The Spirit reproves him more sharply, and saith, "This is the way; walk thou in it." (7) He turns away from the painful voice of God, and listens to the pleasing voice of the tempter. (8) Evil desire begins and spreads in his soul, till faith and love vanish away: He is then capable of committing outward sin, the power of the Lord being departed from him.

This lengthy quote from the sermon, "The Great Privilege of Those that are Born of God," provides an amazing insight into how a temptation unfolds in the life of a believer, and almost diagrams in stop-action the process of how one can lose the battle in temptation. If only King David had heeded the leading of the Spirit he might have been a wonderful example of how to win. Instead he reminds us only of how easy it is to fall.

I might add that before that memorable evening David had it all: God's favor, the subjugation of all his temporal enemies, all the pleasantries that mortal man could desire. But after that night, it's a long downward spiral as we trace rape, murder and anarchy at the hands of Amnon, Tamar, Absalom and Adonijah. Unfortunately, we read the remaining history of his life with this over-arching theme: "It might have been." Sanctified or not, we must heed the warning voice of the Holy Spirit and learn to live victorious lives over temptation.

Students often fall into the error of assuming that entire sanctification is so wonderful that somehow it must preclude the possibility of being tempted. We always remind them, however, that if a perfect Adam and Eve were tempted (they having no sin nature or even a knowledge or memory of sin) why should we expect to be free from temptation?

Above we have discussed the temptation of Christ in the Wilderness. Let us consider also his temptation in the Garden of Gethsemane. Throughout his entire public ministry our Lord knew he would face a showdown with his humanity as the hour of his betrayal and crucifixion drew closer. Even with that knowledge, however, once he entered the garden to pray, it became necessary for him to win in a battle of temptation over whether or not to "drink the cup" that he faced.

As we read a composite of all four Gospel writers we find strong language of the human suffering of Jesus. His spirit was troubled, his physical body so stressed that blood escaped through the capillaries and skin pores so that he appeared to be sweating drops of blood. The temptation for him was to turn away from the cup of suffering that confronted him. No less than three times he prayed, "If it be possible, let this cup pass from me" (Matthew 26:39, 42, 44). Clearly he felt the impulse to turn from the Father's will for him. Knowing the outcome that must materialize, if he were to be the sin-bearer of the world (thus, employing a teleological method of making the choice as we discussed in chapter four) he yielded to the fate that awaited him. Thus we see the Son of Man tempted in all points like as we are, yet without sin.

Temptations, as we have noted above with King David, generally follow a pathway through us that begins with a thought or a visual that we are either thinking about or are actually seeing. The five senses come into play in some manner and to some degree. The object of temptation could be something we see with the eyes, hear with the ears, sense or feel with our sensory faculties, taste or other sensory receptors. What is critical for the believer is to discern as early as possible, is it a thought of evil or is it an evil thought. Let me illustrate from discussions with students.

Temptation and Walking in the Light: You Cannot Stop Seeing

The college student stops by my office to seek some counseling. He is under a burden of concern and needs help. His problem is that as he was driving down the main street of the community, he noticed on the sidewalk a very attractive woman who was quite inappropriately and immodestly clothed — or unclothed. Being a healthy, normal young man with fully functioning hormones, in a flash he saw her and then, with the help of the Lord, he turned away and continued on to class. His question to me was whether or not he had sinned during those few brief milliseconds.

To help him to analyze his own situation I ventured a question or two, basically to help him solve his own dilemma. After he saw her, did he linger with his eyes on her; did he attempt to look again, perhaps in the rearview mirror? Obviously he was tempted to look at her—even to gaze upon her. Such would be a natural reaction for a fellow. But did he gain the mastery over his masculine impulse, and for the sake of purity, did he look away and push it out of his mind?

Many times I have told students in the classroom, and the laity from the pulpit, you cannot help what you see, but you choose what you look at.

The human eye, the magnificent organ of sight, is much like the lens on a fine camera. Whatever object to which it is pointed appears. All that is required is for some light to reflect off the object and that lens will take it in. So whenever our eyes are open, whatever object in our field of vision has light on it will be picked up by the eye, pass through the pupil and will penetrate to the optical nerve and then will be passed on to the brain for processing. Those facts are certain. We cannot help what we see, but we choose what we look at, and that determines whether or not we become guilty of sin. The will must become part of the process as the temptation plays out. How we pass the test will determine whether or not we have sinned. When David first looked down from the palace roof, he could not help seeing the woman, but engaging his will he chose to continue to gaze, and as we noted above, he lost the battle and incurred sin.

I recall sitting in a restaurant eating breakfast with a former student of mine. Years had passed. Now he was a pastor and we decided to meet for some fellowship. As we were visiting, I noticed a van pull into a parking space outside the place and a very attractive woman dressed in tight-fitting clothes slid out from behind the wheel. In a split second, my eyes took that visual in. Knowing the temptation from the devil would continue, I explained what was happening and I shifted in my seat in order not to have her in my field of vision when she entered the restaurant and was seated with her friends. I did not want to compromise myself, or to give place to the devil. And I was victorious. I have told students, every time you are victorious in the place of temptation, you are stronger for the next one. Unfortunately, the converse is true; every time you get defeated in the place of temptation you are weaker for the next encounter.

A Spiritual Virus Protection Program

To the above example of the temptation that could have developed, I point out something I share with students. Once the Holy Spirit resides in your heart, his influence reminds me of a virus protection program on a computer; it is always running in the background searching for harmful viruses and immediately flags the issue for the operator as soon as something threatening appears. The blessed Holy Spirit, just like the virus protection program, is always on duty and is faithful to warn whenever moral danger is near. Blessed be God!

The above incident in the restaurant illustrates what it means to walk in the light. When God gave his opinion on what not to look at, as soon as I assented with my will, I gained the victory and thereby walked in the light.

Satan the Arch Deceiver

Students often struggle to understand that entire sanctification does not end temptation. That is perhaps the result of them listening to testimonies of victory from the saints, without having the benefit of hearing how the victorious person endured a real battle with temptation before coming out on top. Satan, the master of trickery and the art of seduction, sets up the temptation through something good.

The account of Eve illustrates this for us. What did he use to tempt her? It was fruit, and it was good because God had created it. It's helpful to note that this account did not happen on the outskirts of hell, but in the very Garden of Eden— a veritable Paradise. Adam and Eve, made in the very image of God, were not in some questionable situation, but apparently right in the center of God's will, but temptation still came.

Let us note, also, that Satan did not suggest some heinous deed to Eve, nor did he give the idea that he was to become her master. Instead of remaining in obedience to God's will she permitted the call to self-interest and the process of sinning moved along to the bitter result. Thus, we observe how important it is to remain in obedience to the leadership of the Lord. Even the entirely sanctified must remain subservient to the Master. The beautiful thing is that overcoming your temptation will become what defeats the enemy because the experience will draw you closer to Jesus. God uses temptation to conquer the kingdom of evil and bring his children through victoriously.

Desire in itself is obviously not sin. It is when desire has "conceived"— that is, when it has been taken in and cherished and impregnated by the consent of the will— that it gives birth to sin. The handling of impure thoughts is a case in point. Our exposure is almost constant. Someone has compared the presentation of an impure thought to the exposure of a photographic film. When the impure thought or suggestion is presented, it is possible either to develop the film and retain the picture permanently, or to flood the exposed film to light— the light of Jesus— in which case the picture is washed away.

Temptations of the Entirely Sanctified

Spiritual pride and complacent self-righteousness— Satan fell due to this and he will tempt you to become overconfident when you are gaining spiritual ground. Over fifty years ago, while I was serving in a military hospital, a fellow airman quipped to our group, "I may be a little overconfident, but I know I'm good." I laughed then and I still smile when I share this with students. His attitude illustrates what can happen when Satan attempts to puff you up with your spiritual progress, and in so doing, he sets you up for a fall: "Wherefore let him that thinketh he standeth take heed lest he fall" (I Corinthians 10:12). No, the entirely sanctified, while he may enjoy the smile of God as he is walking in the light, understands that all of his help has, and is, coming from the Lord, and will avoid any thoughts of his own importance or superiority.

Another temptation is to confuse opinions with principles and incidentals with essentials. It is quite easy to confuse these. Keep in mind that not all opinions of godly men— not even our own— are eternal principles of right and wrong. Across the centuries godly, insightful men have recognized the difference between cardinal truths about which there can be no debate, e.g., the inspired Word of God, the virgin birth of Christ, his atonement at Calvary, belief in his resurrection, etc., versus matters that are necessary to make it to heaven, e.g., whether or not to wear a necktie, the correct method of baptism, and other matters. Church fathers, reformers and theologians referred to these secondary matters as *adiaphora,* which essentially means "things indifferent."

It is easy for the sanctified believer to get hung up on things that belong in the realm of personal convictions and, in general, have nothing to do with being a sanctified child of God. Dr. R. T. Williams gave good advice when he wrote, "I should hate to choke to death on a piece of ice. I would always think if I could have held on a little longer it would have been gone." Another stated that such dogmatism on nonessentials runs the risk of surrendering the essential, while making a last-ditch stand for the incidental. How many well-meaning saints have painted themselves into a spiritual corner by confusing their opinions with principles, and incidentals with essentials!

The sanctified will be solicited by Satan to hold an unbalanced view of one's own capabilities. To yield to such thinking will result in viewing one's abilities and service more highly than the facts justify; or it may lead to limiting and crippling one's effectiveness by failing to use to the full those talents and gifts that God has given.

Then there is the temptation to be unduly critical of differing opinions. Sanctified people are by nature sure people. One may be convinced of his position without being cocksure and recognize that certainty does not guarantee infallibility. None of us have the ability to know the whole of God's infinite truth. Intolerance has never been listed as one of the fruits of the Spirit.

Another area I have observed as a pastor is the temptation to judge others by light we possess. We tend to be impatient with those who are either immature or not yet established in the sanctifying grace of God. Light is given to us to walk in, not to judge others! Sometimes the Lord says, "What is that to you? Follow thou me" (John 21:22). I recall many years ago when my parents visited us in our new pioneer church. That Sunday morning one of the new converts in the congregation gave a testimony. Unfortunately, she was not dressed to my father's ideals of how believers ought to dress. At lunch that afternoon he asked, "Is she supposed to be a Christian?" I informed him that she was a relatively new convert who had already made tremendous strides in following Jesus and was still learning new things as she, her husband and daughters walk with the Lord. Then I gently reminded him that when he got saved when I was eleven, he didn't change his life overnight and he had grown up in the church. So we dare not judge other folk by our light. Leave them with the Lord and rejoice as they develop.

Satan will tempt you to insist on having your own way. You simply cannot pick up your marbles and go home. One prominent layman was overruled on a matter by the board of his church but then graciously accepted the assignment to carry through the project he had opposed. He was a big man and a saint!

At some point in your sanctified walk you will confront the temptation to substitute external standards for sincerity. The sanctified have a built-in horror of moral compromise. Their personal ideals and standards are the highest, but they can drift into legalism in supposing that cleanness of "the outside of the cup" is the major concern. They may even come to suppose that they receive and retain the favor of God because of what they do *not* do. They forget that holiness is always more than the absence of sin, just as light is more than the absence of darkness.

Beware of the temptation to let good intentions take the place of good actions. We agree that the primary measure of a sin is the motive of the heart, but right performance is just as important. Blundering goodness can cause almost as much havoc in the church as intentional evil. Most problems come from those who "meant well."

Temptations of the sanctified, as of all believers, are many and varied. Temptations are not sin, but they open the door to sin. Remember, "There hath no temptation taken you but such as is common to man: but God is faithful, who will not suffer you to be tempted above that ye are able; but will with the temptation also make a way to escape, that ye may be able to bear it" (I Corinthians 10:13).

"Blessed is the man that endureth temptation: for when he is tried, he shall receive the crown of life, which the Lord hath promised to them that love him" (James 1:12).

Chapter Summary

1. Perfect love does not remove temptation; Adam and Eve were as perfect as a holy God could make them, yet they were tempted.
2. Not only was the Son of God tempted, he provides a beautiful example of how we should respond when tempted.
3. Wesley's step-by-step analysis of David's temptation with Bathsheba demonstrates a stop-action portrayal of how the process of temptation plays out.
4. One need not feel guilt when passing through a temptation; to emerge successfully, is to walk in the light.

11
What about Competition in Sanctified People?

"But the fruit of the Spirit is love, joy, peace, longsuffering, gentleness, goodness, faith, Meekness, temperance: against such there is no law. And they that are Christ's have crucified the flesh with the affections and lusts. If we live in the Spirit, let us also walk in the Spirit. Let us not be desirous of vain glory, provoking one another, envying one another." —*Galatians 5:22-26*

WHEN DISCUSSING THE LIFE of holiness in the classroom, students raise the question as to whether or not competition might be a sign of pride, or might it lead to pride. The answer to that depends upon some variables. Men who love to fish or hunt delight in showing photos to their friends the length and weight of their trophy fish, or the size of the rack on their latest buck. I know some ladies who are pleased to share the results of their beautiful quilting project, the daughter's bridal gown, and the magnificent wedding cake they designed, and so it goes.

Then there is the competition on the ball field: "I can hit the ball farther than anyone on either team"; "my team really skunked those other guys"; "we really showed them how we play basketball around our school." I have heard those comments around the school and so have you. It may even be found in the classroom when the exam grades or the course grades are given.

Do Preachers Ever Compete?

And so the question arises: what about competition and the sanctified person? Is it possible that it could appear in the church? Among those in the ministry the statement is heard that so-and-so tried to out-preach his co-worker in the camp meeting. Interestingly, Dr. Dennis Kinlaw shares an account that I have heard from a number of different sources across the years.

> As a seminary student, I found myself with the privilege of hosting one of the great Methodist preachers of the twentieth century, Dr. John Brasher. He was lecturing at Asbury Seminary, which was founded by Henry Clay Morrison, another Methodist giant. As we talked, Dr. Brasher said to me, "Son, Henry Clay Morrison was a great man." I nodded in agreement. Dr. Brasher responded, "No, son, you don't understand. Morrison was a great man." Then he told me a story.
> Morrison and Brasher were preaching at a camp meeting. With an unusual anointing, Brasher preached to a large crowd on Sunday morning. He said that it was a glorious service with numerous people seeking God. That evening Morrison preached. His text was on the giving of the Law at Mount Sinai. Morrison had a flair for the dramatic and, as Brasher recalled, "The lightning flashed,

the thunder rolled, and the ground shook under our feet." As Morrison preached, Brasher became uneasy and began to suspect that Morrison was trying to outdo the morning service. He told himself, "Morrison knows that he is a greater preacher than I am.

"We had a great service this morning, and he thinks that we must have a greater one tonight." After the service Brasher slipped into his tent and went to bed. Slowly the lights on the campground went out as people ended their Sabbath. In the darkness Brasher heard a noise outside his tent. It was someone fumbling for his tent flap. The person found the flap, entered the tent, and stumbled around until he found Brasher's cot. He knelt at the foot of the cot, buried his head in the covers over Brasher's feet, and wept as though his heart would break. It was Morrison. Brasher did not say a word. Nor did Morrison. Spirit spoke to spirit.

Brasher said to me, "Son, it is one thing to walk in the Spirit, but it is another thing to live continuously in the Spirit. The best thing to do when you have slipped into the flesh is to choose again to walk in the Spirit." Then he thoughtfully affirmed, "Son, Henry Clay Morrison was a great man." What is the flesh? It is just putting my finger in things. Morrison knew that he had sinned and felt he had to make it right. That sensitivity was and is the key to greatness.[1]

To evaluate this account I enlisted the help of numerous holiness preachers, conference leaders and college professors. I sent them a copy of Kinlaw's observations and asked them to share their thoughts. The

---

1. Taken from *This Day with the Master: 365 Daily Meditations* by Dennis F. Kinlaw with Christiane A. Albertson Copyright © 2004 by Francis Asbury Society. Used by permission of Zondervan. www.zondervan.com

response of these respected men was quite enlightening. These respondents were men that many of you would know. You have heard them speak in revivals, camp meetings, conventions and in the classroom, all across the holiness movement.

Nearly every respondent agreed with me relative to Kinlaw's statement: "As Morrison preached, Brasher became uneasy and began to suspect that Morrison was trying to outdo the morning service." The main problem with Kinlaw's comment is it places Brasher in the position of judging the motives of Morrison, and that is something we cannot know to be the case.

One danger that sanctified people must avoid is to assign motives to what other persons are doing or saying—indeed, the Spirit will be faithful to check them when they are tempted. Satan will entice believers to do so, and the failure to stay close to the Lord could lead to disaster. None of us can possibly understand what motivates people to do or say what they do. God alone knows the motives, thus he warns his children, "Judge not, that ye be not judged" (Matthew 7:1). The fact is that a sanctified person will always give the benefit of the doubt when tempted to question another's motives. Relative to the story, only Brasher knows what was going through his mind as he observed the powerful preaching of his colleague. It is dangerous to attempt to assign a motive to his thoughts. Sanctified persons know well to avoid that trap with due diligence.

Sanctified People are Quick to Apologize for an Offense

All of the respondents concurred that the actions of Morrison wonderfully illustrate the attitude of someone who feels that they may have in some manner grieved or unwittingly offended another. If you learn nothing else from this discussion, let the humility of a great preacher of the Gospel serve as your model— God will lead you how to react in any situation in which there is a possibility of hurting or wounding another person.

I like to tell my students, "I can afford to be wrong, but I cannot afford to be unkind." In any situation where you are tempted to judge another's motives, always give the other person the benefit of the doubt. Attribute to them the best possible motive for their actions and leave the results with God.

Several of the respondents agreed with me that to state that "Morrison knew that he had sinned and felt he had to make it right," would have been better for Morrison to acknowledge that he had grieved the Spirit, rather than to label his response as "sin." Our second collective conclusion was that to label Brasher's actions as sin would require us to infer two possibilities: (1) that God had dealt with Brasher during the sermon warning of judgmental thoughts, or (2) that he had refused to heed the Spirit's warning not to judge the speaker, and came to his own erroneous conclusion. Remember, "to him who knoweth to do good, and doeth it not, to him it is sin" (James 4:17). In this case, Brasher knew he should not be judging and did it in spite of the Spirit's instruction, thus resulting in sin. As with most carnal traits, judging another's motives will grieve the Spirit but will not necessarily cause one to break fellowship with God, unless one refuses to listen to Him.

An Inferiority Complex may Cause You Problems

One other factor, often overlooked, is that Brasher may have struggled with an inferiority complex. Many souls in our world today have reached adulthood feeling that their best is never good enough— often the result of poor parenting during the formative years of their life. Poor parenting can predispose children to develop an inferiority complex. In adulthood such people often lack confidence and struggle to get established spiritually. We have prayed and counseled those types; they tend to lack confidence that they can ever fully please God since they could never please their parents. In the spiritual arena, some get overconfident and that produces problems; under-confidence can be just as problematic. The Holy Spirit and some godly counseling can help those to develop some stability.

Of course, we have no way of ascertaining Brasher's personality. It is possible that he may have been feeling inferior to Morrison. If that were the case, we can count on Satan to attempt to convince him that his best just wasn't good enough. Inferiority feelings should not be identified as carnal, but such persons need to be on guard lest the enemy render them weakened and less useful when their complex has nothing to do with spirituality. It is quite possible that Brasher struggled in that area, as many of us tend so to do.

I also asked the group to comment on the matter of competition and bragging on one's hunting trophy, one's sewing or baking project, one's construction results, etc. Again, there was a general consensus that there is nothing wrong with striving to be the best you can be and to perform at your best. Since we are social creatures, there is nothing inherently wrong with sharing the achievements that God has enabled us to accomplish, but we should do so without puffing up our accomplishments. Kinlaw suggests that all human relationships have a built-in rivalry that God permits to stay there so we can learn how to lose— whether the victor wins justly or unjustly. He wants us to reach the place where we do not have to come out on top every time and we do not have to have the last word. We can face defeat without being shattered by it.[2]

2. Ibid.

Sanctified persons, led of the Holy Spirit, will readily know when sharing positive accomplishments have become carnal boasting. There was a general agreement among my respondents that rejoicing in one's achievements can be done without sacrificing one's walk with God, and maintaining a close relationship with the Spirit will provide the proper corrective.

Chapter Summary

1. Many well-intentioned people who desire to be like Jesus in all that they do, can develop the idea that to excel in activities must be carnal and must be evidence of a proud heart. Not necessarily so.
2. The desire to be an overachiever could lead to pride.
3. The sanctified heart is slow to assign wrong motives to others.
4. Sanctified people are quick to apologize, especially in the case where their motives might appear to be wrong.
5. Poor parenting can predispose children to develop an inferiority complex. In adulthood such people often lack confidence and struggle to get established spiritually.

12
What are the Various Kinds of Filling With the Spirit?

STUDENTS IN CLASSROOM DISCUSSIONS eventually bring up the fillings of the Spirit in Old Testament saints, judges, leaders and prophets. How are we to understand passages that speak of Bazalel, Sampson, the seventy elders and a host of other OT persons who are said to have been recipients of the Holy Spirit. How can that occur before Pentecost? Were these entirely sanctified in the New Testament sense? Had they experienced some kind of cleansing? If so, how do we account for some of the aspects of their lives that clearly do not reflect a pure heart, e.g., Samson slays a thousand Philistines with the jawbone of a donkey, only to go in to a harlot a few verses later? Let us consider what is actually happening in these cases.

A number of theologians have attempted to analyze such instances and scholarly research papers have explored this seemingly confusing matter. In the late nineteenth century, Dr. Daniel Steele, the Methodist theologian, wrote some helpful comments and suggested a possible solution. Dr. Delbert Rose at Asbury and others have picked up on his ideas and further developed a helpful way to view the situation. Let us begin with exploring three possible fillings of the Spirit throughout Scripture. In our quest we shall include some New Testament individuals who lived prior to Pentecost, e.g., Zachariah, the father of John the Baptist.[1]

We will begin by pointing out that often, a word may be used in one context in the Bible, and in another section the same word has a different meaning, e.g., the word "prophesy" is used in Numbers 11 to express some type of ecstatic utterance that happened to the elders when they were anointed to assist Moses in matters of judgment, but in Ezekiel and Daniel, the same word means "to foretell the future," and in I Corinthians, it refers "to preaching" or "to forth-telling" the Gospel. Thus words and biblical terms must always be interpreted in context, both in their narrower textual settings, and in their broader literary, historical, and theological settings.

The biblical use of the words "fill," "filled," or "full," and "sanctify" or "sanctified," must be understood in each given context within Scripture or confusion will result. Also, progressive divine revelation within each of the Testaments, as well as progressive movement from the Old Testament into the New, must be recognized by the student in order to properly understand what the text means.

Let's consider two phrases that appear in both testaments. The phrase "filled with the Spirit" is a much broader and inclusive concept than the phrase "baptized with the Holy Spirit." The former phrase is applied to the Spirit's working under both covenants, whereas the latter phrase applies only to those under the new covenant,

---

1. Daniel Steele, *A Defense of Christian Perfection* (New York: Hunt & Eaton, 1896), 108-11; Delbert Rose, "Distinguishing the Things That Differ," *Wesleyan Theological Journal* vol. 9, 1, (1974): 5-14.

i.e., after Pentecost (Exodus 31:23; 35:31; Acts 1:5; 2:4; 4:8, 31; 11:15-17). It is essential that students notice that the phrase "filled with the Spirit" or "the Holy Spirit" does not always denote the same experiential reality within those biblical characters to which it was applied. There was certainly a difference between the Holy Spirit's filling Bezalel to assist Moses in building the Tabernacle (Exodus 31:23; 35:30-34) and Jesus' being filled with the Holy Spirit at his Jordan baptism and his subsequent wilderness temptation, (Luke 3:22; 4:1; and Acts 10:37, 38). Thus, the filling with the Spirit that occurred to Bezalel and Jesus must be distinguished from the experience of those in the Upper Room who were "filled" on the Day of Pentecost. Let us now consider three possible "fillings" with the Spirit.

Years before the rise of the modern Pentecostal movement and the more recent charismatic movements with their distinctive emphases upon the baptism of the Holy Spirit (which generally includes speaking in tongues), Steele was one of the first to examine these interesting phenomena. He has classified the various fullnesses of the Spirit as follows: a charismatic fullness, an ecstatic fullness, and an ethical fullness (i.e., a fullness of the fruit of righteousness, Matthew 5:6; Philippians 1:11). While these incidences need not be mutually exclusive, they are not identical in nature or content, nor do all believers necessarily experience them and certainly not at the same time.

Kinds of Fullness Examined: Charismatic Fullness

As we noted above, we find in Scripture many fillings of the Holy Spirit before the Day of Pentecost, but these were not the Pentecostal baptism with the Holy Spirit. He was not yet given, because Jesus was not yet glorified (John 7:37-39) so these were different from what happened in Acts 2. It was only after Jesus' ascension to the Father's right hand that He obtained for His disciples the long-promised Pentecostal gift of the Holy Spirit. Peter declared, "Therefore being by the right hand of God exalted, and having received of the Father the promise of the Holy Ghost, he hath shed forth this, which ye now see and hear" (Acts 2:33).

Actually, the first person in the New Testament to be "filled with the Holy Spirit" was John the Baptist, who was filled from birth (Luke 1:15). Later Luke declared that both Elisabeth and Zacharias, John's parents, were filled with the Holy Spirit (Luke 1:41, 67). Obviously, they were not filled in the sense of Acts 2:4; 10:44-46; and 15:8-9; for Jesus had not yet come to perform his earthly work and return to the Father to obtain for the Church the promised Pentecostal gift of the Holy Spirit (John 7:37-39; 14:15-17; Acts 2:33).

The fullness known by Elisabeth, Zacharias, and their son, John, was termed by Steele a charismatic filling, because they were under the full influence of the gift of prophecy and doubtless of discernment as well. Old Testament prophets manifested this type of fullness on certain occasions. This charismatic fullness of special enablement became the experience of the twelve apostles and the seventy disciples. We read of that when Christ sent them out to heal the sick and cast out demons and to cleanse the lepers and raise the dead (Luke 10:1, 9, 17; cf. Matthew 10:1, 8). Another example will prove helpful. When the parents brought Christ to the Temple for Mary's purification, we are told that Simeon, a righteous and devout saint, met them, "and the Holy Ghost was upon him" (Luke 2: 25-26).

Although John had a charismatic fullness from birth, he did not have the baptism with the Holy Spirit that he prophesied that Jesus alone could bestow (Luke 3:4, 16). John's own confession to Jesus when the latter came to Jordan to be baptized with water reveals much. At first he declined to baptize Jesus saying, "I have need to be baptized of thee, and comest thou to me?" (Matthew 3:14, NASB). If John's fullness from his birth had been identical with the baptismal fullness that Jesus bestows, John would have recognized he already possessed that spiritual reality and would have rejoiced in it. Instead, he confessed his remaining need of Jesus' baptizing work, which was initiated on the Day of Pentecost.

It is important for students to note that from the experiences of several New Testament persons it is evident that a charismatic fullness is not to be equated with or necessarily linked with that fullness of the Holy Spirit which was promised to the waiting disciples in the Upper Room (Acts 1 and 2). It is clearly evident that a charismatic fullness, e.g., a gift or gifts (special enablement) bestowed by the Holy Spirit can precede the Pentecostal baptism, or it may accompany, or possibly follow that Spirit baptism bestowed by Christ. It is clearly evident that being under influence of any one or more of the gifts of the Spirit is not the same reality as the dispensational baptism with the Holy Spirit, nor are the two inseparably linked with each other. None of the Spirit's many gifts is unmistakable evidence or proof that a believer has received from Christ his personal Pentecost, nor is the absence of any one or more of the gifts a witness against a believer possessing this baptism.

Both within the scriptural account and through the history of the Christian Church, men have exercised gifts of the Spirit. Men such as Samson and Balaam, for example, lacked that heart purity which the Holy Spirit creates when he comes upon believers in Pentecostal fullness. Even in his Sermon on the Mount, Jesus cautioned against possessing "gifts of the Spirit" and performing mighty deeds in His name, yet lacking the "fruits of righteousness" (Matthew 7:20-23).

Ecstatic Fullness

Steele defined ecstatic fullness as "a temporary emotional fullness of the Spirit which in and of itself leaves no permanent moral effect." The dictionary defines *ecstatic* as "an overpowering emotion or exaltation; a state of sudden intense feeling of rapturous delight." This ecstatic fullness doubtless accompanied Elisabeth's charismatic fullness as she responded to the Virgin Mary's testimony (Luke 1:41-45). Mary herself felt a joyous exaltation as she exclaimed in her Magnificat, "My soul doth magnify the Lord" (Luke 1:46).

John the Baptist also experienced ecstatic fullness, according to his personal testimony to his own disciples. For, said he, "He that hath the bride is the bridegroom: but the friend of the bridegroom, which standeth and heareth him, rejoiceth greatly because of the bridegroom's voice: this my joy therefore is fulfilled" (John 3:29).

Returning from their brief mission, the seventy disciples seem to have experienced this kind of fullness as well. However, Jesus cautioned them not to rejoice over the charismatic power to cast out demons.

> And the seventy returned again with joy, saying, Lord, even the devils are subject unto us through thy name. And he said unto them, I beheld Satan as lightning fall from heaven. Behold, I give unto you power to tread on serpents and scorpions, and over all the power of the enemy: and nothing shall by any means hurt you. Notwithstanding in this rejoice not, that the spirits are subject unto you; but rather rejoice, because your names are written in heaven.
> —*Luke 10:17-20*

Their joyous report also gave Jesus an occasion to feel a similar manifestation of joy within himself. Of that moment Luke declares, "In that hour Jesus rejoiced in spirit, and said, I thank thee, O Father, Lord of heaven and earth..." (Luke 10:21). On a later occasion the Savior told His disciples to ask of the Father in His name, that they might receive fullness of joy, obviously an ecstatic fullness (John 16:24).

Christian biographies and histories of revivals corroborate the fact that an ecstatic fullness can precede, accompany, and/or follow the crisis of the Pentecostal baptism. Consequently, overflowing joy or "an emotional high" is neither proof nor necessary ingredient of the baptism with the Holy Spirit. It is essential that students understand this truth, or they will find themselves in confusion in seeking after an emotional high.

Ethical Fullness

The third kind of fullness that Steele notes may be called "ethical fullness" and can be equated with the heart being made perfect in love or entire sanctification. This is the filling that most students think of when they discuss the fullness of the Spirit. When Peter stood up in the Jerusalem Council in Acts 15 and told of his experience in the Jerusalem Pentecost for the Jews and in the Gentile Pentecost at the house of Cornelius, he, as an inspired apostle, was giving the official interpretation of the meaning of Acts 2:14 and 10:44-47.

What happened in each instance was this: The resurrected and ascended Christ was baptizing the Jewish believers with the Holy Spirit (Acts 1:5, 8; 2:14) and doing the same for those Gentile believers (Acts 10:44-47; 11:15-17), just as John the Baptist had prophesied Jesus would do (Luke 3: 16-17), purifying their hearts by faith.

Interestingly, we also read of subsequent fillings following the Holy Spirit's descent on the Day of Pentecost upon the 120 in the Upper Room (Acts 4:8, 31). It seems evident that what occurred within Peter's heart in Acts

2:4 was not the same as the filling in Acts 4:8 and 31. In Acts 2, Peter's heart was cleansed as well as his life empowered for service, whereas in Acts 4:8 and 31 a fresh infilling of power entered the already cleansed heart of the apostle (2:4; 4:8, 31; 15:8-9).

It is noteworthy that in the Book of Acts only the risen Jesus and Peter use the phrase "baptized with the Holy Ghost [Spirit]" (Acts 1:5; 11:15-17). While Jesus talked of power connected with that event in the Christian's life, Peter stressed the purity of heart (1:5, 8; 15:8-9). In a word, to be baptized with the Holy Spirit is a fullness of a specific kind. Such an experience may or may not be accompanied by "an emotional high," or by one of the spiritual gifts. Neither ecstasy nor any one of the Spirit's special graces is essential to, or evidence of, the Savior's baptizing work. Even though the Corinthians were "not lacking in any spiritual gift" (1 Corinthians 1:7), they were yet spiritual babes with carnal hearts, still infected with jealousy and strife, and puffed up and still proud of themselves (5:2) when they should have been humbled at the disgraceful behavior of their fellow member.

Whatever the truth is about the baptism spoken of by Paul in 1 Corinthians 12:13 — namely, "For by one Spirit are we all baptized into one body, whether we be Jews or Gentiles, whether we be bond or free; and have been all made to drink into one Spirit" — it seems definitely not to have been identical with the baptism with the Holy Spirit (and with fire) which John the Baptist prophesied Jesus would bestow, and which Jesus himself promised to disciples, and which Peter personally possessed and preached. That is because the Spirit baptism Jesus administered cleansed the heart and bestowed power for holy living and service.

The Corinthian babes in Christ lacked that filling of the Spirit, for Paul uses stern reproof and earnest exhortation to move them forward into full cleansing. "Having therefore these promises, dearly beloved, let us cleanse ourselves from all filthiness of the flesh and spirit, perfecting holiness in the fear of God" (2 Corinthians 7:1). Although Paul counts these as believers, these Corinthian Christians lacked that heart purity which the Pentecostal baptism that Jesus bestows and brings to believingly obedient disciples (Acts 5:32; 15:89).

So it is clear that the phrase "filled with the Holy Spirit" is not a certain proof text of entire sanctification. Yet there is a kind of fullness of the Spirit which must imply entire sanctification, i.e., the *ongoing* gracious presence of the Holy Spirit in the soul in his fullness, not as an extraordinary gift but as a Person having the right of way through the believer's soul and body, having the keys to even the inmost rooms, illuminating every closet and pervading every crevice of the nature, filling the entire being with holy love. This Steele terms an ethical fullness, or fullness of righteousness, to distinguish it from the ecstatic and the charismatic fullness.

So in conclusion we have learned that whenever we find the term "filled with the Spirit," or language similar to that, we must determine in our mind under which dispensation are the words being used, what is the spiritual condition of the one so mentioned and then we can more accurately determine if the person is an entirely sanctified Christian or if the "filling" is something more temporary— perhaps to accomplish something for the Kingdom— or if it is merely an overflowing of joy in one of God's humble servants.

Chapter Summary

1. Many students are confused when reading of Old Testament characters to whom the Spirit gave supernatural abilities, e.g., Bezalel to oversee the construction of the Tabernacle, Samson to kill lions and Philistines, etc.
2. That presents two problems: the Holy Spirit had not

yet been given, and also, some of these were not living for God, e.g., Samson chasing Philistine women, etc.
3. Three types of fillings may be found in Scripture: charismatic fullness, ecstatic fullness and ethical fullness.
4. A charismatic fullness was not dependent upon one's spiritual condition; it was temporary and was given by God to accomplish God's immediate purpose.
5. An ecstatic filling was simply the emotional overflow of God's servants in both the Old and the New Testament; these occasions also were temporary.
6. The filling of those in the Upper Room at Pentecost were the first of those in a long line of faith that continues to this day for those whose hearts are made perfect in love. This filling is best described as an ethical filling and is to be equated with entire sanctification.

13
Fletcher on Progressive Revelation and Degrees of Perfection

Were Old Testament Saints Sanctified?

BLAMELESSNESS IS AN oft-recurring concept in the New Testament. Moral perfection is not faultlessness before one's friends, companions or acquaintances; it is blamelessness before God. Any discussion on this aspect of Christian perfection needs to consider the life of Job. While his book addresses the problem of unjust suffering, it is also somewhat of a treatise on perfection. It opens with the categorical claim that Job was a man "blameless ['perfect,' KJV] and upright, one who feared God and eschewed [turned away from] evil" (1:1).

Keeping in mind that the life of Job probably places him in the same era as Abraham, we need to remember that the Mosaic Law had not yet been given. There were neither Ten Commandments nor any form of Levitical sacrifices. And yet, the Lord informs Satan that Job was a "perfect," or blameless person: "And the LORD said unto

Satan, Hast thou considered my servant Job, that there is none like him in the earth, a perfect and an upright man, one that feared God, and escheweth evil?" (1:8)

Here we have the Judge of the universe pronouncing an Old Testament person as "perfect." Students ask how that is possible in view of Job's lack of any scriptural teaching, no Sermon on the Mount or any of Paul's teaching on holiness? The answer must be found in the fact that Job was walking in all of the light he possessed — which, admittedly, wasn't much. Another student questions, would Job have gone to heaven if he had died? Without a doubt the answer is, Yes!

What, then, can we learn from Job's case? It is simply this: it is possible with the leadership of the Spirit to live a life that is blameless before God. Job was not faultless, but according to God he was blameless. He lived a life free from condemnation in all that he did. Did he misspell words, forget appointments, fail to recall someone's name, etc.? Of course he did. No one is free from those infirmities, but thanks be unto God, we can live blamelessly before God and our fellow man!

As we trace the struggles of Job through his story, we see a man who sought for answers, along with his friends, but we also encounter one who never wavered in his ultimate faith in God. After his encounter with the Lord, when he (Job) beheld God in his majestic holiness, his lips were silenced. He could only say, "Now my eye sees you; therefore I despise myself, and repent in dust and ashes" (42:5-6). The final proof of Job's perfection was the admission of his folly and shortcomings. To see and feel the full weight of this paradox is to acknowledge with Charles Wesley, "Every moment, Lord, I need the merit of Thy death."

Consider an interesting, but necessary, phenomenon that can be discerned in Scripture; I term it "degrees of perfection," and we can thank the saintly Methodist apologist John Fletcher for pointing these out to us. Let us begin in the Garden of Eden with our first parents, Adam and Eve.

In their innocence, they had only their conscience to guide their ethical decision-making. Of course, the Holy Spirit, the ever-present guide was present in their lives, but there was no external law given at that time. By that we mean that they had no written moral code, no Levitical offering instructions, no priests or prophets, to assist them in their spiritual walk. Life for them was quite simple— their entire legal system consisted of one law: do not eat of the Tree of the Knowledge of Good and Evil. We can term their situation as the lowest rung on the spiritual ladder of our discussion of morality and perfection.

Noah and Job: Perfect Gentiles

Next, ascending to the next higher step, we note Noah and his family and we may term them as *"perfect Gentiles."* Genesis 6:9 states that "Noah was a just man, and *perfect in his generation*" (emphasis added). Keep in mind that his generation also had no Mosaic teaching, no Decalogue or sacrificial system of worship. That would include all who lived until the time of Abraham, including Job, whom most scholars view as a contemporary of the father of the Jews.[1]

Abraham: the Perfect Jew

When God called Abraham to become the progenitor of the Jewish nation, he was a Gentile, but upon his obedience to God, his faith was accounted unto him for righteousness and he walked before God and was "perfect," (Genesis 17:1). That brings us to the next

---

1. John Fletcher, "The Last Check to Antinomianism," in *Works of John Fletcher,* Vol. II, (Salem, OH: Schmul Publications, 1974), 521-29.

level of God's progressive revelation and we may term Abraham a *"perfect Jew."* Thus the patriarch was living on a higher spiritual level than Noah and his era. He had more light than they, so in a sense he was held to a higher standard than Gentiles.

At this point it is essential that students understand that in the progressive revelation of God's plan of salvation, the progress is never from error to truth, but is from a dimly perceived light to more plainly revealed light. So as we move through the Bible, we see God gradually unfolding his plan of salvation to succeeding generations. Thus, we move up the ladder of his divine plan as God led his people to a higher level of spirituality.

After the sojourn of Israel in Egypt, things unfolded just as God had spoken to Abraham.

> And he said unto Abram, Know of a surety that thy seed shall be a stranger in a land that is not theirs, and shall serve them; and they shall afflict them four hundred years; And also that nation, whom they shall serve, will I judge: and afterward shall they come out with great substance. And thou shalt go to thy fathers in peace; thou shalt be buried in a good old age. But in the fourth generation they shall come hither again: for the iniquity of the Amorites is not yet full.
> —*Genesis 15:13-16*

The Perfection of the Mosaic Covenant

Then God raised up his chosen leader to institute the Mosaic Covenant at Mt. Sinai. With the institution of that covenant we ascend to the next rung of the ladder of God's revelation: the teaching on sin and steps needed to be taken in the sacrificial system to achieve acceptance with God. Thus, we may term those who entered into the covenant with the Lord as "perfect under the Mosaic Covenant."

The Perfection of the Prophets Internalizes the Law

With the rise of Israel's prophets we observe another step up the rung on the spiritual ladder in God's progressive revelation: the call to internalize the law of Moses. The Hebrew writer informs us that these laws "could not make him that did the service perfect, as pertaining to the conscience," i.e., those offerings fell short of God's desired goal for the offerer, Hebrews 9:9. Observe how Isaiah excoriated the Mosaic system by the eighth century B.C.

> To what purpose is the multitude of your sacrifices unto me? saith the LORD: I am full of the burnt offerings of rams, and the fat of fed beasts; and I delight not in the blood of bullocks, or of lambs, or of he goats.
>
> When ye come to appear before me, who hath required this at your hand, to tread my courts?
>
> Bring no more vain oblations; incense is an abomination unto me; the new moons and sabbaths, the calling of assemblies, I cannot away with; it is iniquity, even the solemn meeting.
>
> Your new moons and your appointed feasts my soul hateth: they are a trouble unto me; I am weary to bear them.
>
> —*Isaiah 1:11-14*

With that deadness of that system, the prophets began to call for the Law to be internalized and written on the hearts of the people of the covenant. Such preaching leads us to the next rung on the ladder of the progression of Yahweh's will for his people.

That progressive unfolding of God's will came through the call of Isaiah, Jeremiah and other prophets who urged the people to have the law of Moses written on their hearts, and not to just grind out a ritual from year to year. Jeremiah provided the foundation for much of the New Testament teaching about grace. He was watching the old covenant of Moses come apart and the old legal relationship that bound the people of God together break into pieces, but Jeremiah realized that this was not the end. A new covenant would come, and it would be written not on tablets of stone but on the human heart. Then humanity would do the will of God, not because of an external force, but because they knew God. Though cured of their idolatry by the Exile, the Jews needed a better plan of salvation as the Old Testament came to an end. The whole of this perfection is thus summed up by Micah 6:8, "O Israel, what does the Lord thy God require of thee, but to do justice, to love mercy, and to walk humbly with thy God?"

The Perfection of the Disciples of John the Baptism

The next step in progressive revelation can be seen in the life of John the Baptist, who preached and administered the *baptism of repentance* to his hearers. Thus the least of his disciples achieved a level beyond the standard of the Old Covenant. With the baptism of Christ, John's level of spiritual attainment gave way to the Lamb of God, so that, as Fletcher informs us, the least of Christ's disciples apparently moved beyond the followers of John the Baptist. Had not Jesus taught, "The law and the prophets were until John: since that time the kingdom of God is preached, and every man presseth into it" (Luke 16:16).

The perfection of infant Christianity, which is called in the Scriptures "the baptism of John," is thus described by John and by Christ:

"...He that hath two coats, let him impart to him that hath none..." etc. (Luke 3:11).

"...If thou wilt be perfect, sell what thou hast, give to the poor, and follow me" (Matthew 19:21).

"If any man come to me and hate not [i.e., is not willing for my sake to leave] his father, and mother, and wife and children... yea, and his own life also, he cannot be my disciple. And whosoever doth not bear his cross, and come after me, cannot be my disciple" (Luke 14:26).

The Perfection of Those in the Upper Room at Pentecost

With the advent of our Lord's death at Calvary and his resurrection, the way is prepared for the top rung of the ladder in God's progressive revelation of his plan of salvation: the Baptism of the Spirit on the Day of Pentecost. On that day, with the birth of the Church, the full attainment of God's progressive revelation became a reality. Thus we can observe how, starting with the "perfect Gentile" of the antedeluvian world, we trace the unfolding of God's perfect plan all the way to Pentecost.

Fletcher sums these steps thusly:

...a *perfect Gentile* sees God in his works and providences; but wanting a more particular manifestation of his existence and goodness, he sighs, O where shall I find him? A *perfect Jew* ardently expects his coming as Messiah and Emmanuel, or God with us; and he groans, O that thou wouldst rend the heavens and come down! A *perfect disciple of John* believes that the Messiah is come in the flesh, and prays, O Lamb of God, that takest away the sins of the world, restore the kingdom to a waiting Israelite: baptize me with the Holy Ghost: fill me with the Spirit! And *perfect Christians* can witness from blessed experience that He who was "manifest in the flesh," is come in the Spirit's power to establish within them his gracious "kingdom of righteousness, peace, and joy in the Holy Ghost."

...We can see the progress from the perfection of a lower, to the perfection of a higher dispensation in the spiritual world. Do we not see a similar promotion, even among the lowest classes of animals in the natural world? Consider that beautiful insect, which exults to display its crown, and expand its wings in the sun; it is a perfect butterfly. Nevertheless, three weeks ago it was a perfect Aurelia, quietly sleeping in its silken tomb. Some months before, it was a perfect silkworm, busily preparing itself for another state of existence, by spinning and weaving its shroud. And had you seen it a year ago, you would have seen nothing but a perfect egg. Thus, in one year, it has experienced three grand changes, which may be called metamorphoses, births, or conversions. Each change was perfect in its kind: and, nevertheless, the last is as far superior to the first, as a beautiful, flying butterfly exceeds a black, crawling worm; and such a worm, the invisible seed of life, that lies dormant in the diminutive egg of an insect.[2]

Thus, Fletcher illustrates the various degrees of perfection from the perfect Gentile to the New Testament perfect follower of Christ who follows the leadership of the Spirit into Christian perfection. Such an analogy enables students not only to grasp the concept of progressive revelation in the plan of salvation, but to more fully understand how these Old Testament saints did not live on the high spiritual plane of Christ's children after Pentecost, yet they were ready for heaven because they walked in all the light available to them

---

2. John Fletcher, "The Last Check to Antinomianism," in *Works of John Fletcher*, Vol. II, (Salem: OH, Schmul Publications, 1974), 521-29.

in their dispensation. Lawrence Wood provides a helpful overview of Fetcher's contribution.

> Fletcher expanded Wesley's *via salutis* with a concept of four stages (or dispensations) of faith which believers pass through in the course of their lives. These personal and progressive stages of faith are abstracted from the public history of salvation as typified in the age of Noah (Gentilism), where there is a general awareness of God; the dispensation of Moses (Judaism), where there is an awareness of the personal character of God in special revelation; the dispensation of John the Baptist (and the disciples of Jesus during his earthly life), where there is God's *self*-revelation and the offer of redeeming grace and forgiveness of sins; and the dispensation of the risen Lord (culminating on the day of Pentecost which marked the birthday of the church) where believers are enabled to love God with a pure heart through the agency (baptism, infilling, or sealing) of the Holy Spirit. Wesley applauded Fletcher's concept of dispensation: "Mr. Fletcher has given us a wonderful view of the different dispensations which we are under. I believe that difficult subject was never placed in so clear a light before. It seems God has raised him up for this very thing" ([6:136-137] "Letter to Elizabeth Ritchie," January 17, 1775).[3]

Once the student recognizes how Yahweh gradually revealed the steps that Israel needed to take to recover all that was lost by Adam in the Garden, he can better understand how Old Testament saints lived on a lower spiritual level than what God ultimately introduced through Jesus and the Holy Spirit under the New Covenant.

3. Laurence W. Wood, "John Fletcher: The First Wesley Scholar," Perspectives for Wesleyan Methodist Seminarians and Leaders, https://www.catalystresources.org/john-fletcher-the-first-wesley-scholar/ (April 1, 2009).

Chapter Summary

1. Many students are confused when reading of Old Testament characters who were termed "perfect." How can anyone be so designated prior to the New Covenant and Pentecost?
2. With the writings of John Fletcher, one of the most important of the early Methodist writers, we learn of various degrees of perfection that can be ascertained in the progressive revelation of God's plan of salvation.
3. Certain Gentiles, e.g., Noah and Job, were thus designated as perfect to the extent that they walked in all of the limited light that they possessed. As we tell students, they were performing spiritually at one hundred percent of their potential.
4. With the call and response of Abraham until the giving of the law, we can use the term "perfect Jew." All those who fall under the covenant that God made with Abraham are included. This is a step higher on the spiritual ladder than the Gentiles era.
5. The Levitical system, while still in effect, had practically become useless by the time of the prophets. They pointed Israel to a higher spiritual plane by internalizing the Law.
6. John the Baptist initiated a ministry of repentance; his baptism called the people to an even higher plane of spiritual life.
7. Christ's ministry summoned the people to new heights; his Sermon on the Mount positioned his hearers even higher. For example, whereas the Law condemned adultery, his law of love condemns looking with lust. His standard reached the summit of spiritual life and all that remained was for the Holy Spirit to be poured out at Pentecost.

14
Sanctification and Danger of Feelings

What Was "Prophesying"?

IN THE PREVIOUS CHAPTER we have reviewed the various kinds of fillings by the Spirit. Now we will examine a somewhat related topic and consider the influence of the Holy Spirit in the Old Testament. One of the three "fillings" that we examined we referred to as an "ecstatic filling." Let us turn to some Scriptures in which the KJV uses the phrase, "to prophesy" and learn how such an emotional or ecstatic filling can affect the one who experiences such a phenomenon.

Godly Leaders in Israel Prophesy

In the eleventh chapter of Numbers, Moses, the Lord's faithful servant, had been laboring under the entire weight of getting the Children of Israel out of Egypt and onto the way to Canaan. In this chapter the Lord informs Moses of his plan to develop some assistance for him.

> And the LORD said unto Moses, Gather unto me seventy men of the elders of Israel, whom thou knowest to be the elders of the people, and officers over them; and bring them unto the tabernacle of the congregation, that they may stand there with thee. And I will come down and talk with thee there: and I will take of the spirit which is upon thee, and will put it upon them; and they shall bear the burden of the people with thee, that thou bear it not thyself alone.
> —*Numbers 11:16-17*

The key here that the same spirit that had been "upon" Moses, will now descend upon these national leaders. Sure enough, "And the LORD came down in a cloud, and spake unto him, and took of the spirit that was upon him, and gave it unto the seventy elders: and it came to pass, that, when the spirit rested upon them, *they prophesied,* and did not cease" (v. 25, emphasis added).

When Joshua discovered two men in the camp also "prophesying" he complained to Moses, whose response is instructive: "And Moses said unto him, Enviest thou for my sake? Would God that all the LORD's people were prophets, and that the LORD would put his spirit upon them!" (v. 25)

This chapter is the first time this interesting Hebrew word "to prophesy" appears in Scripture. Scholars are generally agreed that it is some type of ecstatic utterance that can vary slightly in its usage, depending upon who is doing it and the situation in which it occurs. We will look at several examples of this elusive verb and then draw some inferences that should enable students to better grasp its meaning. Let us consider another situation where we find the word, I Samuel 10.

The Newly Anointed Saul Prophesied

Israel had demanded Samuel to appoint for them a king, like all the other nations. Against his better judg-

14-SANCTIFICATION AND DANGER OF FEELINGS | 187

ment, he agreed and God directed him to anoint Saul. When the new king-to-be appeared at his home seeking lost donkeys, Samuel informed him of the plan and poured the anointing oil on Saul's head. He then informed him what would happen when he left.

Upon leaving the prophet's house, he stated,

> After that thou shalt come to the hill of God, where is the garrison of the Philistines: and it shall come to pass, when thou art come thither to the city, that thou shalt meet a company of prophets coming down from the high place with a psaltery, and a tabret, and a pipe, and a harp, before them; and *they shall prophesy:* And the Spirit of the LORD will come upon thee, and *thou shalt prophesy* with them, and shalt be turned into another man.
> —*I Samuel 10:5-6 (emphasis added)*

Would-be Murderers Prophesy

Once again we find individuals, in this case a company of prophets, being filled with some type of ecstatic utterance. Here it is the result of Saul being changed into "another man," some type of Old Testament religious experience. Then next time we find the word prophecy, however, it's an entirely different matter. Saul became king and initiated his reign as a genuine leader of Israel, but in time he became madly jealous of young David, the shepherd boy with great skills in killing bears, lions, and giants. He also apparently was gifted playing the harp. On occasion, David served Saul as a musician to ameliorate Saul's troubled mind. I Samuel 16: 23 recounts, "And it came to pass, when the evil spirit from God was upon Saul, that David took an harp, and played with his hand: so Saul was refreshed, and was well, and the evil spirit departed from him."

The situation deteriorated, however, until Saul's jealous heart turned to murder. Notice what the sacred writer says about him.

> And it came to pass on the morrow, that the evil spirit from God came upon Saul, and *he prophesied* in the midst of the house: and David played with his hand, as at other times: and there was a javelin in Saul's hand. And Saul cast the javelin; for he said, I will smite David even to the wall with it. And David avoided out of his presence twice.
> —I Samuel 18: 10-11 *(emphasis added)*

The challenge confronting the student now is to explain how an insanely jealous Saul can prophesy. Again, scholars generally agree that Saul has been overcome with a severe depression that in some manner produces a melancholy fit that manifests itself in ecstatic, perhaps incoherent speech patterns.

Another point to be understood is that while the text states that the evil spirit was from the Lord, students must remember that in Old Testament thinking, what God permits, he is viewed as doing. In this case, the Lord's restraining grace is removed and Satan has full control of Saul's mind. Such is similar to the case when Judas left the upper room and the Passover meal and "Satan entered into him" (John 13:27).

Battle-hardened Soldiers Prophesy

Saul's irrational pursuit of David leads him to send some of his men to locate David, whom he has heard was hiding with Samuel's school of the prophets at Naioth.

> And Saul sent messengers to take David: and when they saw the company of the *prophets prophesying,* and Samuel standing as appointed over them, the Spirit of God was upon the messengers of Saul, and they also *prophesied.* And when it was told Saul, he

sent other messengers, and *they prophesied* likewise. And Saul sent messengers again the third time, and *they prophesied* also. Then went he also to Ramah, and came to a great well that is in Sechu: and he asked and said, Where are Samuel and David? And one said, Behold, they be at Naioth in Ramah. And he went thither to Naioth in Ramah: and the Spirit of God was upon him also, and he went on, and *prophesied*, until he came to Naioth in Ramah. And he stripped off his clothes also, and *prophesied* before Samuel in like manner, and lay down naked all that day and all that night. Wherefore they say, Is Saul also among the prophets?
—*I Samuel 19:20-24 (emphasis added)*

By this late hour in Saul's life, God has entirely departed from him, leaving him open to practically becoming a pawn in Satan's hand. In this situation, to protect David, God has enabled some type of ecstatic trance to descend not only upon Saul's arresting men, but also upon the apostate king, himself.

Methodist circuit riders and camp meeting preachers during the Great Awakening of the nineteenth century record similar instances where a group of drunken troublemakers would invade the camp meeting just to make trouble. As they approached the speaker's stand some invisible force would hit them and knock them to the ground. Peter Cartwright recounts such incidences during his ministry which included people barking, also what he termed the "jerks," and other strange reactions to their overheated emotions, all of which would be classified as "prophesying." Here in Saul's case, he fell under some debilitating spasm or fit that rendered him motionless and unable to move— God's method to protect David and the others.

False Prophets of Baal Prophesy

The next instance of this strange activity surfaces with Elijah and the false prophets of Baal on Mt. Carmel. With all Israel witnessing their actions, the prophets try to summon fire to descend on their sacrifice.

> And they cried aloud, and cut themselves after their manner with knives and lancets, till the blood gushed out upon them. And it came to pass, when midday was past, and *they prophesied* until the time of the offering of the evening sacrifice, that there was neither voice, nor any to answer, nor any that regarded.
> —*I Kings 18: 28-29 (emphasis added)*

Here, again, students understand this action to be some type of frenetic screaming, doubtlessly uttering strange sounds akin to those of witch doctors and voodoo worshippers. Notice they are leaping over their altar and cutting themselves with knives and lancets. It causes one to note that Satan is in the business of counterfeiting spiritual people.

We will consider one more passage relative to false prophets, I Kings 22:10: "And the king of Israel and Jehoshaphat the king of Judah sat each on his throne, having put on their robes, in a void place in the entrance of the gate of Samaria; and *all the prophets prophesied* before them" (emphasis added).

These instances will suffice to illustrate that all references to prophesying in the Old Testament are not speaking about the same phenomenon. In the case of godly persons doing this, what shall we understand it to be? Let us now discover a key to such usage.

Even Musicians Can Prophesy upon Their Instruments

These occurrences in the Old Testament did not cease with the advent of the New Testament church. When the

Spirit was poured out at Pentecost and in other places we read of in Acts, a new phenomenon of speaking in tongues appeared on the religious scene. In those instances, of course, different language groups were present, e.g., in the Upper Room; perhaps as many as fifteen different language groups could have been represented. Anyone who has observed modern day instances of such manifestations recognizes that it almost always is accompanied by highly charged emotions. While we of the holiness movement do not practice seeking the gift of *glossolalia* (speaking in tongues), we do understand that when the Holy Spirit is present in public worship services, we can sense his Presence in the atmosphere of worship. Since we are emotional beings, we do resonate and respond to emotional stimuli. Let us examine this matter of emotions and the extent to which they can influence us.

We Can Be Conditioned to Respond to External Stimulus

External stimulus to the body and mind can produce significant response within us. Psychologists have analyzed human response to emotional stress utilizing numerous clinical studies. In seminary I first learned of the work of William Sargant, M.D., a psychiatrist in the British army during World War II.[1] I had written a research paper on prophetism in ancient Israel, and my professor recommended Sargant's work for my inquiry into the study of emotional response in religious settings. His fascinating study will guide some of our thinking.

Battlefield Stress can Break a Person

British soldiers had retreated across northern France and were facing almost certain disaster at Dunkirk. Churchill urged every boat in England to rescue their

---

1. William Sargant, *Battle for the Mind: The Mechanics of Indoctrinations, Brainwashing and Thought Control*, (Baltimore, Penguin Books, Inc., 1957).

boys before the Luftwaffe could bomb them into oblivion. Those troops were weary, scared and battle-worn. Many of them later manifested emotional symptoms that today are referred to as post-traumatic stress syndrome, PTSD. Dr. Sargant studied the cases of hundreds of those men and his findings comprise part of his volume. What causes men to undergo such extreme mental and emotional changes as a result of battle fatigue?

Next Sargant turned to the laboratory findings of Ivan Pavlov, the Russian physiologist, who had completed numerous studies on how dogs can be conditioned to respond to certain stimuli. Most students of college psychology have read of his laboratory dogs. Pavlov would ring a bell at the same time the dogs were fed. The animals learned to associate the ringing of the bell with food, and after days of such classical conditioning, he discovered that when the bell was rung, the dogs would secrete saliva, a direct result of their conditioning process.

Even Dogs Have a Psychological Stress Limit

His critical findings occurred during a season when the river that flowed through Leningrad flooded and threatened to drown all of the dogs in his laboratory that was located half a story below street level. In the middle of night, Pavlov and his lab assistants freed the animals from their cages, dragging them partly under water as they extracted them out of their cages and released them to fend for themselves until the floodwaters receded.

Rounding up the dogs hours later, they discovered that some of them, reacting to their near brush with death by drowning, had lost their classical conditioning of the ringing bell. Based upon their personality, some dogs behaved quite differently after the flood. Their response was somewhat similar to that of the soldiers who had a near-death experience at Dunkirk. Whenever a dog or a person was subjected to extreme emotional stress, at the point of breaking psychologically, Pavlov coined the term *abreaction* to describe that mental snap. He then adapts that term throughout his book to describe an emotional response to extreme pressure, whether in humans or in animals.

From Dogs to Evangelical Preaching

Sargant had been studying Wesley's Methodists and Whitefield's extemporaneous preaching that mightily moved their hearers in eighteenth century England and America. He concluded that such preaching conditioned the people to respond with strong emotions to the sermons. Being a staunch Anglican with no appreciation for the moving of the Holy Spirit, he decided that revival preachers "worked" their congregation, psyching them up to a fever pitch. He suggested that the evangelists knew how far to push their hearers (to the point of *abreaction*), just before offering them a way to avoid hell. Of course, his was a humanistic analysis, but one that did identify the overt emotional response of the hearers. Next, Sargant decided to visit some of the frontier churches in America.

Snake Handlers and Tongues

Arriving in America in the early 1950s, the psychiatrist found his way into some rural churches in Appalachia. Visiting wild charismatic services in the mountains, he observed a revival meeting in which there was "rhythmic beating, hand-clapping, music and dancing to heighten the excitement"[2] until the emotional level of the crowd had peaked. Just as the crowd had reached frenzy, the cages were opened and the snakes were passed around the energized worshippers. Sargant shares photographs of some of the young ladies at the very moment they grasped the poisonous snakes and reached a point of ec-

---

2. Sargant, 165.

stasy (*abreaction*). In their altered state of mind, they collapsed onto the floor.

Later he visited the island country of Haiti to observe the voodoo practitioners and again, he photographed their worship as they jumped and yelled and worked themselves into frenzy, under the influence of demons and perhaps alcohol and drugs. As with the groups mentioned above, these wild-eyed men would leap and dance until they reached *abreaction*, and some would collapse onto the ground, completely under a demonic spell.

Young People under the Spell of Drums, Drugs and Drink

For his last sampling, Sargant returned to England to visit the nightclubs and discothèques where he observed and photographed youth who experienced the same ecstasy "by the use of rhythmic drumming and dancing" to the sounds of recent popular music, until they would collapse onto the floor.[3]

Well aware of the strange behavior of the drinking scene, he photographed many young people as they partied, drank and danced into the early morning hours at the bars and clubs. Again, he observed as the music pulsated louder, the strobe lights flashed brightly and the liquor flowed freely. Once again he photographed young folk with a glassy-eyed, ecstatic expression that betrayed they had reached a point of *abreaction*, a state in which they are only vaguely aware of their actions. (I find it fascinating that a humanistic medical doctor would connect and find a commonality with snake-handling, tongues-speaking, voodoo witchcraft and young people under the spell of music and alcohol.) So what are we to learn from these findings of humanistic psychologists?

3. Sargant, 164.

What Do the Findings Teach Us about Emotions?

We certainly would not agree with Sargant in some areas of his analysis, e.g., Whitefield and Wesley attempting to stimulate their hearers with scary stories and by preaching the fires of hell, and such like. We would agree, however, to this extent: it is possible to stimulate the emotions of congregations in order to motivate them to seek at the altar. Song evangelists, also, can lead a crowd into an emotional response. We wish to be extremely careful at this point not to criticize or to judge, but a word of caution might be in order. Pastors and evangelists must be extra careful not to play on the emotions of the crowd for the sole purpose of manipulation. Sometimes, in our evangelical circles, we prolong the altar call in order not to cut off that one soul who is almost persuaded. On the other hand it is possible to "get into the flesh," just to get a response. With that word of caution, we will suggest one other area of possible confusion.

Can Altar Workers Interfere with the Spirit?

With a desire to see seekers find spiritual victory, it is imperative that counselors at the altar do not pressure seekers in an emotionally charged situation to claim victory when, in fact, all they received was an emotional high. We have all witnessed those instances when the tide had risen, the seeker, urged on by well-meaning altar workers, jumped or shouted for joy, only to discover later that the spiritual goal had not been achieved.

One prominent evangelist of yesterday rather humorously informed his hearers, "If you go to the altar, weep and blow your nose, you are bound to feel somewhat better." The true witness of the Spirit to one's victory, more often than not, has been a calm assurance, a sensing that everything was clear. We will have more to say about the witness of the Spirit in another chapter.

Facts, Feelings and Faith

Unfortunately for many today, a tendency has developed across the years to place a premium on high emotional feelings and overt demonstrations of the Spirit. This, I am sure, is by default, not by design. Evangelists and powerful preachers can easily leave the impression that entirely sanctified people will manifest some emotional response to the singing, testimonies or preacher, or else there is something missing. We humans tend to mimic those whom we admire and without meaning to we tend to judge and grade ourselves by how high or emotional our response is. If we don't jump as high as our neighbor in the service, then we get discouraged and might even give up. Satan appears to be well aware of such responses and will use our diminished emotions to accuse us of not being spiritual. Many testify to his tactics and to how successfully he has employed such against them. Thus, we see the danger of running on feelings.

Perhaps for you it is not your public response when in the congregation; it is how you feel in private when not among fellow worshippers. Is there constant joy, happiness, euphoria and great tranquility of spirit? Did, as the songwriter suggests, your problems all flee away and all your night turned to day? Probably not. Again, we dare not judge our condition by whether we are undergoing pressure and reverses at home or the office. If so, you will become easy prey for Satan's attacks.

I have often counseled folk who tend to place much emphasis on how they "feel" that they are setting themselves up for easy discouragement. On those gloomy or frustrating days when they have no religious feelings, it becomes necessary to exercise faith. And then things get even worse and it seems the heavens are brass and faith doesn't seem to grasp any assurance.

On those occasions when feelings are gone and you

feel numb, when faith seemingly goes nowhere, then all you can do is to fall back onto the facts. Of what facts are you certain? You have been saved and are God's child; you have been walking in all your light and have been obedient to the voice of the Spirit; you have not sinned in any manner. The facts are that you are still God's child and the testimony of thousands who have been in the same place is this: if you hold steady, faith will once again take hold and yes, the wonderful sense of his Presence will resonate once again in your heart.

Martin Luther's observations on the danger of relying on feelings for determining one's status is timeless advice for those who tend to evaluate their spiritual condition on how they feel.

> Feelings come and feelings go,
> And feelings are deceiving.
> My warrant is the Word of God;
> Naught else is worth believing.
>
> Though all my heart should feel condemned
> For want of some sweet token,
> There is One greater than my heart
> Whose Word cannot be broken.
>
> I'll trust in God's unchanging Word
> Till soul and body sever;
> For though all things shall pass away,
> His Word shall stand forever!

Chapter Summary

1. Many students are confused when reading of Old Testament characters on whom the Spirit fell and "they did prophesy." We discovered that such occasions were the result of an emotional outburst. In the case of God's people, it was probably an overflowing of joy and praise.
2. In the case of Saul, his prophesying occurred when he

was anointed to be king. Later in his backslidden state, it was tantamount to being seized by an evil spirit that motivated him to murder.
3. Saul and his men were similarly overtaken by a spirit that rendered them paralyzed. In this case, it appears to have been God's way of preventing them from harming God's servants.
4. False prophets in their wild orgies were leaping, dancing, cutting themselves in a frenzy — something akin to voodoo worshippers and what has been observed in some charismatic worship services.
5. Such prophesying can even take place in musical worship by those performing on instruments.
6. Since we all have varying degrees of emotional responses, it is imperative that we do not judge our spiritual walk by how we "feel." Many times it is necessary to rely on our faith and on the facts of our case.

15
Sanctification and Choices

LIFE IS MADE UP of choices and we have a motive for everything that we do. Choices are not made in a vacuum. Throughout the course of a day's activities you will make hundreds, if not thousands, of choices. Many choices have no moral value attached to them.

Some examples show the truth of this fact. For instance, if you are standing in your closet trying to decide if you should wear the blue shirt or the white shirt, nothing in your decision is going to affect your walk with the Lord; it simply makes no difference. Now there may be some good reasons to choose one color over another, e.g., blue might not match well with your purple trousers, but either choice won't call for a moral decision. In the classroom I often have shared a sequence of decisions that the typical person makes in the first hour after awakening in the morning.

Most of Your Choices Have No Moral Value Attached

We begin with the sound of the alarm clock as it sends forth its awakening sound on the nightstand by your bed.

Upon hearing that awful clanging, buzzing, or chirping, you are confronted with your first decision of the morning. Will you reach out and turn it off or will you continue to let it ring? You reach a decision so you reach out and shut it off. That is your first decision of the day. Whether you try to ignore it or whether you reach out and quiet it, nothing will affect your conscience or your walk with God. The choice was amoral, i.e., it had no moral value attached to it.

Once you have turned off the alarm, you have another choice to make: do you get out of bed and get moving, or do you continue to lie in bed? There is another choice to be made, and again, it has no moral value attached to it. Whether you arise or whether you sleep will not affect your walk with the Lord. True enough, it may mean you will be late to work or to class and you need to face those consequences, but it won't affect your walk with God.

More decisions await the sleepy you. In the bathroom, a choice needs to be made as to cold water or hot water. In the clothes closet, styles and colors must be selected for that day's apparel. In the kitchen the choice for breakfast awaits you; will it be bacon and eggs, oatmeal, a health bar, or nothing? Again, no moral value attaches to those decisions.

Now, it's off to the job and you must decide if you will walk to work or drive. Since your workplace is six miles away, you decide to drive. There's another choice, but again no moral value is attached to it because it matters not to anyone else whether you walk or drive and it certainly wouldn't affect your walk with the Lord. Next you grab your car keys off the hook and head for the garage.

Once in the car, you start the engine and make the choice to place the car in "R" rather than "D" and you also decide to push the button to open the garage door, since you have learned that it's always better to exit the garage with the door open. You back down the driveway and out into the street and placing the car in "D," you head toward the first intersection.

You have just completed a whole sequence of decisions, and again, none of your choices had any moral value attached to them. It matters not one bit to anyone else if you eat a health bar for breakfast, drive to work, open your garage door, or whatever. None of those choices will affect your walk with God. But now, you are about to make a decision that will affect you morally.

Moral Choices are the Ones that Count

Approaching the intersection you observe the big red sign that reads STOP. How you respond this time involves a choice that does have moral value attached to it and how you choose will impact your spiritual walk. Christians clearly are instructed in Scripture to obey the laws of the land and those who have the rule over you. Municipal and state laws leave no doubt; you must stop at all stop signs. Now I have college students who talk about doing what is known as a "rolling stop," but that is impossible — one either rolls or one stops! And the traffic officer can certainly enlighten you on the difference. To fail to stop could mean damage and bodily injury to motorists coming from the other direction. It might be your best friend or your relative in that other car that you may hit by refusing to obey the law.

Walking in the Light Keeps You in the Clear

Can one walk a morally pure life? Yes, it is possible. One may do so by simply walking in the light. I John 1:7 states, "If we walk in the light as he is in the light, we have fellowship, one with another, and the blood of Jesus Christ, his Son, cleanseth us from all sin." To enable students to understand the concept of light, I offer this definition: "Light is God's opinion on any matter." God does have an opinion on just about any matter on which you will consult him. In the above example of making choices we mentioned choosing clothes to wear. Actually, if you will take time to ask, God will give you an opinion on how you should dress. Perhaps you have some items of dress that might be borderline as to modesty, and asking the Lord his opinion will enable you to dress to please him. In doing so, you will feel a wonderful satisfaction knowing that you are honoring the Lord. To do so will also boost your confidence in walking in the light. For the believer, one of the greatest rewards you can enjoy is to have the Holy Spirit's approval. Permit me to make one other point on this matter of consulting with God in order to get his opinion.

As a father of two daughters it was my duty to instruct them in the ways of the Lord and to give them counsel to properly prepare them for adulthood. Years have now passed and they are grown women. On occasion they will consult with me about some matter in their life, about some decision they must make. Even though they have long since reached their maturity and are no longer under my roof, it does please me that they have enough confidence in my advice that they want to hear my opinion. Surely it must warm the heart of our heavenly Father when we go to him for his opinion on choices. If earthly fathers are pleased when their grown children still seek their advice, how much more must God be pleased when his children so honor him?

Sanctification and Motives

While many choices have no moral value attached to them as we saw above, they do have a motive behind them. Motives are the best measure of one's character according to the teaching of our Lord. Within the heart of the carnal Christian we often observe the desire to do things for the wrong reason. In the entirely sanctified, however, the desire to do something is not contaminated with the wrong reason. Satan may tempt you to do something good, but not so much to help others as to make yourself feel good, to somehow demonstrate that you are a dedicated Christian.

That kind of behavior fell under our Lord's strong rebuke. In his warning against giving alms for the wrong reason, he clearly instructs his children to do good, but always with the right motive and for the proper reason. Hypocrites give their alms, not from any love of the needy and the poor, but rather to be seen of men. Unsanctified individuals also do seemingly good things for the wrong reasons. An apparently benevolent person can manipulate circumstances or people in order to impress others with their great compassion and generosity— all of which falls under our Lord's special condemnation. With the Holy Spirit reigning within the heart of the entirely sanctified, such temptations from the enemy are immediately rejected. Their motives have been purified and they no longer do things just to be noticed by others. We observe then, that motives will ultimately determine the rightness or wrongness of every choice. That is why the Early Methodists always maintained that the motive is more important than the deed. God is more concerned with why you did something than what you actually did. Let me illustrate.

A Compliment or a Cheap Shot?

Suppose you were talking to someone and meant to give them a compliment, but as the conversation continued, it became apparent to you that the person didn't catch your intended kind words. But, God who rightly judges the motives of every word you utter and deed you perform, understood that you meant for your words to be kind, whether properly understood or not.

On the other hand, let us suppose that for some reason, you intended to give a little dig or put-down in a thinly disguised manner, and the one to whom you had directed it failed to catch the intended thinly-veiled snide remark. Outwardly, you might walk away and think that you had gotten away with your unkind goal, and because he didn't catch it, you might think you were in the clear. However, the Lord knew your intended barb and even if your victim failed to comprehend your evil motive, you will answer at the judgment for your malevolent intentions.

Entire sanctification will perfect your motives; perfect love will seek only to be kind to others. Many times I have shared with my students this old aphorism: "I can afford to be wrong, but I cannot afford to be unkind." With the help of the Holy Spirit, you can travel the road of life as a caring person who is known for your compassion to others.

Shading the Truth with Wrong Motives

Bill took up running in college. His dad had been quite an athlete in his youth and Bill wanted to please him. So he went out for track and really threw himself into it. There was one other fellow who was also quite a runner and one day they decided to have a match race between just those two men. He later wrote home the results: "Today I ran against the best man we have and, I came in second and he came in next to the last."

Here is one who manipulated the wording to appear better than he really was. It serves as an illustration of how the carnal heart operates and will influence one's choices. By carefully shading the truth, he chose to leave his dad with a totally different impression of what happened. Omitting the fact that only two men were in the race, he left his father with the impression his son was quite an athlete. God hates deception. How wonderful is the heart purity that awaits every child of God! He alone can purify your motives and make of you a radiant, useful Christian—one whose only goal in life is to live a transparent life for the Lord.

Chapter Summary

1. The number of choices that are made in the course of a day is staggering. The vast majority of those choices have no moral value attached to them, i.e., they are not "right" or "wrong."
2. Choices that involve morality will determine whether or not one is walking in the light.
3. It is wrong to judge others by your light.
4. Almost every time you speak, you have a motive—either it's good or evil—whether or not others catch your motive.
5. An unsanctified heart will cause you to say and do things with a defiled motive; the result will be less than actions motivated by perfect love.

16
The Road to Maturity

Living and Growing in the Life of Perfect Love

IT IS COMMONLY ACCEPTED that essentially three aspects of salvation are found throughout the New Testament: regeneration, full salvation (entire sanctification), and final salvation (glorification). Curiously, the epistles of Paul and the other writers have far more to say about maintaining the life of holiness (process) than they do about getting or finding a pure heart (crisis).

This sanctification is both the divine act of heart cleansing and the resulting life of holiness. The following passage makes this clear: "But now being made free from sin, and become servants to God, ye have your fruit unto holiness, and the end everlasting life" (Romans 6:22). In an earlier chapter we have discussed that complete self-giving which makes possible this full release of God's sanctifying power is beautifully foreshadowed in the self-dedication of the Hebrew slave who, not choosing to go out free in the Year of Jubilee, declares, "I love my master, my wife, and my children; I will not go out a free person" (Exodus 21:5). He then presents himself to his master, who pierces his ear with an awl, making him a "love slave" for life (see vv. 2-6). This is the servitude of perfect freedom. It is in such an act of self-donation that Christ establishes his sanctifying reign in my heart, enabling me to say in all humility and praise to God, "I have been crucified with Christ; and it is no longer I who live, but it is Christ who lives in me" (Galatians 2:20).

Even though I may have experienced a radical death to sin, and Christ now reigns in me in the power of the indwelling Spirit, my continued victory is guaranteed only as I maintain this vital relationship. "I have been crucified with Christ" is the perfect tense in Greek and has the force, "I have been and am now crucified with Christ." The holy life is a moment-by-moment relationship maintained as I submit to the disciplines of the Spirit. "This I say then, Walk in the Spirit," Paul writes later in Galatians, "and ye shall not fulfil the lust of the flesh" (5:16). Not only will you maintain that relationship, but also you will grow as a result of retaining it. In an interesting letter to Adam Clarke, Wesley wrote, "Last week I had an excellent letter from Mrs. Pawson, a *glorious* witness *of full salvation,* showing how *impossible* it is to *retain pure love* without *growing* therein."[1] Thus, in order for you to retain the blessing of entire sanctification, you must constantly aim at adding to what God has done for you, i.e., growth in grace.

Is Holiness Improvable?

Wesley himself taught that while having the heart made perfect in love proved to be a wonderful event in the life of the believer, it could be improved and deepened as one walked with the Spirit. In his *Plain Account of Christian Perfection,* he wrote about the blessing, "It is *improveable*

---

1. J. A. Wood, *Perfect Love,* (Nicholasville, KY: Schmul Publishing Co., 2008), 188.

[sic]. It is so far from lying in an indivisible point, from being incapable of increase, that one perfected in love may grow in grace far swifter, than he did before."[2]

Furthermore, the holy life is a life "in the flesh." When Paul says, "The life I now live in the flesh [but not according to the flesh] I live by faith in the Son of God, who loved me and gave himself for me," he means that he lives the holy life in a flesh-and-blood body, with all its passions and desires— the same kind of body, incidentally, that the Son of God assumed in the Incarnation. It was as a true man that Jesus was "tempted in all points, like as we are— yet was without sin" (Hebrews 4:15). As He lived a holy life in a physical body with all its urges, drives, and desires, so may we— by the power of the same Spirit who indwelt Him! The apostle asks, "Or do you not know that your body is a temple of the Holy Spirit within you, which you have from God, and that you are not your own? For you were bought with a price; therefore glorify God in your body" (1 Corinthians 6:19-20).

The Scriptures clearly contain a doctrine of both counteraction and suppression, not of sin (which is destroyed by sanctifying grace) but of our bodily impulses that may lead to sin. In Romans 8 Paul admonishes, "For if ye live after the flesh, ye shall die: but if ye through the Spirit do mortify the deeds of the body, ye shall live" (v. 13). That we may term, scriptural counteraction. Again Paul writes, "But I keep under my body, and bring it into subjection: lest that by any means, when I have preached to others, I myself should be a castaway" (1 Corinthians 9:27). That is scriptural suppression.

Adam Clarke says to this very point, "As God requires every man to love him with all the heart, soul, mind, and strength, and his neighbor as himself; then

---

2. John Wesley, *A Plain Account of Christian Perfection*, (Nicholasville, KY: Schmul Publishing Co.), 105.

he is a perfect man that does so; he answers to the end for which God made him." Entire sanctification is to the end or purpose of perfect love. Love in the sanctified person governs the will; such persons cannot grieve those whom they love. As one saintly scholar put it so well, "Keeping love at full tide will be the greatest safeguard a holy man can have."[3]

The Apostle Paul as we have seen wrote that justification and sanctification are intimately related, just as Christ's death and resurrection are two phases of one event. To die with Christ is to be simultaneously raised with Him to "new life [in] the Spirit" (Romans 7:6; see 6:1-4). Galatians 2:20 reminds us that God's purpose in our salvation is to one end: that in some divinely mysterious way Christ may be reincarnate in our human flesh, living out His holy life in us! (See Romans 8:29.)

Matthew 6:33 instructs the believer to "Seek ye *first* the kingdom of God..." (emphasis added) That is the key. All the other things that seem so necessary need not be neglected; it's just that they won't occupy first place. Martha, the busy hostess, came under Christ's gentle reproof for being encumbered by food preparation and serving. While those duties seemed necessary and proper, she let them take first in priority, ahead of the more essential matters: listening when Jesus sat and taught with Mary at his feet. That admonishment to Martha serves as our guide. Though we have many tasks and duties to accomplish in life, none of these should ever be permitted to become our top priority when placed alongside our spiritual duties.

Thank God, we may be kept "blameless at the coming of our Lord Jesus Christ" (I Thessalonians 5:23). Blamelessness is not to be taken as something to be

---

3. T. M. Anderson, *After Sanctification: Growth in the Life of Holiness* (Nicholasville, KY: Schmul Publishing Co., 2002), 76.

reserved for the moment of Christ's appearing. The word translated "kept" has a double connotation, including not only the idea of conservation and preservation, but also the idea of shielding, defending, and protecting. According to Gordon Pitts Wiles, the term asserts that the current state of the believer in entire sanctification will be sustained to the moment of the Second Coming. If they are "blameless at the coming of our Lord Jesus Christ" they must necessarily already be entirely sanctified prior to that event.[4]

In this vein, Ernest Best also affirms that such spotlessness will not come into sudden effect at that moment if the believer is not already holy. If they are blameless in that Day, it is because they already enjoy entire sanctification prior to it.[5]

John Wesley's comment is well known, "What the eye is to the body, the intention is to the soul… 'If thine eye be single,' singly fixed upon God, 'thy whole body' …shall be filled with holiness and happiness." The "perfect" Christian is one who does "everything for the glory of God" (I Corinthians 10:31). Singleness of intention is a classic definition of perfection.

The Status Quo will Never Suffice

So in order that we might avoid losing our spiritual momentum, let us keep a few basics in mind. There is a natural tendency to settle down a bit after winning a great victory. We dare not bask in the afterglow. The biblical example of Israel will be helpful. The nation had struggled for forty long, weary years. Yes, they celebrated the death of their oppressors at the Red Sea, but through their own hard-heartedness they had traversed the hot, dry wilder-

---

4. William M. Greathouse, *Love Made Perfect: Foundations for the Holy Life* (Kansas City: MO, Beacon Hill Press, n.d.), Kindle Edition.
5. Ibid.

ness. Finally, Joshua led them across the Jordan and they celebrated a genuine Passover. They had sanctified themselves, followed the Ark of the Covenant and the priests over the Jordan and victory was theirs. It would have been easy to rest on their laurels. This however was no time to sit back and rest.

To continue with the analogy of Israel, we observe that they got careless early on. Yes, they rejoiced at getting across the Jordan into Canaan, and indeed, they celebrated the singular, miraculous victory at Jericho, but they proceeded to become overconfident and careless and were resoundingly defeated at Ai. While entire sanctification is the establishing grace as Paul points out in I Thessalonians 3:13, "…he may establish your hearts unblameable in holiness before God, even our Father, at the coming of our Lord Jesus Christ with all his saints", as wonderful as that may be, it does not cause one to be infallible. The safety of Israel— and for us— is not the crisis that took place, it is the ongoing relationship that we must insure takes place every moment of every day.

So while the entirely sanctified may fall into sin (as Israel was defeated with an Achan in the camp), he is much more safe than he was in his former unsanctified condition. Again, however, that is not proof positive that failure is not possible. Consider Adam and Eve, as perfect morally as a holy God could make them, with no knowledge of previous sin, but when tempted, they were careless and fell into sin and lost everything God had given to them.

We must take courage, however, as Peter has stated, "He that lacketh these things is blind, and cannot see afar off, and hath forgotten that he was purged from his old sins. Wherefore the rather, brethren, give diligence to make your calling and election sure: for if ye do these things, ye shall never fall" (II Peter 1:9, 10). While we as Wesleyan-Arminians understand the possibility of forfeiting our walk with God, such is not the case with Reformed theologians, i.e., Calvinists. Here is an actual example of what some teach.

Years ago while I was serving as the pastor of a growing church I felt the Lord was leading me to further my education for future teaching on the college level. I contacted a large seminary within commuting distance and discussed with the staff about enrolling in their masters program. The academic catalog did state inside the front cover that all students must agree with their articles of faith which stated their belief in eternal security. When I spoke by phone with the academic dean, I inquired as to how essential it was that I sign that statement of faith. He informed me that it was required and then put the question to me, "Do you believe in eternal security?"

I answered quoting Peter's statement, "If ye do these things, ye shall never fall."[6]

To my utter amazement he countered with the strangest theological comment I ever heard from a Ph.D.: "Well, we both know better than that!" To this day, I am at a loss as to how to explain what the dear man meant by that statement. Peter not only suggested the possibility of losing out with God, he gave us encouragement that it need not ever happen, if we give due diligence to walk with the Lord.

Based upon years of observing college students and congregations, I can affirm the very clear possibility of falling from grace. I could cite many examples of students, laymen and preachers who allowed themselves to become careless and lost out with God. Some fell and unfortunately they have never recovered themselves.

A Pure Heart is Ever the Goal

After a person is converted, the Holy Spirit begins to work in his or her heart with the purpose of remov-

6. II Peter 1:10.

ing or cleansing remaining inward sin and filling the heart with divine love. God is faithful in this work, readying the heart for sanctifying grace. In some cases, finding sanctifying grace takes years, in others, weeks or days. How quickly it happens is not the point. Going on to perfection is the point. Make this hymn your prayer:

> O glorious hope of perfect love!
> It lifts me up to things above;
> It bears on eagles' wings;
> It gives my ravished soul a taste
> And makes me for some moments feast
> With Jesus' priests and kings.
>
> Rejoicing now in earnest hope,
> I stand and from the mountain-top
> See all the land below:
> Rivers of milk and honey rise,
> And all the fruits of Paradise
> In endless plenty grow.
>
> O that I might at once go up!
> No more on this side of Jordan stop,
> But now the land possess:
> This moment end my legal years;
> Sorrows, and sins, and doubts, and fears,
> A howling wilderness.
>
> Now, O my Joshua, bring me in!
> Cast out Thy foes; the inbred sin.
> The carnal mind remove;
> The purchase of Thy death divide!
> Give me with all the sanctified
> The heritage of love!
> —*Charles Wesley (1742)*

In this sense entire sanctification is what one has described as the actualization of our conversion. To be truly sanctified is not to be a "super" Christian; it is to be a true Christian. W. E. Sangster has a helpful passage in his book *The Pure in Heart*, in which he insists that "Life, as it bubbles out of the subconscious, is amoral, and should be regarded merely as instinct or 'reaction' until the conscious self identifies itself with the end desired." He continues:

> When I feel a sudden stab of jealousy, is it I?— I, in the very instant that I feel it? Is it I, when some surge of pride stiffens my spirit? Is it I, in the moment when some carnal appetite stirs in my flesh?
>
> Certainly, in that split second, it feels like me... Is that carnality, pride, jealousy, self-pity or any other member of the dirty litter— is it mine?— mine the second that I feel it; mine whether I disown it or not?
>
> I cannot feel that it is. As a conscious moral being, it is not mine till my will makes it mine. I have an amoral nature, with race and family memories and tendencies... No more of it need be admitted to my moral life than fellowship with God in Christ allows. In the moment it stirs in me, trying to wrest my moral life to what I judge to be evil, it is still only temptation... If I finger it awhile and glut my imagination in it, it becomes sin, and sin though it has not issued in a deed, but because I have taken it as my own...
>
> I will not take it as my own... is how to assess it swiftly in the light of God and, seeing it to be evil, blast it with a prayer.
>
> It was never mine. It was amoral instinct. It was only an impulse bidding for moral stature. It was recognized in the white light of God in its evil tendency, and never passed the moral guard.[7]

7. W. E. Sangster, *The Pure in Heart* (Salem, OH: Schmul Publishing Co., 1984), 235-236.

By the power of the indwelling Spirit we may subjugate, master and control, all our impulses to the glory of God! This is suppression, but not of sin; it is the control of amoral human nature, by the Spirit. The Spirit-indwelt Christian is not exempt from temptations to the flesh, but he has within him the divine and all-effectual "Counteragent" to the subtlest of all his foes. Filled with the Spirit, he is able to defeat temptation.[8] That is how the process of purification develops in the life of the believer. That is why entire sanctification is both a process and a crisis. We will develop more of this process in the next chapter.

Chapter Summary

1. Entire sanctification is not an end in itself; it is just a beginning.
2. Perfect love is improvable; the earnest Christian is always praying for and searching for ways to improve his walk with God and with his fellow man.
3. The failure to seek for more of God and for a larger capacity of divine love leads to a religious plateau. In that state the soul will shrivel, dry up and ultimately backslide. The only safe approach is to seek an even higher plane. That's the natural drive of the truly sanctified.

---

8. William M. Greathouse, *Beacon Bible Exposition*, (Kansas City, MO: Beacon Hill Press, 1975), 6:132.

17
If It's Both Crisis and Process, What About the Process?

"Wherefore, my beloved, as ye have always obeyed, not as in my presence only, but now much more in my absence, work out your own salvation with fear and trembling. For it is God which worketh in you both to will and to do of his good pleasure. Do all things without murmurings and disputings: That ye may be blameless and harmless, the sons of God, without rebuke, in the midst of a crooked and perverse nation, among whom ye shine as lights in the world." —*Philippians 2:12-15*

IN THE CLASSROOM, PROBABLY the liveliest discussions are generated when we discuss the growth that takes place after the crisis of entire sanctification has taken place. In so many different venues we hear comments made by those who had been brought up to believe that once one is sanctified, he or she has arrived; that death to self will solve everything. It's like, mission accomplished; now let's get on with enjoying life. That notwithstanding, what a thrill it is to listen to mature saints of God speak about new lessons that God is teaching them, testifying in ways in which they are discovering how to be less earthly and more heavenly minded and thrilling to new growth in grace as they endure some new burden that has laid them low.

In a recent phone conversation with a seasoned saint, I was blessed as he shared how he was tempted to feel sorry for himself. It appeared that a door of ministry was closing to him. As he took the whole matter to the Lord, he witnessed a miracle unfold in such a manner that what appeared to be a closed door, ended up being an even wider field of service than he could have hoped. Yes, he was tempted to self-pity, but in the place of prayer God vindicated his servant, and he exited the dark place a stronger, more useful servant of the Lord as a result of his discouraging encounter.

Will the Spirit Really Lead You?

Perhaps the matter of how the believer can know the leading of the Spirit has generated some of the greatest amount of classroom discussion. Every sincere Christian desires to know God's will in every area of life, but how can we know when God is speaking and when it is just some thoughts that come to the mind?

No man can tell another when he is becoming a glutton, but the Holy Spirit knows. No man can tell another when his sensitivity is becoming self-centered to the point of enmity against God, but the Holy Spirit always does. When religion becomes envy; when encouraging words of others are being accepted by an inordinate love of praise; when righteous anger gives way to an ugly temper, the Spirit will provide the faithful needed reproof.

That notwithstanding, into the confusion will come, if

we will listen, the still small voice, that gentle pressure of the Spirit in tones of conviction assuring, "This is the way, walk ye in it." To know when we are exercising leadership for the thrill of power, or when the enjoyment of the presence of one of the opposite sex is becoming a thing of danger or disloyalty, when the admiration of beauty has shifted to the lustful look— all this is possible only by the guidance of the Spirit. Our Christian experience will be barren unless it is made a living thing through the guidance of the Holy Spirit. "As many as are led by the Spirit of God, they are the children of God" (Romans 8:14).

How the Spirit Leads: Everett Cattell's Illustration

Everett Cattell, president of Malone University (former Cleveland Bible College) from 1960-1972 and missionary to India for many years, claimed as a boy that his besetting sin was talking too much. Speech is a gift from God. What would teachers and preachers do without it? Yet how easily it gets out of hand! His social life was pretty much confined to a group of church young people, and their socials were full of fun. He seemed to be able to talk non-stop in these socials and somehow people would always laugh at his humor. Still he was trying to be an earnest Christian and the incessant frivolousness began to bother him. It was not that there was anything inherently wrong in what was said; no one was being run down, there were no dirty or even off-color stories, nor were there falsehoods. But the very lightness and silliness of so much that was said sent him home with an awful sense of emptiness. Night after night he returned home and prayed about it. Unfortunately, the next party resulted in the same thing and the emptiness returned.

At last he became desperate and decided to take the bull by the horns. He went early to the next gathering and took a back seat in the corner where he would be able to sit out the gathering in silence. The party got started and the chatter began. Then someone asked for Cattell; where was he? Then somebody else spotted him in a corner. So the group headed over and wanted to know what was the matter— was he ill? Obviously, from his perspective, this would not do. His apparent solution to his talking problem was now getting for him too much attention. He decided to move around a little within the group— just enough to divert the attention from himself and then he planned to retreat to a quiet corner again. The move proved to be fatal. A little talk led to more talk. Pretty soon he was the life of the party again and found himself going home with the same empty, aching heart. He cried and prayed over the situation. With patience the Spirit seemed to teach him a lesson. He no more wanted to remove the fun from a young person's life than he wanted to cut out his tongue.

But the Spirit did want to control him. He seemed to say that if in the midst of the fun Cattell would listen, he would speak. And he found it to be true! He continued to go to the same socials with the same crowd but with a new victory. It was gloriously true that if he would listen the Spirit would speak! He later stated that he quickly learned to hear that gentle pressure that seemed to say, "Take care. Let up now. Don't tell that one! Time to change the subject now." So his life went. Obedience brought victory and the joy of going to bed and reviewing an evening in which there had been intense joy but without loss of the Spirit's affirmation in his life.[1]

The More Sensitive You are to Him, The More He will Lead

Constant obedience in this area brings a growing sensitiveness to the voice of the Spirit. When God evaluated the life and character of King Asa's life he concluded that his "heart was perfect all his days" (II Chronicles 15:17),

---

1. Everett Lewis Cattell, *The Spirit of Holiness*, (Grand Rapids, William B. Eerdmans Publishing Company, 1963), 60-61.

even though he still manifested human infirmities, e.g., "In his disease he sought not the Lord, but to the physicians" (II Chronicles 16:10-12). No doubt the king's contemporaries observed these imperfections in the outward acts of the king, these mistakes in judgments, but the Lord who looks at the heart states that Asa was "perfect in all his days."[2]

It is so imperative that seekers after holiness of heart understand that when God removes the vestiges of the carnal heart, new vistas of growth will open up to them. Now instead of feeling the need to put others down in order to elevate oneself, there is a desire to put the best construction on the actions of others. John Wesley pointed out for himself that he had often repented of judging people too severely, but rarely of being too merciful. How true!

How many times have you heard someone blurt out, "I know what she meant when she said that"? How can you possibly judge the intended meaning when someone speaks? The carnal person will always look for a negative motive in another. It takes a magnanimous person to state that while not knowing the motive, he will opt for assigning a positive intention. It's the way Jesus would have it.

Sometimes when the other person speaks it is possible to view either a positive or a negative motive. The sanctified heart will always opt for assigning a positive motive in others. If it is not clear, he will consistently give others the benefit of the doubt.

We have just looked at an example of how the Holy Spirit will lead you in your relationship with others. Now let's observe how the Spirit will lead you as you attempt to reach out to others with the Gospel.

---

2. Daniel Steele, *Milestone Papers*, (Salem, OH: Schmul Publishers, 1976), 40-41.

How the Spirit Can Lead in Witnessing

Some of the greatest thrills of those who are seeking to serve the Lord with all their heart are those times when the leadership of the Spirit is so apparent. One of those special occasions took place in my life when I turned into the parking lot of a Subway to pick up a sandwich. Parking my car I noticed a young mother and a little girl going into Subway. At that moment the Lord prompted me to speak to them about him. After I picked up my sandwich I saw the two sitting in the almost-empty dining area. Knowing that an older man like me would probably scare a child, I felt led of the Spirit to make my granddaughter the focus of a little discussion that I hoped would follow.

"Hi there, you remind me of my granddaughter Mackenzie; she's five. How old are you?"

Holding up two fingers, "Two."

"Really? You look bigger than that. What's your name?"

"Trinity."

"Oh, that's a nice name!" To her mom I added, "That has a biblical ring to it."

Mom responded, "Yes… you know, the Father, the Son and the Holy Spirit." I had to smile within, thinking, *Yes, I do teach systematic theology and we do study the Trinity.* I pressed on.

"Oh, yes… with a name like that, you probably like to sing songs in Sunday school, like Mackenzie does. Do you go to Sunday School?"

Mother responded, "No, we don't go."

"Really? Oh, a nice girl like this really would enjoy singing those great songs with the other kids like Mackenzie. Where do you live?"

"In Clinton."

"Really? I was just there a few weeks ago. There is a camp meeting that is held there."

"Yes, I know. I live just across the road from the camp ground. I can hear them in the summer when they are doing their thing." (I had to smile within myself at her description of a holiness camp meeting.)

I replied to her, "Do you know, I have a former student who serves as the pastor of a church just a couple of miles from your house. And he just got married to a lovely lady, also a former student of mine. I know they would really love to meet Trinity and you! And they could teach her the same songs Mackenzie sings in Sunday school. Why don't you give me a phone number and I'll have them get in contact with you?"

And do you know, she wrote down her name and her phone number on her napkin! I later phoned the pastor and his wife, who then had a lead with which to invite them to their church that is located only a few minutes away from Trinity's home.

Do you see how God led me to speak to them? How he prompted me to focus on my granddaughter in the conversation, and how he's going to lead my students to help Trinity and her mother to find Jesus? I want to continue to learn how to hear his voice and to be responsive to him. And the next time you find a child, try a similar strategy and see how the Spirit will enable and lead you! That illustrates how the Spirit will lead you in witnessing, if you will have the courage to follow Him. Dennis Kinlaw's account of how God led him illustrates this thrilling component to attempts to share the Gospel

While on a flight he had an opportunity to witness to the stranger who was his seatmate. As the plane prepared to land, the man asked Kinlaw if he thought their conversation had been an accident. Kinlaw laughed and said, "No, I don't think this is an accident because I am not supposed to be on this plane." Curiously, the other man stated that he had been rerouted by the airline and wasn't to be on that particular flight either. He didn't think the flight or the conversation was an accident at all.

As the plane touched down Kinlaw later expressed his feelings of deep remorse knowing that just as he was at the point where he could present Christ to his fellow passenger, he was out of time. Sharing his dismay with the Lord in a silent prayer, the Spirit answered him, "I am doing very well with him on my own." He went on his way praying for a man he would very likely never see again, but rejoicing that the Lord who arranged their time together, would be just as faithful to send another witnessing believer across the path of this hungry individual. That is how the Spirit leads people to those who will be faithful to witness; that is how He will lead you, if you are willing.[3]

Using Compliments for Sharing the Gospel

All new students in most holiness colleges must sign up for freshmen orientation, a course designed to familiarize students with life in a new setting. In addition to learning how to study, to manage their time, to take lecture notes, to prepare for tests, i.e., all the basics that will enable them to be successful in the academic arena, they are introduced to some social skills. Frequently, I am invited to give some lectures on how to develop interpersonal relationships. I have observed over the years just how difficult it is for many students even to initiate a conversation. Even more challenging is for them to keep a conversation moving. Eric Berne authored a book entitled, *What Do You Say After You Say Hello*. I am not familiar with the work, but its title makes my point here. Students seemingly have no problem greeting a stranger, but they are at a loss as to how to follow up their initial

---

3. Taken from *This Day with the Master: 365 Daily Meditations* by Dennis F. Kinlaw with Christiane A. Albertson Copyright © 2004 by Francis Asbury Society. Used by permission of Zondervan. www.zondervan.com

"hello" and initiate a real conversation. That ability is so essential if we are to reach out to the lost.

If students are to become successful pastors, missionaries or teachers, they will discover the importance of such skills. If they are to reach out to others with the Gospel, they must be able to converse with strangers. So I spend considerable time with them, to help them to learn to speak to others.

For me, the best way to initiate a conversation is by offering a compliment. I practice this method in all types of settings— when shopping, in a restaurant, and visiting after the church service. It is particularly rewarding to speak to strangers when traveling, especially in the airport and on the airplane. Permit me to share some methods that work for me. After all, I want to move the conversation to spiritual matters. Isn't that the real goal for believers who desire to share the Good News of Jesus?

What's Your Witnessing Strategy?

One compliment that works for me occurs when I am sitting in the airport across from a couple of strangers. After making eye contact, I will say to them, "You two look like honeymooners." Almost without fail, they will both smile, or even laugh, and ask why I think so. They end up telling me how long they have been married, where they live, what they do in life, where they are traveling, etc. It all started with a compliment.

Here is another opening that I use with regularity. Once we have boarded the plane and are aloft the attendants will pass through the plane to take drink orders. When one stops by my seat and takes my order, my lead-in line is always the same: "Before I tell you, I have a question for you." Looking quizzically at me, they ask what is my question. I then ask them, "Do you like your job?"

Not knowing who I am and what I might be up to, they reply, "Why, yes, I do."

My next statement is always the same: "Well, it shows," (meaning I can observe that they like their job).

Invariably, the attendant smiles and thanks me for my remark. At that point, I have made a friend. Many times I have done that, and without fail I receive a very positive response. I spoke that to a male attendant who appeared to be in his middle thirties. He sort of hunkered down in the aisle of the plane and we just chatted for several minutes — a very pleasant and warm conversation.

On another occasion, after my little conversation opener, the lady responded with a very pleased expression. Somewhat later, she walked specifically to our seat and asked what else she might get me. My wife was seated beside me, and I told the lady how much we enjoyed the little biscotti cookies they had served us along with our drinks. "You know," I said to her, "we have a granddaughter who loves to come to grandma's house and they like to do tea times together. If you could get me several of those cookies, that would really add to their next tea." She promised to see what she could do and returned a little while later with a whole bag of the packaged cookies. She was happy to do it and I was delighted. It all began with my compliment. You can devise a strategy that works for you if you will try.

Learn to be Others-Oriented and God will Open Doors for You

Now if you will ask the Lord to help you, learning to give a compliment for the express purpose of initiating a conversation with a spiritual goal can become a habit, one that you can develop for the glory of God. And it will open immense doors of opportunity for service. Such goals will add depth to your prayer life as you pray for those to whom you have spoken, and it will take your mind off of your own problems and make you an "others-oriented Christian."

Keep in mind this chapter is about the process of dying out to self and living for Christ. As you witness to others, you will notice that your focus begins to move away from yourself and on to those you are attempting to help. As you play down self, you lift others up, and that is so beneficial in your seeking for God's fullness. Also, as you make this a practice in your life, you are lifting up the Savior who promised, "And I, if I be lifted up from the earth, will draw all men unto me" (John 12:32). Learn to exalt the Lord and you will see results from those you are attempting to reach.

As we said to the college orientation class, you will develop excellent social skills and will cause others to respect and like you if you practice giving compliments. In fact, after I lecture on this topic for the first class meeting, I give students an extended assignment. Each student must give a compliment to a pastor, a Sunday School teacher, the song leader, the one who sang the special song, the college professor, the cooks in the cafeteria, the ones scraping lunch trays, and others with whom they interact in throughout the week. The next class finds us discussing the responses they received as they offered their compliments. Whatever else they learned from their assignment, they discovered that everyone likes a compliment. Mark Twain once stated, "I can live for two months on a good compliment." Abraham Lincoln observed, "Everyone likes a compliment."

So develop the practice as you interact with others, and you will discover not only will you feel good when you do it, but you will appreciate the positive reaction your comments elicit from others. Keep in mind, however, you are not doing this just to manipulate people for something you want from them— what the world calls "buttering them up"— but your goal is to open a conversation and use it to reach others. God will honor your attempts, and you will develop confidence as you mature in this all-important area of reaching out.

Chapter Summary

1. Entire sanctification is both a process and a crisis, i.e., it is both preceded and followed by a steady growth in grace.
2. The process of growth is Spirit directed; nothing is more rewarding to a believer than to be aware of the Spirit's leading.
3. It's not just in the large areas of life that he desires to lead; it's in the smaller details as well — even in interpersonal relationships.
4. To be an others-oriented believer is to be involved in witnessing to those with whom we interact along the way of life.
5. Witnessing is a skill that can be learned and improved with practice.
6. Witnessing brings rich rewards to those who put forth the effort. We must leave the results of our attempts with God.
7. The use of compliments provides an excellent pathway to initiate a conversation with people.
8. The more success that God gives you in this area the more you will be further motivated to be bold for the Lord.

18
Misconceptions about Holiness and Christian Perfection

TRAVELING AROUND THE holiness movement as an evangelist, I enjoy a unique opportunity to observe people as they converse at camps, conventions, meetings, and even during informal discussions. Of particular interest to me as a college/seminary professor, and as a former pastor for more than twenty years, are the ideas people have about entire sanctification. At times the conversations I hear lack clarity and even contain misconceptions.

This chapter is an attempt to clear up some areas of confusion by addressing some of these misconceptions—to examine what the Scriptures say and what do they not say about this vital Christian doctrine. Also we will explore some evidence for this great work of God and what the child of God might expect after receiving it. Keep in mind that the greatest gift God can give us is to share his divine nature with us, and that the greatest expression of our gratitude for this unspeakably great gift is to accept it! So let us look more closely into the matter.

The Holy Spirit is Not in the Life of the Regenerated

Frequently, I have said to a congregation: "I am not going to heaven because I have been entirely sanctified; I am going to heaven because I have been justified and have walked in all the light I have received since then." Some folks have argued with me that the Holy Spirit is not given at all in the new birth, but such claims run counter to some rather plain passages of Scripture, e.g., "If any man have not the Spirit of Christ, he is none of his" (Romans 8:9). Also the Apostle Paul states, "And hope maketh not ashamed; because the love of God is shed abroad in our hearts by the Holy Ghost which is given unto us" (Romans 5:5).

Jesus promised his disciples that "If a man love me, he will keep my words: and my Father will love him, and we will come unto him, and make our abode with him" (John 14:23). His disciples' security and fulfillment were to be in the abiding presence of the Father, the Son, and the Spirit within them. The wonderful thing is that when Christ comes into a life, he brings the Holy Spirit with him. That Holy Spirit is the Spirit of holiness, and he comes into us with his holy power to transform us and to enable us to walk in Christ's ways. Thus Paul can say, "Therefore if any man be in Christ, he is a new creature: old things are passed away; behold, all things are become new" (2 Corinthians 5:17)!

Once one has been granted the new birth, he enjoys a wonderful new relationship with the Lord. He is no longer the unwilling servant of sin, but revels in his new status as a child of God. If such a person were to die at this point, would he make it through to the City of God? Most assuredly, because he can testify to a justified state. Since his record of sin is gone, he can rejoice with the other children of God.

In time however — and for some individuals sooner

rather than later — one who has been granted the new birth comes to learn of a deeper need, a lingering impairment, a besetting sin, a problem for which he is not responsible. As he continues to walk in the light, the Holy Spirit will lead him to full deliverance from all the contaminants of his inherited depravity. Amazingly, the Spirit is more willing to do this than most can imagine! Remember, "This is the will of God, even your sanctification" (1 Thessalonians 4:3).

Dividing the Holy Spirit into Two Parts

Some have raised this question: "How can one receive the Holy Spirit at the new birth and then, in some manner receive him again when he is sanctified?" Perhaps this analogy will be helpful. Let us imagine that we have a large-mouth jar with a number of fair-sized rocks and stones in it. Now, let us fill the jar with water until it overflows. Is the jar truly full of water? We are tempted to answer, "It must be since it's running over." But is it really full? No, it cannot be because rocks are taking up space — space that could contain more water. Let us, however, remove the rocks and stones and fill the jar until it overflows. Now, we can rightly say, "The jar is full of water."

Such an analogy reflects in rough form what happens when God saves a sinner and puts his Spirit within him. The new believer is "filled" with as much as he can contain of the Spirit. However, the Spirit cannot completely fill the new believer due to the rocks and stones of carnal traits. Not until the moment of entire sanctification, when the residue of inherited depravity is removed, will he really be filled. Thus, we can understand that although the Spirit is indeed given to the new believer, that same believer will receive a fuller, more complete filling when the Spirit enters him in his fullness when his heart is made perfect in love.

Can Saved People Live on a Lower Level until Entirely Sanctified?

Many folk in some of the churches where I have served seem to operate under the assumption that after they have been born again, there are certain things that they can still do since they are "merely saved." In their erroneous thinking, once they are wholly sanctified, then they will deal with those other matters. Such reasoning will surely lead to cooling off and backsliding. The true child of God will want to walk in every ray of light that he has and will make no allowances for doing anything that does not have the complete approval of God. I have had parishioners say to me, "Well, I still do thus and so because I am not sanctified." No, my friend, you must walk in all your light (which I refer to as "God's opinion on any matter") or you cannot maintain a saved relationship. God's Word is quite clear that "if we walk in the light, as he is in the light" we will enjoy God's fellowship and blessing (1 John 1:7). To do any less is to invite spiritual disaster. Is there anything in your life that you know does not measure up to God's Word?

Can Believers Postpone Seeking Holiness?

Another area of misunderstanding concerns the lack of pressing on to entire sanctification. The simple fact is that holiness of heart stands as not only a glorious privilege of the believer but also the duty of every believer to pursue. While a person might never say, "Well, now God has saved me, and I will just enjoy this new salvation; and eventually, when the time seems right, I will seek for holiness," their actions may reveal this is their thinking. They can end up "kicking the can down the road" rather than getting down to business and seeking a pure heart. Such reasoning is fatal for the child of God. Those who truly have been converted and desire a healthy walk with God will be shown by the Spirit that a pure heart is God's will for them. Furthermore, since Jesus has "suffered without the gate" that he might sanctify them (Hebrews 13:12), stopping short of all that has been purchased for them at Calvary will grieve the Spirit out of their life and they will forfeit their saved experience.

For that reason, we urge believers to begin seeking for a pure heart just as soon as they understand their need. I have stressed to students that not only is entire sanctification a privilege; it's also a duty. To neglect to seek earnestly for it is gross negligence and will soon negatively impact your walk with God. If you are thinking that sanctification can be put off until an optimum time, let me counsel you— as soon as you understand that you have a carnal heart, for you, "now is the day of salvation" (2 Corinthians 6:2). Begin pressing forward in prayer, and do not stop until God assures you that he has finished his new creation in holiness.

Entire Sanctification will Radically Change your Lifestyle

Another area of misunderstanding that I have observed is that great change will accompany the experience of entire sanctification. While it certainly is true that aspects of your life will witness change, most of that change will be internal. I have counseled students who seem to have the idea that many great changes will accompany holiness— change in the areas of dress, deportment, lifestyle issues, etc. Such thinking reflects a measure of misunderstanding about the new birth. Permit me to explain.

When the Lord takes up residence in the heart of the new believer he gives direction by shedding light upon the areas of the believer's life that need to be addressed— both externals that I mentioned above, as well as internal concerns. The believer takes the necessary action as rapidly as God's light reveals changes that he desires to see. Therefore, when the believer's heart is purified by faith, most of those matters—external and internal—have already been adjusted in ways that are pleasing to God.

So you ask, what changes at the moment of entire sanctification? Actually, when the believer's heart is cleansed, those who are closest to him will notice changes in attitude, mood, and response that more clearly reflect the Savior's meek and gentle nature. Usually, very little will change in external lifestyle issues. Those have already been dealt with in the new birth. Fellow students, fellow workers, employers, life's companion, children, family pets, etc., will notice a new demeanor, but not radical changes as far as externals are concerned. Those were taken care of in the new birth.

I am Not Ready for Heaven until I am Entirely Sanctified

Many of my students seem to struggle to understand that holiness actually begins with the new birth. In their minds, salvation is one thing, and entire sanctification is something totally different. Actually, when God saves a sinner, at the moment he believes, four things happen to him: justification, regeneration, adoption, and initial sanctification. Permit me to comment on these.

Justification

Justification is a forensic or legal term whereby one's record of sin in heaven is wiped clean. In God's eyes, it is just as if the person had never sinned. Interestingly, this process is even better than a pardon. Let us say that a governor or a president pardons a criminal and that person is released from prison. By that process the criminal gets out of prison early, but the crime is still on his record. When God justifies an individual, it is as though the crime had never been committed! But there is more that happens.

Regeneration

At the moment of salvation, the seeker is regenerated, changed into a new person in Christ. Whereas justification does not actually change the seeker, only his record, in regeneration, all things have passed away and all things become new. He now seeks only to live for the Lord and to please him in everything that he does. In this process all of his relatives, friends, classmates, and fellow employees— the whole world— will know that he is a different person. But there is more that happens.

Adoption

In that same moment of salvation, the new convert becomes a member of the heavenly family of saints. He has been adopted into the family of God, whereby God becomes his father, Jesus Christ his elder brother, and every other Christian becomes his spiritual relative.

Initial Sanctification

As wonderful as these three happenings are, we want to notice especially the fourth event that transpires at the new birth. The newly saved person receives the Holy Spirit in initial or beginning sanctification. Just like the thief on the cross apparently made it to heaven without a second work of grace, such a person now qualifies for Hebrews 12:14, "Follow peace with all men, and holiness, without which no man shall see the Lord." Holiness has begun in his heart. He has begun living a new life free from known sin with the loving image of Christ initially imparted to his soul as a positive, life-changing dynamic. Now he can keep walking right on into the blessed experience of entire sanctification just as rapidly as he seeks and believes God to do it for him.

Wesley, early in his leadership of the Methodists, felt that heart purity only was possible after a long period of seeking, probably near the time of death. As he visited the societies and bands of Methodism, however, he listened to the testimony of many who testified to a pure heart after only a matter of a few days, weeks or months. He also wrote of his observations at one of the societies and later reported that he spoke with forty who had professed to have been cleansed and made perfect in love. He stated, "Some of them said they had *received that blessing* [emphasis mine] *ten days,* some *seven,* some *four,* some *three days,* after they found peace with God, and *two of them the next day.*"[1]

From those observations he stated that heart purity could be found just as soon after conversion as the seeking person made the perfect consecration. As he stated in typical John Wesley fashion, "Since it is of faith, then why not now?"[2]

Thank God for his faithfulness in leading believers into the holiness of heart that Christ purchased for his children who obey him!

Confusing Keeping the Law with Having God's Presence

So many in our churches today operate under the notion that if they keep enough of the rules and dos and don'ts, somehow that is satisfactory. The holiness movement does have a plethora of preachers and pastors who maintain great stress on keeping externals— almost to the point where the new convert thinks that just adhering to the rules will somehow assure them of salvation and ultimately, get them into heaven. This type of thinking surfaces in churches, revival services, around the altar, and is especially prominent in the classroom. Unfortunately, it is misguided thinking.

Keeping all the biblical injunctions and the commandments is not enough; we must have his Presence.

---

1. *Works,* Vol. IV: 135.

2. Taken from *The Works of John Wesley.* Thomas Jackson, ed. Third edition. 14 vols. Letter #373, 12:362. Reprint 1959. Used by permission of Zondervan. www.zondervan.com.

Remember, Israel was helpless against the Egyptians at the Red Sea. It was God's Presence that made the difference, not their keeping some rules or laws. Moses understood such to be the case and that is why at the golden calf incident, he refused to lead Israel any farther unless God would give the assurance that he would send his Presence with them.

When Christ comes into the heart of the new believer, he brings his Holy Spirit with him and takes over the life of the new convert. That is what salvation really is; it's the active Presence of Christ within. John 14:23 makes this abundantly clear, "If a man love me, he will keep my words: and my Father will love him, and we will come to him, and make our stayed with him."

It's the law that spells out the conditions of Christ's continued abiding presence in the heart and life. That is the reason Jesus focused so much in his Upper Room Discourse (John 14-17) on the necessity of the believer remaining (abiding) in Christ; it was the believer's security. It's another way of reinforcing what John states when he stressed our walking in the light, so that the blood of Christ may continually cover us. We must walk and abide; therein is the believer's security!

One of the mistakes that Israel frequently made was to presume that as long as they were performing the rituals of the Mosaic Law, somehow God's Presence was with them. Remember how Israel took the Ark of the Covenant into the battlefield against the Philistines, assuming that having the sacred chest with them would somehow gain them the victory of the enemy. What a disaster that proved to be.

God's Presence means everything and makes all the difference between a successful, achieving walk with the Lord, and an empty, dry profession that means only defeat and spiritual destruction.

Chapter Summary

1. The subject of entire sanctification has produced many misunderstandings and strange ideas among the holiness folk.
2. Some teach that new believers do not have the Holy Spirit; that he is given only when one is entirely sanctified.
3. Some teach that salvation is a defective work that doesn't count for much, that it's the second work of grace that prepares you for heaven.
4. A believer has found glorious deliverance from the burden and guilt of sin but is not free to continue certain questionable activities by assuming they are permissible since he is not yet entirely sanctified.
5. Many have the erroneous view that it's entire sanctification that settles the lifestyle issues, such as dress, hair, worldly attractions, etc. Actually, the changes are almost all internal; probably only those closest to you will notice the changes that are wrought within you.
6. Many students assume that a perfect heart or entire sanctification can be sought when they are really ready to settle down and be serious about their religion. Actually, holiness of heart for the believer is not an option— it's a duty. You must begin seeking as soon as you understand your need and the cure that is available.

19
The Four Pentecosts in the Book of Acts

TRAVELING THROUGHOUT HOLINESS churches as an evangelist I hear discussions, conversations and even preaching that reveals a certain lack of clarity as to what did transpire at Pentecost. In this chapter I will attempt to clarify some areas of confusion by addressing several of these misconceptions— to examine what the Scriptures say, and what do they not say about this vital event in Church history. Since the greatest gift that God can give us is to share his divine nature with us, then the greatest expression of our gratitude for this unspeakably great gift is to accept it! Let us look more closely into the matter as Scripture records it.

What did Actually Happen at the Jerusalem Pentecost?

In order to evaluate the events recorded in Acts 2, students of the Word must first be clear on the spiritual condition of those one hundred and twenty people who were present when the Spirit came. As we know they were in that Upper Room in response to the instructions given them by the angel on the Mount of Olives at the time of

Christ's ascension. The Gospels record that Jesus appeared on earth for forty days after his resurrection. Since there are fifty days between Passover and Pentecost, apparently those tarrying in the Upper Room must have been there for nearly ten days. As a former pastor, I would submit that to get a group together for a few hours of prayer would be challenging, to say the least— not to mention ten days! "And they worshipped him, and returned to Jerusalem with great joy: And were continually in the temple, praising and blessing God" (Luke 24:53). Luke then continued the narrative, writing, "These all continued with one accord in prayer and supplication" (Acts 1:14). To the thoughtful reader, their diligence in prayer says much about their spiritual status.

Were Those in the Upper Room Believers?

Many have argued that those in the Upper Room were not believers, but were born again at Pentecost. These folk advocate a teaching known as "Pentecostal regeneration." Such a position is contrary to facts found in the Gospels. For example, John the Evangelist quotes Jesus as saying about the Twelve, "but ye know him; for he [the Holy Spirit] dwelleth with you, and shall be in you" (John 17:14). The same writer asserts that "greater works than these shall he do; because I go unto my Father" (John 14:12). But the writer stressed their status even more clearly when he uttered, "I pray for them: I pray not for the world, but for them which thou hast given me; for they are thine" (John 17:9).

Luke added his testimony about their spiritual condition when he wrote, "...rejoice, because your names are written in heaven" (Luke 10:20). Other writers indicate that these men had been casting out devils and performing other miracles ever since they had been ordained and commissioned by the Lord (Matthew 28:19; Mark 3:14-15). Any fair reading of the relevant

Scriptures certainly paints a picture of believers who were happily engaged in serving the Master; hardly a description of unsaved sinners!

While the evidence speaks clearly to a saved body of believers, waiting and praying in the Upper Room during the ten days leading up to Pentecost, it is evident that these had some rather deep-seated spiritual needs. Mark indicated that they were sometimes unstable and disloyal, and on one occasion, "they all forsook him [Jesus], and fled" (Mark 14:50). At times they were given to a vindictive spirit (Luke 9:54-55) and were carnally selfish and ambitious (Mark 10:28; 10:37-41; Matthew 19:27). Whatever level of spirituality they had achieved, it obviously fell short of the work of entire sanctification.

Let us look now at what Luke recounted as transpiring in the Upper Room.

Did they Experience a Spiritual Change?

The historical facts of that important event are familiar to all:

> And when the day of Pentecost was fully come, they were all with one accord in one place. And suddenly there came a sound from heaven as of a rushing mighty wind, and it filled the entire house where they were sitting. And there appeared unto them cloven tongues like as of fire, and it sat upon each of them. And they were all filled with the Holy Ghost, and began to speak with other tongues, as the Spirit gave them utterance.
>
> —*Acts 2:1-4*

What is significant to some students is that nothing is said about any change wrought in the heart of these waiting, praying people. Let us search for a solution to this apparent dilemma.

As we read the accounts of these disciples following

their spiritual baptism, we observe men who act with a new boldness, eagerly spreading the message of the risen Lord among the dwellers and visitors in Jerusalem. The religious and political leaders unleashed a wave of severe persecution on them. These Early Church leaders endured imprisonment and threats, but they could not be silenced.

The Samaritan Pentecost: Jewish "Half-Breeds"

We learn in the Book of Acts of four different episodes where believers, disciples, pious non-Jews and even the much-maligned Samaritans received the infilling of the Holy Spirit. Jesus had informed the disciples just as he was departing to return to the Father, "But ye shall receive power, after that the Holy Ghost is come upon you: and ye shall be witnesses unto me both in Jerusalem, and in all Judaea, and in Samaria, and unto the uttermost part of the earth"(Acts. 1:9). As Luke traces the flow of the Gospel, he shows how it affected people in not only Jerusalem, but in Samaria, Caesarea and Ephesus.

The writer also includes the conversion and cleansing of Saul, the radical Pharisee. Some scholars have adopted the description of Saul's experience as a personal Pentecost; others tend to avoid such terminology for the experience of entire sanctification. Above we have considered the Jewish Pentecost that actually ushered in the dispensation of the Holy Spirit. It is important to note that of all those involved in the Upper Room event, none of them were non-Jews (Gentiles).

Let us now consider the half-Jews, e.g., the Samaritans, as Luke writes it in Acts 8:4-8.

> Therefore they that were scattered abroad went everywhere preaching the word. Then Philip went down to the city of Samaria, and preached Christ unto them. And the people with one accord gave heed unto those

things which Philip spake, hearing and seeing the miracles, which he did. For unclean spirits, crying with loud voice, came out of many that were possessed with them: and many taken with palsies, and that were lame, were healed. And there was great joy in that city.

It is clear that those to whom Philip preached in Samaria had already received knowledge of the Gospel. Jesus himself had conducted a two-day revival in one of their towns. In fact, it was to the woman at the well that he first revealed to any mortal person that indeed, he was the Messiah. That knowledge, along with her personal testimony, brought about the glorious gospel to their area. Since the preaching of Jesus to them, they had clear Messianic expectations. Thus it is clear that when Philip went there to preach, he was going to a group which had prior knowledge of Christ, and indeed many had accepted him as their Messiah.

Some would argue that at the time when Philip left the city his hearers were not saved. This they argue because they have a problem with these converts being sanctified when Peter and John come to instruct them.

Wesley, however, agrees with us that these folk were indeed believers. Of the Samaritans, he interpreted their baptism in Acts 8:12 to mean that "they then saw and felt the real power of God, and submitted thereto." He further shows in his comment on verse 14 that they experienced the word of God "by faith" through the preaching of Philip. As Wood states, "hence, for Wesley, the Samaritans had saving faith prior to their reception of the Spirit."[1] Other Wesleyan scholars also agree that no matter what one's position on the matter, and how they may choose to interpret this account of the Holy Spirit's com-

---

1. Laurence W. Wood, *Pentecostal Grace* (Grand Rapids, MI: Francis Asbury Press, 1980), 225.

ing upon these Samaritans, there is no denying the "secondness" of their experience.[2]

The results of his preaching were immediate and dramatic. Many were cleansed of unclean spirits, they gave heed to the preaching of Philip, the leading sinner of the community was converted and baptized, many men and women accepted the teachings of the evangelist, and there was great joy in the city. With those results, it's very difficult to believe that these were not enjoying a saved relationship with the Lord.

Let us now observe the sequel of this amazing account as Luke records it in verses 14-17.

> Now when the apostles which were at Jerusalem heard that Samaria had received the word of God, they sent unto them Peter and John: Who, when they were come down, prayed for them, that they might receive the Holy Ghost: (For as yet he was fallen upon none of them: only they were baptized in the name of the Lord Jesus.) Then laid they their hands on them, and they received the Holy Ghost.

The news of the revival reached the apostles in Jerusalem and produced no small stir. The reputation of people of Samaria, a community of half-breeds, was less than stellar. "The Samaritans were worse than aliens. They were heretics, schismatics, more to be hated than infidels."[3] No wonder the leaders at the headquarters were filled with wonderment. The situation called for evaluation. Peter and John were immediately dispatched to the city. Notice the sequence of their activities when they arrived. The first thing they did was to pray for them "that they

---

2. Donald S. Metz, *Studies in Biblical Holiness* (Kansas City, MO: Beacon Hill Press, 1971), 115; Charles W. Carter and Ralph Earle, *The Acts of the Apostles* (Nicholasville, KY: Schmul Publishing Company, 1973), 115.

3. Richard B. Rackham, *The Acts of the Apostles* (London: Methuen and Co., 1951), 112.

might receive the Holy Ghost." Since we know that all spiritual work done within the heart is accomplished by the Spirit, these folk must be considered to have been believers when Peter and John arrived. Apparently the apostles have in mind some type of repeat of what had transpired in the Upper Room at Pentecost. They then proceeded to lay hands upon them and they received the Holy Ghost. As one writer stated, if no other reference occurred in all the New Testament to a second work of grace, this would suffice.[4]

The Gentile Pentecost: The Case of Cornelius

Luke records another fascinating account of a second, instantaneous crisis experience in Acts 10. The broad outlines of this event are generally well known to students. Let us now look more fully into the account of Cornelius, an officer in the Roman army who was stationed in the coastal city of Caesarea, essentially the capital of Palestine, as far as Rome was concerned. We are introduced to this Gentile officer with these details.

> There was a certain man in Caesarea called Cornelius, a centurion of the band called the Italian band, a devout man, and one that feared God with all his house, which gave much alms to the people, and prayed to God alway. He saw in a vision evidently about the ninth hour of the day an angel of God coming in to him, and saying unto him, Cornelius. And when he looked on him, he was afraid, and said, What is it, Lord? And he said unto him, Thy prayers and thine alms are come up for a memorial before God.
> —*Acts 10:1-4*

The church world has always had those who oppose two separate distinct works of grace. When Wesleyan

---

4. Metz, 116.

scholars use the account of Cornelius to illustrate two installments in the process of becoming a New Testament Christian, they are met with the argument that Cornelius was not a proper candidate for entire sanctification because he wasn't saved until Peter preached in his house. Let us consider the facts as Luke records them to gain an understanding of his spiritual status.

Whatever else can be said about Cornelius it becomes clear that he enjoyed some type of relationship with the Lord that was comparable to regeneration. In verse 2 we find he was a devout man, he feared God (reverential awe) with his entire household, he gave much alms, i.e., was a liberal giver to the needy, and enjoyed a strong, continuous prayer life. He was not only an exemplary head of his household, but had an influence upon his servants and family. Any pastor would love to have him as a member of the congregation!

In view of this godly life, the Lord with a heavenly vision honored him. The crowning support for the spiritual state of this one occurred when Peter arrived and stated, "Of a truth, I perceive that God is no respecter of persons; but in every nation he that feareth him, and worketh righteousness, is accepted with him" (Acts 10:34-35). While Peter doubtlessly has in mind his surprise that the door to New Testament Christianity is now open to Gentiles, he surely is making some reference to Cornelius and his life of "fearing God" and "working righteousness."

When the hesitating Peter finally arrived at the place, we see another indication of the spiritual stature of this man in his narration to Peter of the angel's explanation to him: "And Cornelius said, Four days ago I was fasting until this hour; and at the ninth hour I prayed in my house, and, behold, a man stood before me in bright clothing, And said, Cornelius, thy prayer is heard, and thine alms are had in remembrance in the sight of God" (vss. 30,

31). Peter then preached a basic salvation message with amazing results.

> While Peter yet spake these words, the Holy Ghost fell on all them which heard the word. And they of the circumcision which believed were astonished, as many as came with Peter, because that on the Gentiles also was poured out the gift of the Holy Ghost. For they heard them speak with tongues, and magnify God. Then answered Peter, Can any man forbid water, that these should not be baptized, which have received the Holy Ghost as well as we?
> —*Acts 10: 44-47*

When Peter later reported to his colleagues in Jerusalem about the events that had transpired at the house of Cornelius, he essentially stated that whatever happened to this Gentile and his household, it was the same as what had happened to the apostles at Pentecost, "purifying their hearts by faith."

> And God, which knoweth the hearts, bare them witness, giving them the Holy Ghost, even as he did unto us; And put no difference between us and them, purifying their hearts by faith.
> —*Acts 15: 8-9*

Perhaps one other item needs to be pointed out to students and that is the word choice of Peter to the apostles: "Forasmuch then as God gave them the like gift as he did unto us, who believed on the Lord Jesus Christ..." (Acts 11:17) which reinforces the fact Peter speaks of the Pentecostal blessing, not to their conversion. But some argue Peter used the word "saved" in his account at Jerusalem, "Who shall tell thee words, whereby thou and all thy house shall be saved" (11:14). Students of Wesley are well aware of the fact that he and other early Methodists used the terms "saved" and "fully saved," in a way that might seem strange to students today, when they are discussing "justification" and "entire sanctification." The point is, we dare not build a case for or against a second work of grace for Cornelius based upon the word "saved," that we tend to use for the first work of grace. That is not how Early Methodists tended to use the term. It seems clear that the second crisis in the experience of Cornelius came to him instantaneously, interrupting Peter's sermon, and as such was "lifted to the New Testament norm of Spirit-filled Christian living by an unforgettable experience."[5]

Was Cornelius a Proper Candidate for Holiness?

Many Reformed theologians argue that Cornelius the centurion was not a believer when he first appears in Acts 10. They commend him for his many prayers to God, his charitable alms giving and his devout ways and then proceed to argue that a person can do all of this and still not be a Christian.

On the other hand, the Wesleyan-Arminian student sees in Cornelius a man of limited teaching and instruction in spiritual things who is walking in all of the light he has received and is "therefore accepted of God." The Lord said as much when he informed Cornelius that "Thy prayers and thine alms are come up for a memorial before God" (Acts 10:4). Here is a man who has followed the general revelation of nature and conscience as far as they can lead him and God, who knoweth the hearts of all men, will see to his further instruction from the newly Spirit-baptized Peter. The account reaches its climax when Peter arrives and speaks to their spiritual status. "Then Peter opened his mouth, and declared, Of a truth I perceive that God is no respecter of persons: But in every nation he that feareth him, and worketh righteousness,

---

5. Metz, 121.

is accepted with him," (Acts 10:34-35). The narrative concludes with the familiar words, "While Peter yet spake these words, the Holy Ghost fell on all them which heard the word. And they of the circumcision which believed were astonished, as many as came with Peter, because that on the Gentiles also was poured out the gift of the Holy Ghost" (Acts 10:44-45). Again, the reader is left without a clear explanation of what all transpires when the Spirit is poured out on believers. Any confusion will be resolved if we visit the Jerusalem Council that is presented by Luke in chapter fifteen.

When the Gentiles in the house of Cornelius received the Holy Spirit it sent shock waves throughout the Church. Keep in mind that until the case of Cornelius, all new converts and recipients of the Holy Spirit had been Jews. To think that such outsiders should be counted worthy to enjoy the benefits of Christianity was more than they could conceive! Between chapters ten and fifteen, the reader of Acts can feel the tension and skepticism of the Jewish believers. How could unclean Gentiles share in this glorious Gospel? So the leaders of the Early Church, under the leadership of James, convened its first general conference to discuss how to proceed.

Peter Resolves the Confusion to the Apostles

It was the speech of Peter that finally answers our ongoing question in this chapter: What had happened spiritually to those in the Upper Room at Pentecost? Peter indirectly answers the question by explaining what had happened in the house of Cornelius the Gentile. After he lays out the scenario of his being summoned to Caesarea, he informs his doubting fellow Jews, "And God, which knoweth the hearts, bare them [those of the house of Cornelius] witness, giving them the Holy Ghost, even as he did unto us" (Acts 15:8). Fortunately for our question, he informs his hearers that God did the same for them as he did at Pentecost, "And put no difference between us and them, *purifying their hearts by faith*" (Acts 15:9, emphasis added). Now the dilemma is solved; now we know with confidence what the Holy Spirit did in the Upper Room— he cleansed those believers of their indwelling sin! This leads to the question, what evidence is there that those newly entirely sanctified souls were changed as a result? Let us consider the facts.

Whereas the unsanctified believers had been man-fearing and rather unstable in their demeanor before Pentecost, they were changed into bold, courageous witnesses for the Lord (Acts 2:14). Their factionalism and narrow sectarianism left and in its place a beautiful unity resulted, "and all that believed were together, and had all things common" (Acts 2:44). The former unstable, fearful and quarrelsome selves were gone! Whatever had transpired at Pentecost, their inner spiritual response and their outer spiritual expression had been dramatically altered!

As these hardy souls allowed the Spirit to flow through their lives and their message they dramatically impacted their world. They became Spirit-directed ones who are recorded as those who "turned the world upside down." It was not the resurrection of Christ, as marvelous as was that event. It was the crisis of Pentecost that made the radical change in their lives— and that change awaits, today, every sincere seeker. As I often admonish my students, a pure heart is not only your privilege; it is your duty! The personal cleansing of Pentecost will produce dramatic effects on those who seek until God witnesses to a pure heart.

The Disciples of John at Ephesus, or the "Ephesian Pentecost"

We have now considered the spread of the message of entire sanctification as it advanced from Jerusalem, to Samaria and Caesarea; from exclusively Jews, to half-breed Jews, to Gentiles. Now let us consider the disciples of John that Paul confronted at Ephesus.

> And it came to pass, that, while Apollos was at Corinth, Paul having passed through the upper coasts came to Ephesus: and finding certain disciples, he said unto them, Have ye received the Holy Ghost since ye believed? And they said unto him, We have not so much as heard whether there be any Holy Ghost. And he said unto them, Unto what then were ye baptized? And they said, Unto John's baptism. Then said Paul, John verily baptized with the baptism of repentance, saying unto the people, that they should believe on him which should come after him, that is, on Christ Jesus. When they heard this, they were baptized in the name of the Lord Jesus. And when Paul had laid his hands upon them, the Holy Ghost came on them; and they spake with tongues, and prophesied. And all the men were about twelve.
> —Acts 19: 1-7

Let us begin with ascertaining the situation at that city and the background of those twelve men. On Paul's second missionary journey, with Aquila and Priscilla, he visited Ephesus after leaving Corinth, and evidently planted the church there (Acts 18:19). While Paul was gone, a man named Apollos came to the city. Luke described him as one who was eloquent and mighty in the Scriptures. Since he knew only the baptism of John, and sensing his potential in the Gospel, they instructed him "the way of God more perfectly" (Acts 18:24-28). Apparently somewhere else in the area was a cluster of twelve men with the same limitations as Apollos. When Paul met them, he examined them as to their spiritual status and upon learning of their deficiency of the Holy Spirit— they had not yet received the Holy Spirit in the fullness of Pentecost— he prayed, laid hands on them, and they were filled with the Holy Spirit.[6]

The problem here for students is to understand the state of grace of these men. Let us look further at the text. Apparently Paul regarded them as believers, v. 2. Notice, when Paul addressed their problem, he did not ask them if they had knowledge of Christ; that appears to be understood. F. F. Bruce understood these to be disciples of Christ. While they had been baptized according to John's baptism, the text does not state that they were his disciples.[7]

Students need to remember that since these men were limited to John's baptism, that does not mean they were unconverted in the full sense of the term. John's baptism was a "baptism of repentance unto the remission of sins" (Mark 1:4). Therefore, it is logical to assume these men, while not completely instructed in the Gospel, did enjoy a relationship with God. As one scholar noted, the very fact that Paul rebaptized them in the name of the Lord Jesus Christ indicates that he was satisfied that they were proper candidates by the time that he met them at Ephesus. Had they not been true believers then the apostle erred in baptizing unconverted persons.[8]

This is key to understanding their spiritual position. Another has summed up this situation that when Paul laid hands on them they were already disciples, they believed on Jesus. Paul acknowledged their conversion and baptism. When the Holy Spirit came upon them he came upon them instantaneously. They were already men scripturally and accurately called Christians.[9] Perhaps another

---

6. W. T. Purkiser, *Conflicting Concepts of Holiness* (Kansas City, MO: Beacon Hill Press, 1953), 39.

7. Metz, 117.

8. Purkiser, 41.

9. Metz, 118.

comment by a Wesleyan scholar will help to put this event in even more clear light.

> ...under the imposition of hands by Paul, they received the baptism of the Holy Spirit and fire in the purification of their natures, as promised by John (Matthew 3:11; Luke 3:16) and provided by the very nature of God (Hebrews 12:29). Thus the complete possession and empowerment of their lives, as experienced by the Christian disciples on the day of Pentecost (cf. Acts 1:8; 2:1-4; and 15:8, 9), as well as by the Samaritans under the ministry of Peter and John (Acts 8:14-17), and the Gentile household of Cornelius at Caesarea under Peter's ministry (Acts 10:44-48; 11:15-17; 15:8, 9), became a reality with these believers.[10]

One other fact should be kept in mind. Jesus informed his disciples that only believers can receive the Spirit when he stated, "And I will pray the Father, and he shall give you another Comforter, that he may abide with you forever; even the Spirit of truth; *whom the world cannot receive,* because it seeth him not, neither knoweth him; but ye know him; for he dwelleth with you, and shall be in you" (John 14: 15-17, emphasis added). Were these twelve men unconverted, Jesus is saying that they could not receive the Spirit.

To receive or to be baptized by the Holy Spirit, it is absolutely essential that one already *know* Him. Thus, in each of these four "Pentecosts" in the Book of Acts, those receiving the Holy Spirit had to have had the Spirit of Christ in some measure in order to be accepted of God. It is obvious then, that one must have the Spirit with him (in justification) before he can have the Spirit in him in full spiritual baptism power. Only believers are candi-

---

10. Charles W. Carter and Ralph Earle, *The Acts of the Apostles* (Nicholasville, KY: Schmul Publishing Company, 1973), 284.

dates for being filled with the Spirit and, as such, are in a suitable position to receive him.

One other phenomenon for students to keep in mind is this: nowhere in these four incidences in the Book of Acts, do believers receive the Holy Spirit gradually — it's always instantaneous, i.e., there is no entire sanctification by growth. And for those who believe that in each of these cases we have examined, that the subjects were experiencing conversions, i.e., a first work of grace, but not entire sanctification, then the reader is left without one example of two works of grace in this entire book.

Students sometimes raise the question as to how Wesleyan-Arminian writers profess to believe in two works of grace and then deny that anyone in the Book of Acts was entirely sanctified as each of the four accounts are written by Luke? It may be that many late nineteenth-century holiness writers sometimes, in their drive to press believers on to entire sanctification, spoke of the first work of grace in an almost disparaging manner. Joseph McPherson noted this trend of those well-intentioned writers, "too often the initial work of grace in a penitent's heart is forcibly minimized in the ongoing effort to emphasize and exalt a second work of grace."[11] With these thoughts in mind, let us consider the unique case of Saul, who became Paul, to determine if what happened to him should be viewed as a second work of grace.

When was the Apostle Paul Entirely Sanctified?

The most significant man in the New Testament, other than Christ himself, was the former Pharisee, Saul of Tarsus. He wrote more books than any other New Testament writer, and his teaching is critical to understanding the application of the glorious gospel of Christ. Let us con-

---

11. Joseph D. McPherson, *Exploring Early Methodism* (Evansville, IN: Fundamental Wesleyan Publishers, 2018), 107.

sider the process of his being filled with the Holy Spirit. It is both unusual and unique. No other biblical character evidenced such a sudden and dramatic change as the future apostle.

We shall consider the narrative of Paul from two contexts: first, the events that transpired on the road to Damascus, Acts 9:3-8, and secondly, the actions in the house of Judas where he was met by Ananias, Acts 9:10-19. Luke also records two other accounts of his conversion that are given in Paul's own words, first to a Jewish mob, Acts 22:3-11, and lastly, to King Agrippa, Acts 26:2-18. Six days of travel would get one from Jerusalem to Damascus, a distance of 135 miles.

> And as he journeyed, he came near Damascus: and suddenly there shined round about him a light from heaven: And he fell to the earth, and heard a voice saying unto him, Saul, Saul, why persecutest thou me? And he said, Who art thou, Lord? And the Lord said, I am Jesus whom thou persecutest: it is hard for thee to kick against the pricks. And he trembling and astonished said, Lord, what wilt thou have me to do? And the Lord said unto him, Arise, and go into the city, and it shall be told thee what thou must do. And the men which journeyed with him stood speechless, hearing a voice, but seeing no man. And Saul arose from the earth; and when his eyes were opened, he saw no man: but they led him by the hand, and brought him into Damascus. And he was three days without sight, and neither did eat nor drink.
> —*Acts 9:3-9*

Almost all evangelical scholars agree that Paul's conversion took place on the road approaching the city of Damascus. John Wesley, however, held the view that Paul was not converted until three days later. Interestingly, even John Calvin, who did not teach two distinct separate works of grace, taught that Saul's conversion took place on the road, and that he was "suddenly changed into a new man, a new man framed by the Spirit of God."[12] The challenge for newer students of Wesley is to understand his usage of eighteenth century terminology. Some of his terminology sounds somewhat foreign in our vernacular, e.g., Wesley often speaks of some who were "saved," (he means justified) and then he speaks of those who are "fully saved," or "fully born," by which he means entirely sanctified. What evidence can we glean from this scriptural account to determine what did happen?

For most, the best evidence for Paul's change of heart (repentance) is that while lying on the ground in a blinded condition he asked what the Lord would have him do (submission), and addressed him a second time as "Lord." (Notice, when Ananias, a believer, received the message to go to Saul, he also addressed Jesus twice as "Lord," vss. 10, 13). Sometimes we are so focused on going forward to the altar to be saved that we fail to recognize that the act of submitting to the Lord with the consent of our will can move us quickly to the inner change we are seeking. It doesn't necessitate protracted seeking.

A good case in point is the day Zacchaeus met Jesus. Is it too much to believe that by the time the tax collector had climbed down from the tree, his heart had been touched and changed? By the time Jesus arrived at his house, Zacchaeus was explaining to the Lord his plan for making restitution. Yes, Saul very likely was a changed man by the time he was led into the city of Damascus.

After his instructions to arise and enter the city, Saul willingly complied. What else would we expect from a new believer but to acknowledge Jesus as "Lord," and

---

12. *Commentary on the Acts of the Apostles* (Grand Rapids, MI: Wm. B. Eerdmans, 1949), 1: 372.

begin to walk obediently in the light? His conversion apparently led him to a three-day fast.

When the rather reluctant Ananias arrived, his greeting provides another clue as to Paul's spiritual progress. He was greeted by strange new words to him. "Brother Saul, the Lord, even Jesus, that appeared unto thee in the way as thou camest, hast sent me, that thou mightest receive thy sight, and *be filled with the Holy Ghost*" (Acts 9:17, emphasis added). Here we observed the saintly Ananias addressing Saul as a brother in Christ, further evidence of his status with God. Immediately, Saul's eyes were opened and he was forthwith baptized. Observe that Luke records not that he "received" the Holy Spirit, but that he was "filled." While these terms appear somewhat interchangeably in the Scriptures, the latter tends to remove all doubt as to its Pentecostal quality of entire sanctification.

Some students inquire as to the extremely short time lapse of three days from Paul's conversion to his receiving the Holy Spirit, and that is a fair question. Metz provides some excellent thoughts on the element of time between Saul's conversion and entire sanctification. He points out that God, presumably, could regenerate and sanctify a person in one work of grace.[13]

While that is true, one searches in vain in the Bible for such examples. After all, man, not God, is the one who necessitates a time element between the two crisis experiences, i.e., heaven will perform the work just as quickly as the seeker sees his need, understands the cure, determines to have it, and then believes God to do it. Wesley puts it so well, "Since it's by faith, why not now?"[14]

It is fair to point out that it took Jesus' disciples three years to find their need met. Peter's preaching at Pente-

---

13. Metz, 119.
14. Wesley, ibid.

cost indicated that the time could be brief (Acts 2:37-39). The same could be said for the Samaritans; Peter and John were sent as soon as Philip returned with news of the revival; Ananias saw no reason for Saul to delay in being filled with the Holy Spirit within days of his conversion; and Paul urged both the Thessalonians (I Thessalonians 4:3), and the disciples at Ephesus (Acts 19:1-7) to immediate action.[15] The important matter for students to understand is that the time issue is relative to one's degree of awakening to his need to be sanctified wholly, his understanding of what God can do for him, and his perseverance in seeking. Those factors often determine the time element in finding a pure heart. Wesley provides an amazing account of just how the lapse of time can be between the first and second work of grace.

He relates the story of a woman, Grace Paddy, who according to him was, "Convinced of sin, Converted to God, and Renewed in Love [entirely sanctified], within twelve hours."[16] He actually interviewed the lady whom he described as a well-bred, sensible young woman in whom he had confidence. Here is her story as she related it.

> I was harmless, as I thought, but quite careless about religion, till about Christmas, when my brother was saying, "God has given me all I want: I am as happy as I can live." This was about ten in the morning. The words struck my heart. I went to my chamber, and thought, "Why am I not so? O, I cannot be, because I am not convinced of sin." I cried vehemently, "Lord, lay as much conviction upon me as my body can bear." Immediately I saw myself in such light, that I roared for the disquietness of my heart. The maid running up, I said, "Call my brother." He came, and

15. Metz, 119-20.
16. Wesley, *Works*, 3:234-35.

rejoiced over me, and said, "Christ is just ready to receive you, only believe;" and then went to prayer. In a short time all my trouble was gone, and I did believe. All my sins were blotted out. But in the afternoon I was thoroughly convinced of the want of a deeper change. I felt the remains of sin in my heart, which I longed to have taken away. I longed to be saved from all sin, to be cleansed from all unrighteousness; and all the time. Mr. Rankin was preaching; this desire increased exceedingly. Afterwards he met the society. During his last prayer, I was quite overwhelmed with the power of God. I felt an inexpressible change, in the very depth of my heart. And from that time I have felt no anger, no pride, no wrong temper of any kind; nothing contrary to the pure love of God, which I feel continually. I desire nothing but Christ; and I have Christ always reigning in my heart. I want nothing: He is my sufficient portion, in time and in eternity.[17]

"Such an instance I never knew before; such an instance I never read," writes Mr. Wesley. "A person convinced of sin, converted to God, and renewed in love, within twelve hours! Yet it is by no means incredible; seeing one day is with God as a thousand years."[18]

Do Non-Wesleyans Believe in Two Works of Grace?

We have focused in the previous sections on examining the four Pentecosts that appear in the Book of Acts. In so doing we have stressed the secondness of each of those events. Students are surprised to discover, however, that many theologians and preachers who would tend to

---

17. Wesley, *Works*, 3:234-35.
18. In Joseph D. McPherson, *Just As New as Christianity*, (Evansville, IN: Fundamental Wesleyan Publishers, 2016), 243-44.

argue quite forcefully against any clear scriptural teaching on two separate acts or crises in the life of true believers, have actually testified and written of two distinct occasions in their own lives when God wrought a special work for them. Let us consider at least one example of such people.

In my years of undergraduate study, I was introduced to an important writer and his book. That volume contains numerous examples of persons who denied two works of grace and then later testified to second events in their lives that parallels Wesleyan teaching. James Gilchrist Lawson gave us these accounts in his *Deeper Experiences of Famous Christians*.[19] He shares a list of terms used by different denominations to designate this "second" event in the lives of already saved people. Many of them were already famous in the religious world by the time the subsequent event transpired in their lives.

Lawson studied many of the spiritual giants in Church history, looking for a common thread in their experiences. All of them, he discovered, had been rather nominal Christians until the Holy Spirit transformed their lives. Each of them used different terminology for what had happened to them: "full consecration," "the baptism of the Holy Spirit," and "entire sanctification." Regardless of the term they used, they all recounted a definite experience with the Holy Spirit subsequent to being saved. For many, it transpired years after their conversion. Keep in mind, these had not been reared under Wesleyan-Arminian teaching, so they were charting a somewhat new course in their spiritual lives. Let's consider one of his subjects, D. L Moody.

---

19. James Gilchrist Lawson, *Deeper Experiences of Famous Christians* (Anderson, IN: The Warner Press, 1911).

Case of D. L. Moody's Second Crisis

The future evangelist had been converted in 1855 and eventually became popular with the Plymouth Congregational Church as a Sunday School worker and went on to be very prominent in the Young Men's Christian Association in Chicago. In 1870 Moody partnered with Ira D. Sankey, who became his song evangelist for the balance of his ministry. While in Dublin, Ireland, he met an evangelist named Henry Varley, who urged Moody to become fully yielded to God. That encounter produced a hunger in his heart for a deeper experience, a yieldedness that he had never experienced.

During a revival in Moody's Chicago church, under the preaching of Henry Moorhouse, the hunger steadily increased. Keep in mind that Moody and these preachers mentioned above were neither Methodists nor Wesleyan-Arminian in their theology. In fact, several of them would oppose such teaching.

Moody continued to hunger for a deepening of his own life. Something was missing and he sensed it. In 1871, two ladies sat on the front pew in his church and they informed him, "We have been praying for you."

His response to them, "Why don't you pray for the people?"

"Because, you need the Spirit."

At that time, he had the largest congregation in all Chicago, but he had felt an inner lack. Something was missing in his spiritual life. In the days that followed, including the burning and rebuilding of the city, he continued to seek for whatever it was he knew he was missing.

Then with no advanced warning, while walking the streets of New York a few weeks later, he stated, "God revealed Himself to me, and I had such an experience of His love that I had to ask Him to stay His hand."[20] From

---
20. Lawson, 246-47.

that day forward, Moody enjoyed peace he had never known and power in preaching that continued until his death in 1899.

Lawson's book is full of such examples— all of folk who had not been instructed in the message of heart holiness. Thus we frequently find those outside the teachings of Wesley who would deny two separate works of grace in the life of the believer, and yet they provide testimony of that very happening in their own lives. Such accounts should serve to underline the validity of Wesleyan-Arminian teaching.

We are now ready to consider in our last chapter how the believer may successfully seek and find this promised blessing that is available to every sincere believer.

Chapter Summary

1. While most are aware of the Day of Pentecost, many students are surprised to learn that the entire second chapter of Acts says nothing about a pure heart for any of the 120 assembled. One must work all the way to chapter fifteen to learn that their hearts were purified by faith in chapter two.
2. As a literary convention scholars often speak of four "Pentecosts" in the Book of Acts: the Jewish or Jerusalem Pentecost in chapter two; the Samaritan Pentecost in chapter eight; the Gentile Pentecost at the house of Cornelius in chapter ten, and the Ephesian Pentecost in chapter nineteen.
3. It's important for students to observe that in none of these cases were the believers entirely sanctified gradually; it was always done in an instant.
4. The case of Paul the Apostle generates discussion because of the short time between his conversion and his being filled with the Spirit. Here we learn that the time element is up to the Lord. As someone has stated, "God can cut short his work in an instant of time."

5. Wesley recounts cases where individuals found salvation in two installments in less than one day.
6. James Gilchrist Lawson's book, *Deeper Experiences of Famous Christians,* illustrates that all through Church history people who have not been taught anything about a second work of grace, have felt a lack or spiritual deficiency, perhaps years into their ministry. Without using Methodist terminology, they have described exactly what we would term a second work of grace.

20
How do I Attain this Glorious Blessing?

SEEKING ENTIRE SANCTIFICATION LEADS to a host of questions in the classroom relative to how one should seek. All who find victory will follow a pathway that includes some basic steps. Begin by having a clear knowledge of what you need for God to do for you. Be sure that you are not seeking some angelic perfection that is not biblically sound or humanly possible. There is no end of excellent resources written by godly people that will keep you from seeking for too much or too little.

It will be helpful to remind yourself of the promises and exhortations from scripture. To be entirely sanctified is a clear command of God, "As He which hath called you is holy, be ye holy" (I Peter 1:15, 16). You have been called to this blessing, "God hath not called us unto uncleanness, but unto holiness" (I Thessalonians 4:7). You have been chosen to this holiness, "He hath chosen us in Him before the foundation of the world, that we should be holy and without blame before Him in love" (Ephesians 1:4). And Paul informs us that we have be chastened by the Lord "…for our profit, that we might be partakers of his holiness" (Hebrews 12:10). The ultimate goal for you is, "To the end He may establish your hearts unblameable in holiness before God, even our Father" (I Thessalonians 3:13). And this blessing is available to you, "Christ also loved the Church and gave Himself for it; that He might sanctify and cleanse it… that it should be holy and without blemish" (Ephesians 5:25-27). What more can you possible need than these promises?

You must be fully aware of your need for a heart made perfect in love. You must have a clear understanding of what you are seeking. Wesley and the Early Methodists generally put it this way: learn your disease, and then seek the cure. So many people hear teaching, preaching and testimonies about this wonderful experience, and they begin to seek for something but are rather unclear on what it is. In their mind, some fantastic phenomenon is going to shake them to their very core.

Once you are clear on what God can do for you, set that as your spiritual goal in life. You will begin to make progress as you journey toward the goal. Determine that this object of your seeking will be the most important thing in life, not just something to do occasionally or haphazardly, but with all your being. Throughout the day and night, let it be your main focus.

As I counsel with some individuals it becomes evident that they are not yet desperate enough to understand that they cannot keep walking with the Lord without a pure heart. It is also apparent that they don't really understand that for which they are seeking. That is why it is so important that pastors, evangelists and teachers make plain to them why they need to be sanctified wholly, and what it will do for them.

Many seek holiness of heart out of a sense of duty. While it is commendable that they do so, unless urgency drives them onward, chances are great that until they grasp that carnality is ruining their walk and their witness, they will make little progress. If you attempt to continue walking with the Lord and are willing to do so without a pure heart, then you are not yet a viable candidate for the blessing. A sense of urgency needs to pervade your seeking.

What Must I Know Before I Begin Seeking for a Holy Heart?

You must take personal inventory and be certain that there is no known sin in your life. It is essential to have a clear testimony of salvation. Are you really enjoying your sonship in the Lord? Are you living victoriously? If not, do not focus on being sanctified until you know without a doubt that you are saved. It is essential that you be on the top rung of the ladder of a saved experience. Little progress will be made until these facts become clear.

Also, it is essential that you have made all the restitutions that you can possibly make. Understand that sometimes, the passing of time and lost contacts preclude your ability to make some of them. For example, I owed a mechanic a fairly small sum for repairing my motor scooter many years ago. When I tried to locate him to pay the bill, his business had shut down, and my best efforts to locate him proved fruitless. That being the case, I put the owed amount in the missionary offering and never gave it another thought. Your credit is good with the Lord until the right time presents itself to make your restitution.

Consider this when making the restitution: turn it into an opportunity to testify to the person why you are making it. Who knows? God may use that to awaken the person and will enable you to be the means of reaching him or her with the gospel.

So to sum up as you begin seeking holiness, be clear in your testimony of salvation, be enjoying a victorious walk with a strong devotional life— do not end up like so many who go forward for entire sanctification, only to discover as they are praying that they are actually backslidden and are really only being restored to their saved experience. A line from an old gospel song was quite helpful to me and to others:

> Ye who know your sins forgiven, and are happy in the Lord.
> Have you read the precious promise, which is left upon record?
> I will sprinkle you with water; I will cleanse you from all sin,
> Sanctify and make you holy; I will dwell and reign within.
>
> Tho' you have much peace and comfort, greater things you yet may find:
> Freedom from unholy tempers, freedom from the carnal mind.
> To procure your perfect freedom, Jesus suffered, groaned and died;
> On the cross the healing fountain, gushed from His wounded side.
>
> Be as holy and as happy, and as useful here below,
> As it is your Father's pleasure, Jesus, only Jesus know.
> Spread, O spread the holy fire, tell, O tell what God has done,
> Till the nations are conformed, to the image of his Son.[1]

That's good theology. Notice how the first line refers to those persons who are already enjoying a saved experience as they are seeking entire sanctification. That assur-

---

1. Walter H. Talcott, "Ye Who Know Your Sins Forgiven," *Wesleyan Heritage Hymns*, (Salem, OH: Allegheny Publications, 2008), 115.

ance of present victory is vitally important. It will enable you to avoid confusion as to where you are in your seeking, and as to what to expect. Do not declare yourself a seeker for heart purity if you are unclear as to your present relationship with God. You need to be on the top rung of the spiritual ladder as you begin your search for the second work of grace in your heart.

My Advice to Seekers of Entire Sanctification

Many illustrations could be given of people who really felt that the blessing of entire sanctification would be nice — even great — but they have sought it rather half-heartedly, and, I might add, unsuccessfully. Perhaps it would be helpful for the reader to reread chapter 18 on the many misconceptions that appear in the holiness movement about the blessing of entire sanctification. I have often observed people at the altar who went forward out of some sense of duty or general feelings of dissatisfaction with their present walk with the Lord, but there was no real sense of urgency and their praying produced nothing but a temporary sense of relief.

I often recommend seekers to ask the Lord to increase their longing for heart holiness. If you are seeking, tell him that you are unsatisfied with your current walk due to all the carnal manifestations that have become evident since you were saved.

One of the greatest gifts that God can give a person, other than the gift of himself, is the gift of a hunger for himself. "Blessed are they which do hunger and thirst… for they shall be satisfied" (Matthew 5:6). The closer becomes your walk with the Lord, the more intense will become your appetite for him. This can serve as a good test of how close your relationship with God really is: how great is your desire for him? Is it increasing as you walk with him? Has your quest for a pure heart reached the point of craving as the beloved song states it?

> Hallelujah, I have found Him,
> Whom my soul so long has craved!
> Jesus satisfies my longings;
> Thro' His blood I am now saved.[2]

Many times it is helpful to verbalize your thoughts to the Lord as you pray. Of course, he already knows your desire and your need, but stating your inner thoughts will help you to focus and give you a sense of progress as you seek. But there is more that you can do.

Over the years, it has been my observation that seekers usually make progress when they are willing publicly to declare their need, either in testimony or to those who are praying with them at the altar. Many altar workers go forward to pray with seekers, but seem to be at a loss as to how to pray with them. On occasion it almost can become humorous when a well-meaning counselor at the altar assumes what is the need and prays completely amiss, almost to the embarrassment of those around him. For the seeker it could be that pride is standing in the way of you acknowledging your need; yielding to pride will certainly hinder any progress.

Something positive seems to result as you share your spiritual need with those in whom you have confidence. Yes, it's humbling, but those praying with you will understand how you feel. Doubtlessly, they would tell you they had similar feelings when they were seeking for a pure heart. Knowing that those counselors have been where you are as you seek, will provide a positive sense of kinship with these true, well-meaning brothers and sisters in the Lord.

Another observation I have made is that naming your

---

2. Clara Teare [Williams], "Satisfied," *Glorious Gospel Hymns* (Kansas City, MO: Nazarene Publishing House, 1931), no. 61.

carnal traits, of which you are so well aware, will help you to make progress. James tells his readers, "Therefore confess your sins to each other and pray for each other so that you may be [spiritually] healed" (5:16). That has proven to be great advice. It almost serves as an early form of accountability, and that is a great source of encouragement as well as a guard against careless living.

Many scholars agree that one of the features that enabled the Early Methodists to be so effective in soul-winning and in establishing a powerful church, was their willingness to mutually share their weaknesses, spiritual needs and faults to one another in the famous Methodist class-meeting. You, too, will make steady progress by acknowledging to trusted spiritual advisors the carnal traits from which you are longing to be free. An old gospel song written many years ago provides excellent advice as to how you might pray as you are seeking:

Have Thy Way, Lord

Jesus, see me at Thy feet, with my sacrifice complete.
I am bringing all to Thee; Thine alone I'll be.

O how patient Thou hast been, with my pride and inbred sin!
O what mercy Thou hast shown, grace and love unknown!

Lord, I loathe myself and sin ; enter now and make me clean;
Make my heart just like Thine own; Come, Lord, take Thy throne.

Lord, Thy love has won my all; let Thy Spirit on me fall;
Burn up every trace of sin; make me pure within.

Praise the Lord, the work is done!
Praise the Lord, the vict'ry's won!
Now the blood is cleansing me; from all sin I'm free.

Chorus:
Have Thy way, Lord, have Thy way, This with all my heart I say;
I'll obey Thee, come what may, Dear Lord, have Thy way.[3]

Those who have successfully found Christian perfection give this warning: do not look at people— they will let you down. Probably one of the greatest hindrances in the holiness movement, as many young people have informed me, is those persons who profess so highly and possess so little. Satan loves to flash before seekers the lives of hypocrites. Such individuals have done enormous harm to the cause of Christ. Many times I have sat in my office with students who have recounted stories of parents, teachers, church leaders, etc., who have proven to be a great disappointment by leading lives that did not measure up to the Bible. Rather than focus on people and their failures, learn to look at the lives of those steady Christian models in whom you have confidence. Best of all, look to Christ, our great Example. Let him be your pattern. Reflect on how he responded in the various circumstances of his life, ministry and ultimately, his trial and crucifixion.

I have found it will be helpful if you share your progress with individuals in whom you have confidence. If you happen to seek publicly and you don't feel clear yet, it is not only permissible, but it will prove helpful to declare

---

3. George Bennard, "Have Thy Way, Lord" *Wesleyan Heritage Hymns* (Salem, OH: Allegheny Publications, 2008), 321.

where you are in your seeking, i.e., share what progress you have made. So many feel obligated to make a profession after they have sought publicly. My advice to you is this: don't let a well-intentioned altar worker talk you into something that has not happened in your heart. Some workers feel they have failed if seekers don't make a profession at the altar. Experience dictates, however, that it is far better to simply state whatever progress you have made. Then declare yourself to be a seeker and keep walking in the light. In his time, God will manifest himself. The beautiful promise of the prophet declares, "The Lord whom ye seek shall suddenly come to his temple" (Malachi 3:1). When the conditions have been met and the Lord has granted you faith to believe, he will come in his refining fullness and take up his abode in the temple of your heart!

And most importantly of all— do not despair! Never give in to Satan's taunt that God is not going to entirely sanctify you, that your case is too difficult for the Lord. He is no respecter of persons and what he has done for others, he longs to do for you— just as fast as you will permit him.

What Does the Experience of Our Saints Teach Us?

In the more recent years of my ministry I have explored the experience of a host of men and women who enjoy positions of leadership in various capacities within the holiness movement. These are people of piety, ones who enjoy high esteem among their peers and with those to whom they minister. My purpose was to elicit from them their account of seeking and finding perfect love. In doing this, my search could come under Wesley's fourth rubric in his quadrilateral— What is the experience of the Church on a given matter? I wanted to hear from them of their own struggles that prefaced their finding entire sanctification, i.e., what does their history, their experience, teach us?

A number of those have related to me how they fell into the trap of seeking it by works. In their earnestness they felt that by eliminating from their lives certain activities, increased fasting, and more self-denial— surely that would convince the Lord to sanctify them. Living a careful, self-disciplined life will enable you to make steady progress toward the desired goal. You would do well to adhere to the well-known advice of Susanna Wesley who warned her sons, "Whatever weakens your reason, impairs the tenderness of your conscience, obscures your sense of God, takes off your sense of spiritual things, whatever increases the authority of the body over the mind, that thing is sin to you, however it may seem."[4] While there is no doubt that the practice of self-denial will raise one's level of spiritual awareness, those are not what will bring the desired work of grace.

Many who enjoy a sanctified experience have shared with me that if they were perfectly honest, they felt that they must seek for a certain period of time; it just somehow seemed presumptuous to expect the Lord to answer their cry until they had sought for some many weeks, months or even years. Interestingly, they concluded by stating that if they had done the first night what they did the last night they could have secured the blessing much earlier. What they were telling me was they didn't really expect to get it as they were seeking, so it's no surprise that they failed. When we come asking of our Father, we must expect to receive from his hand, or we will not.

Others have acknowledged that an element of fear played a prominent role in their inability to trust God for the desired blessing. One of Satan's most effective tools is

---

4. Letter to John Wesley, June 8, 1725.

to convince seekers that even if God did sanctify them, they wouldn't be able to live the life. Such folk have given way to evil reasoning and thereby lost out at that point. My advice would be simply to tell God that you intend to live for him and walk the holy walk with his enablement and not to let Satan distract you by throwing up the unknown future to you. Most are quite weak in their confidence and their fear of failure inhibits them from even trying. Seekers need to remind themselves that they cannot live the life in their own ability, but once the Holy Spirit fully possesses their life, he will enable them to lead a successful, God-honoring life.

I like to encourage seekers with the fact that they need not to convince the Lord to sanctify them; he desires to grant them the blessing even more than they want it. Did not the Lord advise the disciples that, "If ye then, being evil, know how to give good gifts unto your children: how much more shall your heavenly Father give the Holy Spirit to them that ask him?" (Luke 11:13)

What is the Witness of the Spirit? How Will I Know?

Another area which has proven to be a challenge for seekers centers around how they are to "feel" when the moment of deliverance becomes a reality. Without fail, students have conditioned themselves to expect a lightning bolt from heaven that will fall on them from top to bottom. Our earlier chapter on the three fillings of the Spirit discusses the ecstatic emotions that occurred to individuals. Those were unique moments in holy history. However, nowhere in Scripture are individuals exhorted to seek for such a phenomenon. Further compounding the problem for students are the glowing testimonies and demonstrations of some of the saints in their lives. Unless they experience something of that nature, they have conditioned themselves to doubt what God might do for them, i.e., they have predetermined what they should feel, and failing that occurrence, they will not believe what God has done for them.

Here again is where my inquiring of some of the most esteemed saints in holiness churches has proved helpful. One of the godliest men I have ever known recounted to me his experience. William Mydock, one who enjoyed a wonderful saved experience, had been thoroughly awakened to his need for heart purity and had sought several times but to no avail. Then one night in the large tabernacle at Stoneboro Camp, in an emotionally charged camp meeting service, he went forward for prayer. Interestingly, no one came to pray with him. At that point some might be tempted to discouragement, since the enemy would likely tell them they surely deserved some attention from the altar workers. For whatever reason, no one came to pray with him. Undeterred, he prayed on.

After praying for a while longer, he felt that God had granted him the faith to believe that the Holy Spirit had taken up residence in his heart, an enormous sense of relief filled his soul and he sensed the work had been done. He told me that he stood up, backed up a few steps to the front pew, sat down, and really felt nothing in the way of high emotions. I wish to stress that this saint led the midnight prayer meeting in the tabernacle for years — a man of great esteem among all who knew him. He never looked back, and he never doubted what the Lord had done for him. My point here is that even though no great emotional surge accompanied the moment of his sanctification, the work had been accomplished in his heart.

The Witness is Not an Emotional High

Let us now observe some negative effects of relying too much on one's emotions. I was positioned near the front of the large tabernacle and watched as the group of altar workers boisterously urged the young man to yield all to God. He had been praying quite loudly and had attracted most of those in the front of the building.

Suddenly, he jumped to his feet, uttered a loud shout of praise and took off running. He flew out one of the large open side doors and galloped around the tabernacle with arms raised, shouting loudly as we all praised God with him. Three times he encircled that place and then came back in and shouted some more.

Of course, the observers were confident that such an emotionally charged performance must be an indication of his victory. Unfortunately, in a day or two he was back at the altar, defeated and unsure of where he stood spiritually. His error was in assuming because of his progress earlier, along with the emotional high he had enjoyed, he must have gotten the blessing. Often the Spirit will give encouragement to seekers, but such should not be taken for the witness of the Spirit.

Note, there is nothing wrong with enjoying spiritually high emotions. Have you not experienced a wonderful sense of God's Presence when worshipping in the congregation? Nothing can surpass the wonderful sense of the *Shekina* glory, perhaps while singing one of the wonderful hymns of the Church. Who can help but feel God's nearness while lifting Wesley's, "Arise, My Soul Arise" in a large tabernacle with the full organ swelling as you sing? The danger, however, is to assume that because you enjoyed that wonderful feeling that everything must be okay. You take that feeling to indicate that you are just where you should be in your walk with the Lord — when in fact, you are just being swept along with the emotion of the moment. So we must never determine our spiritual acceptance with God by how loudly we sang along with the congregation.

Observe that in the above paragraphs, I used the word that a person "sensed" the presence of the Holy Spirit. Over the years I have tended to opt for that word rather than to say that he or she "felt" something. That choice of words is quite deliberate on my part. I do that to inculcate into my students the danger of running on feelings. As John Wesley, the wise patriarch of Methodism has cautioned us, "None therefore ought to believe, that the work is done, till there is added the testimony of the spirit, witnessing his entire sanctification, as clearly as his justification."[5] With his unique doctrine of assurance, he set his followers onto the pathway of a "know-so salvation." No one needs to wander in a wilderness of uncertainty, never secure in the knowledge whether the work has been done. With an unmistakable clarity, God will enable his seeking child can enjoy an unshakable witness when the heart has been made perfect in love.

Let us consider how the Lord communicated to his people in the Old Testament. When God spoke to Noah, Abraham, Jacob, Moses, the prophets and others in the Old Testament, the question often surfaces as to the manner in which God spoke. Was it in an audible voice or was it merely a "voice" in the mind of the hearer. A clue that might provide us an answer, at least on some of the occasions, can be seen when God "came" to the prophets with a divine message. Consider the case of Jeremiah.

Just as the Word of the Lord "Came" to Jeremiah, He will "Come" and Witness to You

> The words of Jeremiah the son of Hilkiah, of the priests that were in Anathoth in the land of Benjamin: To whom the word of the LORD came in the days of Josiah the son of Amon king of Judah, in the thirteenth year of his reign. It came also in the days of Jehoiakim the son of Josiah king of Judah, unto the end of the eleventh year of Zedekiah the son of Josiah

---

5. John Wesley, *A Plain Account of Christian Perfection*, (Nicholasville, KY: Schmul Publishing Co.), 53.

king of Judah, unto the carrying away of Jerusalem captive in the fifth month. Then the word of the LORD came unto me...

The words of these first four verses of the Book of Jeremiah will suffice as an example of an interesting phenomenon that can be observed in the original Hebrew text of our Bible. Three times in these verses we read that the "Word of the Lord" came to the prophet. Actually, the word "came" does not appear in any of these three verses in the original Hebrew text. That is not because the Hebrew language lacks the word "come" or "came." It does have such a word, and it is used hundreds of times throughout the Old Testament. However, the word "came" is not in these verses.

Instead, what does occur is a form of the verb, "to be" which should be translated by any Hebrew student as, "To whom the word of the Lord 'was' in the days of Josiah...." Such a rendering does translate accurately the words of the text but seems awkward to the modern reader. To my students I suggest a better way of handling the text. I have them supply a word that conveys the intent of the writer— "To whom the word of the Lord 'happened' in the days of Josiah..." That is actually the thought that those verses are conveying to the reader.

In some manner unknown to us today, as Jeremiah was meditating and waiting on the Lord, something beautiful, something transcendent, "happened" to him. He became aware that God, in some mysterious manner, was communicating or speaking to him. Something was "happening" as the divine Presence caused him to become conscious or aware that the Eternal was imparting a message to him. One observes this phenomenon, repeatedly, throughout the Old Testament prophets. The same phrase, "and the word of the Lord came" to Micah, to Jonah, to Zephaniah, appears in almost all of their books. In other words, as these holy men of God dwelt in the presence of the Lord, something beyond this world "happened" to them. They became aware that God was speaking to them, conveying a message that needed to be delivered to the people of Israel.

The same transcendent action occurred to the apostles. Peter informs us in his epistle that "holy men of God spoke as they were *moved* by the Holy Spirit" (II Peter 1:21, emphasis added). How beautiful it would be if every minister contemplating his sermon, waiting before the Lord for something direct from heaven, would become conscious that something was "happening" to him as the Eternal reveals the message that the people need to hear! No doubt, every God-called preacher can testify to those precious times when, sitting in the pastor's study, seeking God's will for next Sunday's sermon, he becomes strangely aware that something almost too sacred for words has "happened" just when that peculiar leading of the Lord was needed.

As a minister I would share that nothing can replace those moments when, just like Jeremiah and other faithful prophets, I could sense God was imparting to me the very thoughts or the message that the people needed to hear. And why should we limit our thoughts to just pastors? Why not to Sunday School teachers, to missionaries, to moms and dads, and to anyone who needs that special direction for life's activities, i.e., any believer who seeks God's will for life's decisions? May God grant those sacred moments when the Eternal Presence "happens" to his children, to those who await his leadership as they navigate their way through this present world! And why not to the seeker at the altar?

What I am suggesting is that when the Holy Spirit speaks to you as you seek him, it is very likely that something will "happen" as I have illustrated above. As you are humbly kneeling in prayer, awaiting the Voice of the Lord to affirm his sanctifying work in your heart, it will probably be that you will "sense" that he has met your need. In a manner not easily described, but unmistakably certain, the Spirit will witness to your heart. You will know that moment; no one can talk you into it, and no one can talk you out of it. The Lord, whom you have been seeking, has suddenly come to his temple— the temple of your heart! If you cannot seem to clear in your seeking, there are reasons.

Often I have prayed and counseled with seekers at the altar who have prayed for a while and then look at me and declare, "I have just done everything I know, but nothing seems to work." A sweet elderly mother-in-Israel once gave a college class good advice. When you are at an impasse in your seeking, the problem can usually be located in one of two areas— a failure to confess clear to the bottom of your carnal heart, or a failure to believe him to do the work. To that excellent advice I would add a further caution. It's easier to believe God to sanctify you down the road; the challenge is to believe him to do it now. "Behold, today is the day of salvation; now is the accepted time" (II Corinthians 6:2).

For the careless, half-hearted seeker, it's always easier to kick the can down the road and put off earnest seeking for a pure heart. To such careless persons I have this word of admonition: finding the perfect love that you so desperately need is not only a privilege— it's a duty. By that we mean just this: you cannot stay justified by refusing to walk in the light of entire sanctification. To do that would be guilty of a sin of omission— knowing to do something and refusing to do it. If Jesus thought your heart purity was worth his suffering without the gate, how can you disregard the great price he paid to secure it for you?

Edwin Hatch, an Oxford graduate and a biblical

scholar of whom few were his equal, must have sensed the need of that vitalizing Presence of God in his life. In 1878 he penned these words that so beautifully express the desire of those who long to be fully possessed by the Holy Spirit.

Breathe on me, Breath of God,
Fill me with life anew,
That I may love what Thou dost love,
And do what Thou wouldst do.

Breathe on me, Breath of God,
Until my heart is pure,
Until with Thee I will one will,
To do and to endure.

Breathe on me, Breath of God,
Till I am wholly Thine,
Until this earthly part of me
Glows with Thy fire divine.

Breathe on me, Breath of God,
So shall I never die,
But live with Thee the perfect life
Of Thine eternity.[6]

Chapter Summary

1. Entire sanctification is not an end in itself; it is just a beginning.
2. It is essential that seekers have a clear understanding of their spiritual disease and of the cure, i.e., what God can and will do for them.
3. Sharing your need with confidential counselors is help-

---

6. Edwin Hatch, "Breathe on Me, Breath of God," *Hymnal of the Church of God*, (The Gospel Trumpet Company, 1963), 178.

ful; it will enable you to make certain progress.
4. Listen to the experience of old saints, but be sure not to seek for the exact same manifestations or witness that occurred to them.
5. Be willing to testify publicly to your seeking— and your progress; it will help you and it will encourage others.
6. Do not expect an emotional high, and do not judge your progress by any lack thereof.
7. God will be faithful to witness to your heart when the work is done; or if need be, He will reveal what is lacking on your part. Just as God's Word "happened" to the prophets, it will "happen" to you.

About the Author

PAUL L. KAUFMAN WRITES FROM a diverse background, having spent over forty years in the Bible college classroom as a professor of Hebrew, Church History, Bible and Theology. He has been a Professional Fellow at Ashland Theological Seminary for over thirty years as a church historian. During those years he has also taught at Malone University, Kent State University, God's Bible College, Hobe Sound Bible College (Chair of Bible/Theology) and taught at Allegheny Wesleyan College for almost four decades. He has served as a college evaluator for the Association for Biblical Higher Education and as academic dean at AWC for almost twenty years.

He holds graduate degrees from Baltimore Hebrew University (M.A.), Antietam Biblical Seminary (Th.M.,Th.D.), Lutheran Theological Seminary, Gettysburg (S.T.M.), and his Ph.D. in American Religious History is from Kent State University. He served a total of twenty-one years as pastor of two congregations in Maryland and Ohio, and has been a general evangelist for over twenty years, speaking in ministerial conferences, camp meetings and local church revivals.

Works Cited

Anderson, T. M., *After Sanctification: Growth in the Life of Holiness,* Nicholasville, KY: Schmul Publishing Co., 2002.

Barclay, William, *A New Testament Word Book,* London: SCM Press, 1955.

Bennard, George, "Have Thy Way, Lord" *Wesleyan Heritage Hymns,* Salem, OH: Allegheny Publications, 2008.

Benson, Joseph, *The Holy Bible, Containing the Old and New Testaments — according to the Present Authorized Version— with Critical, Explanatory, and Practical Notes,* New York: Lane & Tippett, 1846.

Carter, Charles W., and Earle, Ralph, *The Acts of the Apostles,* Nicholasville, KY: Schmul Publishing Company, 1973.

Cattell, Everett Lewis, *The Spirit of Holiness,* Grand Rapids, William B. Eerdmans Publishing Company, 1963.

Cell, George Croft, *The Rediscovery of John Wesley,* New York: Henry Holt and Co., 1935.

Clarke, Adam, *Clarke's Commentary,* Nicholasville, KY: Schmul Publishing Co., 2019.

Commentary on the Acts of the Apostles, Grand Rapids, MI: Wm. B. Eerdmans, 1949.

Cox, Leo, *John Wesley's Concept of Perfection,* Salem, OH: Schmul Publishing Co., 1999.

Croly, George, "Spirit of God Descend Upon My Heart," *Psalms and Hymns for Public Worship,* London: N.P., 1854.

Delbert, Rose, "Distinguishing the Things That Differ," *Wesleyan Theological Journal* vol. 9, 1, 1974.

Fletcher, John, "The Last Check to Antinomianism," in *Works of John Fletcher,* Salem, OH: Schmul Publications, 1974.

———, Familiar Letters, *The Works of Reverend John Fletcher in Four Volumes,* New York: Lane & Scott, 1849.*

Foster, R. S., *Christian Purity*, n.p., 1851.

Greathouse, William M., *Beacon Bible Exposition*, Kansas City, MO: Beacon Hill Press, 1975.

———, *Love Made Perfect: Foundations for the Holy Life*, Kansas City: MO, Beacon Hill Press, n.d., Kindle Edition.

Hatch, Edwin, "Breathe on Me, Breath of God," *Hymnal of the Church of God*, The Gospel Trumpet Company, 1963.

Hills, A. M., *Fundamental Christian Theology*, Salem: Schmul Publishing Company, Inc., 1980.

Jackson, Thomas, ed. *The Works of John Wesley*, Third edition. 14 vols. Reprint. Grand Rapids: Zondervan Publishing House, 1959.

Keefer, Luke L., Jr., *John Wesley: Disciple of Early Christianity*, Wesleyan Theological Journal 19: 1, 1984.

Kinlaw, Dennis F., *This Day with the Master: 365 Daily Meditations*. Zondervan. Kindle.

Lawson, James Gilchrist, *Deeper Experiences of Famous Christians*, Anderson, IN: The Warner Press, 1911.

Matheson, George, "Make Me a Captive, Lord," *The United Methodist Hymnal*.

Mavis, W. Curry, *The Holy Spirit in the Christian Life*, Grand Rapids, MI: Baker Book House, 1977.

McPherson, Joseph D., *Exploring Early Methodism: Discoveries of Spiritual and Historical Value*, Evansville, IN: Fundamental Wesleyan Publishers, 2018.

———, *Just As New as Christianity*, Evansville, IN: Fundamental Wesleyan Publishers, 2016.

Metz, Donald S., *Studies in Biblical Holiness*, Kansas City, MO: Beacon Hill Press, 1971.

Mischel, Walter, *The Marshmallow Test: Why Self-Control Is the Engine of Success*, New York: Little, Brown and Company, 2014.

Nicoll, W. Robertson, ed. *The Expositor's Greek New Testament*, Grand Rapids, MI: Wm. B. Eerdmans Publishing Co., n.d.

Purkiser, W. T., *Conflicting Concepts of Holiness*, Kansas City, MO: Beacon Hill Press, 1953.

———, *These Earthen Vessels*, Kansas City, MO: Beacon Hill Press, 1985.

Rackham, Richard B., *The Acts of the Apostles*, London: Methuen and Co., 1951.

Ruth, Christian Wismer, *Entire Sanctification: A Second Blessing, Together with Life Sketch, Bible Readings and Sermon Outlines*, Chicago: Christian Witness Co., 1903.*

Sangster, W. E., *The Pure in Heart*, Salem, OH: Schmul Publishing Co., 1984.

Sargant, William, *Battle for the Mind: The Mechanics of Indoctrinations, Brainwashing and Thought Control*, Baltimore, Penguin Books, Inc., 1957.

Steele, Daniel, *A Defense of Christian Perfection*, New York: Hunt & Eaton, 1896.*

———, *Milestone Papers*, Salem, OH: Schmul Publishers, 1976.

Talcott, Walter H., "Ye Who Know Your Sins Forgiven," *Wesleyan Heritage Hymns*, Salem, OH: Allegheny Publications, 2008.

Taylor, Richard S., *A Right Conception of Sin*, Nicholasville, KY: Schmul Publishing Co., 2002.

Teare, Clara, [Williams], "Satisfied," *Glorious Gospel Hymns*, Kansas City, MO: Nazarene Publishing House, 1931.

Wesley, Charles, "Wrestling Jacob," *Wesleyan Heritage Hymns*, Salem OH: Allegheny Publications, 2008.

Wesley, John, *A Plain Account of Christian Perfection*, Nicholasville, KY: Schmul Publishing Co., 2015 (meticulously corrected to the fifth edition, 1785).

Wiley, H. Orton, *Christian Theology*, Kansas City: Beacon Hill Press, 1952.

Wood, J. A., *Perfect Love*, Nicholasville, KY: Schmul Publishing Co., 2008.

Wood, Laurence W., "John Fletcher: The First Wesley Scholar," Perspectives for Wesleyan Methodist Seminarians and Leaders, https://www.catalystresources.org/john-fletcher-the-first-wesley-scholar/ April 1, 2009.

———, *Pentecostal Grace*, Grand Rapids, MI: Francis Asbury Press, 1980.

Works of John Wesley, London: Wesleyan Methodist Book Room.

Wynkoop, Mildred Bangs, *A Theology of Love*, Kansas City, MO: Beacon Hill Press, 1972.

* This title now available from Schmul Publishing Co.

MEMBERS OF SCHMUL'S WESLEYAN BOOK CLUB BUY THESE OUTSTANDING BOOKS AT 40% OFF THE RETAIL PRICE

Join Schmul's Wesleyan Book Club by calling toll-free:

800-$S_7P_7B_2O_6O_6K_5S_7$

Put a discount Christian bookstore in your own mailbox

Visit us on the Internet at
www.wesleyanbooks.com

Schmul Publishing Company | PO Box 776 | Nicholasville, KY 40340

www.ingramcontent.com/pod-product-compliance
Lightning Source LLC
Chambersburg PA
CBHW060351190426
43201CB00044B/2001